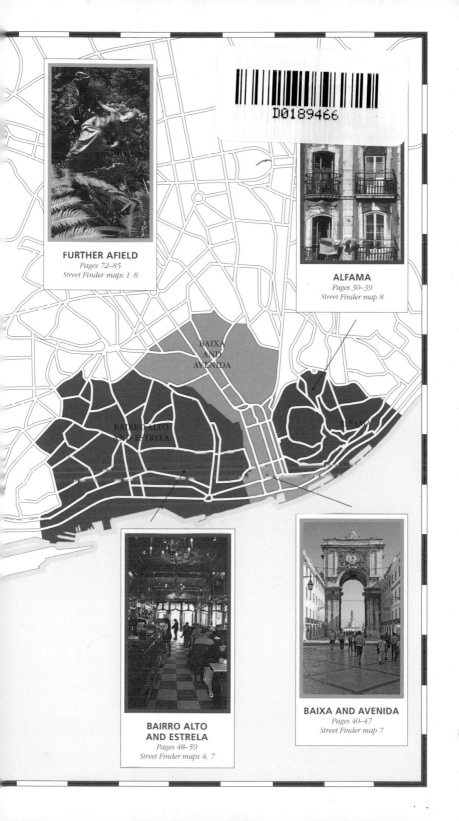

FURTHER AFIELD
Pages 72–85
Street Finder maps 1–8

ALFAMA
Pages 30–39
Street Finder map 8

BAIXA
AND
AVENIDA

BAIRRO ALTO
AND ESTRELA

ALFAMA

**BAIRRO ALTO
AND ESTRELA**
Pages 48–59
Street Finder maps 4, 7

BAIXA AND AVENIDA
Pages 40–47
Street Finder map 7

EYEWITNESS TRAVEL

LISBON

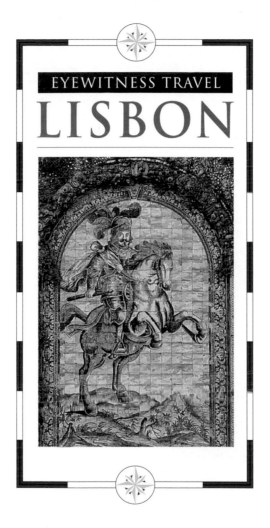

EYEWITNESS TRAVEL

LISBON

MAIN CONTRIBUTOR: SUSIE BOULTON

DK

LONDON, NEW YORK,
MELBOURNE, MUNICH AND DELHI
www.dk.com

PROJECT EDITORS Claire Folkard, Ferdie McDonald
ART EDITORS Jim Evoy, Vanessa Hamilton
EDITORS Francesca Machiavelli, Rebecca Miles,
Alice Peebles, Alison Stace
DESIGNERS Anthea Forlee, Carolyn Hewitson,
Nicola Rodway, Dooty Williams

CONTRIBUTORS AND CONSULTANTS
Clive Gilbert, Peter Gilbert, Sarah McAlister, Norman Renouf,
Joe Staines, Martin Symington, Tomas Tranæus

PHOTOGRAPHERS
Linda Whitwam, Peter Wilson

ILLUSTRATORS
Isidoro González-Adalid Cabezas/Acanto Arquitectura y Urbanismo S.L.,
Paul Guest, Claire Littlejohn, John Woodcock, Martin Woodward

Printed and bound by L. Rex Printing Company Limited, China

First published in Great Britain in 1997
by Dorling Kindersley Limited
80 Strand, London WC2R 0RL

13 14 15 16 10 9 8 7 6 5 4 3 2 1

**Reprinted with revisions 1999, 2000, 2001,
2002, 2003, 2004, 2006, 2008, 2011, 2013**

Copyright 1997, 2013 © Dorling Kindersley Limited, London
A Penguin Company

A CIP CATALOGUE RECORD IS AVAILABLE FROM THE BRITISH LIBRARY.

ISBN 978-1-40938-602-5

FLOORS ARE REFERRED TO THROUGHOUT IN ACCORDANCE WITH EUROPEAN
USAGE, I.E., THE "FIRST FLOOR" IS THE FLOOR ABOVE GROUND LEVEL.

Front cover main image: Torre de Belém

MIX
Paper from
responsible sources
FSC™ C018179

◁ View of the Castelo de São Jorge at night

CONTENTS

Manueline vaulting in the cloister
in the Mosteiro dos Jerónimos

INTRODUCING LISBON

A statue of St Antony, dressed up
for his feast day celebrations

View to the Sé across the Baixa from the Elevador de Santa Justa

The Monument to the Discoveries

Atmospheric houses in the old Moorish district of Alfama

Palácio da Pena, Sintra

HOW TO USE THIS GUIDE

This guide helps you get the most from a visit to Lisbon, providing expert recommendations as well as detailed practical information. The opening chapter *Introducing Lisbon* maps the city and sets it in its historical and cultural context. Each of the five area chapters, plus *The Lisbon Coast*, describe important sights, using maps, pictures and illustrations. Hotel and restaurant recommendations plus features on subjects such as entertainment and food and drink can be found in *Travellers' Needs*. The *Survival Guide* contains practical information on everything from transport to personal safety.

LISBON

Lisbon has been divided into five main sightseeing areas. Each of these areas has its own chapter, which opens with a list of the major sights described. All sights are numbered and plotted on an *Area Map*. Information on the sights is easy to locate as the order in which they appear in the chapter follows the numerical order used on the map.

Sights at a Glance
lists the chapter's sights by category: Churches, Museums and Galleries, Historic Buildings, Parks and Gardens.

1 Area Map
For easy reference, the sights covered in the chapter are numbered and located on a map. The sights are also marked on the Street Finder *maps on pages 166–79.*

A locator map shows clearly where the area is in relation to other parts of the city.

Each area is indicated by a colour-coded thumb tab (see inside front cover).

2 Street-by-Street Map
This gives a bird's-eye view of the heart of each of the sightseeing areas.

A suggested route for a walk is shown in red.

Stars indicate the sights that no visitor should miss.

3 Detailed Information
All the sights in Lisbon are described individually. Addresses and practical information are provided. The key to the symbols used in the information block is shown on the back flap.

THE LISBON COAST

W *ithin an hour's drive northwest of Lisbon you can reach the rocky Atlantic coast, the wooded slopes of Sintra and countryside dotted with villas and royal palaces. South of Lisbon you can enjoy the sandy beaches and fishing towns along the coast or explore the lagoons of the Tagus and Sado river estuaries.*

1 Introduction to The Lisbon Coast

The Lisbon Coast has its own introduction, which provides an overview of the history and character of the coast and countryside around Lisbon and outline what it has to offer the visitor today. The area covered by this section is highlighted on the map of Portugal shown on page 89. It covers coastal resorts and local wildlife, as well as beautiful palaces and historic towns.

Exploring the Lisbon Coast

2 Regional Map

This shows the main road network and gives an illustrated overview of the region. All entries are numbered and there are also useful tips on getting around the region.

The Lisbon Coast chapter is indicated by a green thumb tab.

3 Detailed Information

All the important towns and other places to visit are described individually. They are listed in order, following the numbering given on the Regional Map. Within each entry, there is further detailed information on important buildings and other sights.

Story boxes explore specific subjects further.

For all the top sights, a Visitors' Checklist provides the practical information you need to plan your visit.

Palácio Nacional de Sintra

4 The Top Sights

These are given two or more full pages. Historic buildings are dissected to reveal their interiors; museums and galleries have colour-coded floorplans to help you locate the most interesting exhibits.

INTRODUCING
LISBON

FOUR GREAT DAYS IN LISBON

It is in Lisbon's many hidden nooks and crannies that the city's capacity to surprise and to seduce is felt the strongest. Let yourself be distracted by its inspiring architecture, linger in enchanting squares and explore the city's Moorish legacy in the streets of the

Gold buckle in the Mosteiro dos Jerónimos

Alfama district. Sights listed here are cross referenced to the rest of the guide so you can learn more and tailor the day to your needs. The cost indications include travel, food and admission for two adults or in the case of the Family Day, a family of four.

View of São Vicente de Fora and the dome of Santa Engrácia

HISTORIC LISBON

- The splendid Sé cathedral
- Charming Alfama and city views from the Castelo
- Lunch in the city's oldest streets
- Graça, Lisbon's highest hill

TWO ADULTS allow at least €70

Morning
Begin the day at Lisbon's Romanesque cathedral, the **Sé** *(see p36)*, dating from the 12th century. Its cloister is now the site of an excavation of earlier, Moorish-era buildings. From the quiet of the cathedral set off into the warren of narrow lanes in **Alfama** *(see pp32–3)*, then climb (or catch the 28 tram) to the **Castelo de São Jorge** *(see pp38–9)* and enjoy spectacular views of the city. Restaurants around the castle cater to tourists, but are not necessarily tourist traps. Stop here for lunch or head to cheerful **Restô do Chapitô** *(see p131)*, a restaurant and performing arts school with breathtaking terrace views.

Afternoon
Graça, central Lisbon's highest hill, is a short tram ride or a steep walk away. It has a different feel to Castelo or Alfama – and fewer tourists. Enjoy views from the **Miradouro da Graça** *(see p37)* and stop for a coffee break at the open-air café under the pines by Igreja da Graça. Follow the tram tracks down Rua do Voz do Operário to the grand Renaissance façade of **São Vicente de Fora** *(see p34)*. The adjoining monastery has classic *azulejo* tiled panels. Head to the nearby **Santa Engrácia** *(see p35)*, one of Lisbon's most attractive churches. Then catch the 28 tram across town to **Chiado** *(see pp52–3)*, where you can take a break from history and spend some time shopping, or take in the sombre but attractive ruins of the **Igeja do Carmo** *(see p52)*. Round off the day with a visit to the **Solar do Vinho do Porto** *(see p54)* at the top of Bairro Alto and relax with a glass of one of their 200 types of port.

ART AND BULLS

- Contemporary art at impressive Culturgest
- Restored Neo-Moorish bullring
- World-class art and lunch at the Gulbenkian

TWO ADULTS allow at least €50

Morning
Check out the current exhibition and architecture at Culturgest (Caixa Geral de Depósitos building, 1 Rua do Arco de Cego), an important institution of contemporary culture. For a contrast, visit the delightful Moorish pastiche that is **Campo Pequeno** *(see p80)*, Lisbon's bullring since 1892. In the same space on the south side is the impressive 17th-century Palácio Galveias, once the property of the ill-fated Távora family *(see p71)*. This building now houses the Municipal Library. Walk to the exquisite **Museu Calouste Gulbenkian** *(see pp76–9)* where you can stop for lunch before visiting the stunning art collection.

Classical marble statue, Museu Calouste Gulbenkian

Afternoon

The Gulbenkian deserves a lot of your time as it is has one of the finest collections of art in the world. Within the complex there is also a museum of contemporary art, **Centro de Arte Moderna** *(see p80)*, and a pleasant park. Climb the short distance to the top of **Parque Eduardo VII** *(see p75)* and stop at the delightful outdoor café **Linha d'Àgua** *(see pp136–7)*. Stroll across the street that separates this part from the rest of Parque Eduardo VII and enjoy the view of Lisbon, extending to the river and beyond.

Torre de Belém, one of the city's most recognized landmarks

A DAY BY THE RIVER

- **Treasures old and new in Belém**
- **Dynamic Alcântara district**
- **Art and history at the Museu de Arte Antiga**

TWO ADULTS allow at least €70

Morning

Take the 15 tram to **Belém** *(see pp60–71)*, hopping off early if you want to walk the last section along the riverfront promenade. Set at the mouth of the River Tagus, Belém is particularly rich in history and sights. The **Torre de Belém** *(see p70)* and the magnificent **Mosteiro dos Jerónimos** *(see pp66–7)* are two of its must-see historic gems, while the **Centro Cultural de Belém** *(see p68)* is emphatically and strikingly modern. Belém is full of restaurants, particularly along Rua de Belém and parallel Rua Vieira Portuense.

Afternoon

After lunch, walk or take the tram back to Alcântara. This part of Lisbon has a special vibrancy with many nightclubs, restaurants and exciting urban renewal projects. East of this area, on the fringes of the tranquil Lapa district, is the unmissable **Museu Nacional de Arte Antiga** *(see pp56–7)*.

A FAMILY DAY

- **Explore the impressive, modern Parque das Nações**
- **Study ocean life at the city's enormous oceanarium**
- **Visit animals at Quinta Pedagógica farm**

FAMILY OF 4 allow at least €150

Morning

Begin by exploring **Parque das Nações** *(see p81)*. The cable car ride here offers wonderful views of Europe's longest bridge, the Vasco da Gama. It is also possible to hire bikes, and there is an area for roller-skating and skateboarding. The city's immense oceanarium, **Oceanário de Lisboa** *(see p81)*, is the main attraction, so go early (from 10am) or at lunchtime to avoid long queues. Other highlights include the Pavilhão do Conhecimento – Ciencia Viva, a

The vast Vasco da Gama bridge spanning the Tagus River

hands-on science museum and the promenade along the river. For lunch, there are plenty of eating options in the park itself, from floating restaurants and riverfront esplanades to the fast-food court in the adjoining Vasco da Gama shopping centre.

Afternoon

A short metro ride and walk from Parque das Nações is the Quinta Pedagógica dos Olivais (Rua Cidade Lobito, Olivais Sul), a small city farm located in the middle of an urban residential area. It aims to educate children about traditional rural activities and crafts in Portugal. The main draw is, of course, the animals, which include the usual hens, geese, goats, donkeys, horses and cows. The Quinta is open on weekends until 5:30pm (to 7pm from May–September). Organized activities have to be booked in advance.

Modern art and architecture at Parque das Nações

Putting Lisbon on the Map

Lisbon, the capital of Portugal, is situated on the
Atlantic coast, in the southwest of the country.
It is approximately 300 km (180 miles) from the
Algarve in the south and around 400 km (250 miles)
from the Minho in the north. The political, economic
and cultural centre of Portugal, the city lies on the
steep hills on the north bank of the Tagus. The
greater Lisbon area occupies around 1,000 sq km
(300 sq miles) and has a population of 3.3 million.
The city has become increasingly popular as a holiday
destination and its proximity to the coast makes it an
ideal choice for both sightseeing and sunbathing.

Aerial view of Lisbon, showing the Tagus river

0 kilometres   100

0 miles   50

KEY

✈ Airport

⚓ Port

═ Motorway

▬ Major road

═ Minor road

— Main railway line

-·- National boundary

ATLANTIC

OCEAN

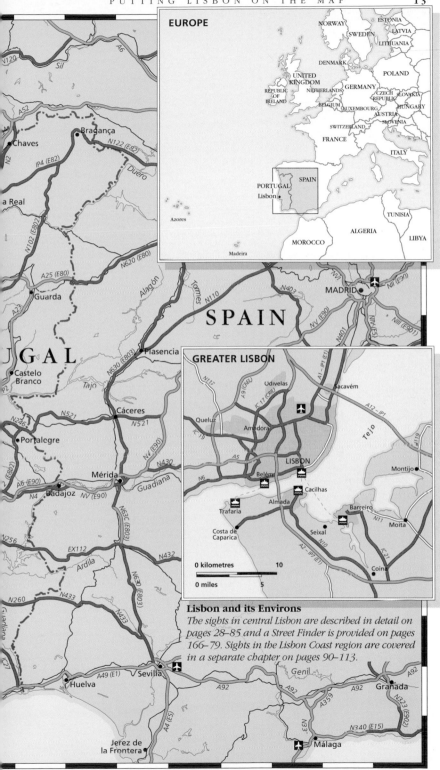

EUROPE

NORWAY
SWEDEN
ESTONIA
LATVIA
LITHUANIA
DENMARK
UNITED
KINGDOM
POLAND
REPUBLIC
OF
IRELAND
NETHERLANDS
GERMANY
CZECH
REPUBLIC
SLOVAKIA
BELGIUM
LUXEMBOURG
AUSTRIA
HUNGARY
SWITZERLAND
SLOVENIA
FRANCE
ITALY
PORTUGAL
SPAIN
Lisbon
Azores
TUNISIA
ALGERIA
LIBYA
MOROCCO
Madeira

SPAIN

MADRID

GREATER LISBON

Udivelas
Sacavém
Queluz
Amadora
LISBON
Belém
Tejo
Montijo
Cacilhas
Trafaria
Almada
Barreiro
Moita
Costa de
Caparica
Seixal
Coina

0 kilometres   10

0 miles   5

Lisbon and its Environs

*The sights in central Lisbon are described in detail on
pages 28–85 and a Street Finder is provided on pages
166–79. Sights in the Lisbon Coast region are covered
in a separate chapter on pages 90–113.*

Rolloguo deregido ao serenissimo i muito pode-
roso primçipe elrey dom manuell nosso senor sobre
ae vidas i excellentes feitos dos Reis de portugall
seus amteçessores, hordenados i escriptos per seu
mamdado per duarte galluam fidalguo de sua
casa do seu cosselho noquall falla do gramde louuor da presemte materia que he o propio i broadei-
ro louuor desse mesmos Reyes de portugall:

Mito deuem serenissimo senor trabalhar os homees por
emsua uida obrarem uistudes por que mereçã a deus no ou-
tro mundo i neste leirem de seu tempo memoria. Nam soo
mente que uiuerã o que as animallias tem per Iguall
com nosco. Mas que bem i louuadamete biuam que he propio do
homem O quall teemdo aiuda em dias breue com uistude a faz

THE HISTORY OF LISBON

*O*ver the centuries, Lisbon has both flourished and suffered. The city is most famous for its history of maritime successes, in particular the voyages of Vasco da Gama who first navigated a sea route to India. In recent years the city has flourished again, and it is now a major European centre of commerce.

According to myth, the Greek hero Odysseus (also known as Ulysses) founded Lisbon on his journey home from Troy. The Phoenicians are known to have established a trading post on the site in around 1200 BC. From 205 BC the town was in Roman hands, reaching the height of its importance when Julius Caesar became the governor in 60 BC.

St Vincent

With the collapse of the Roman Empire, barbarian tribes invaded from northern Europe. The Alans, who conquered the city in around AD 409, were superseded by the Suevi who in turn were driven out by the Visigoths. None of these tribes were primarily town-dwellers and Lisbon began to decline. In 711 North African Muslim invaders, the Moors, overran the peninsula and occupied the city for some 450 years. Lisbon was an important trading centre under the Moors and their legacy is evident today in the Castelo de São Jorge and the streets of the Alfama district.

The first king of Portugal, Afonso Henriques, finally ousted the Moors from Lisbon in 1147. Among those who helped was the English Crusader Gilbert of Hastings, who became Lisbon's first bishop. A new cathedral was built below the castle and, shortly afterwards, the remains of St Vincent, the patron saint of Portugal, were brought there. Lisbon received its charter early in the 13th century, but it was not until 1256, under Afonso III, that it became the capital.

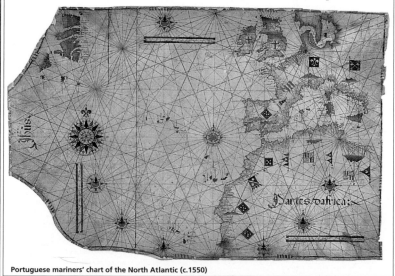

Portuguese mariners' chart of the North Atlantic (c.1550)

◁ Illuminated page from the *Chronica de Dom Afonso Henriques,* showing Lisbon in the 16th century

THE REIGN OF KING DINIS

Under King Dinis, the son of Afonso III, the court at Lisbon became a centre of culture and in 1290 the University of Lisbon was founded. Dinis extended the city away from the castle, developing the Baixa, and Lisbon flourished as trade with Europe grew.

In the 14th century, the city continued to expand westwards along the river, despite the ruin caused by the Black Death, which spread throughout Portugal from Lisbon. In 1373, after Lisbon was sacked by Enrique II of Castile, Fernando I built a new line of fortifications to protect his 40,000 citizens and to redefine the boundaries of the growing city. When Fernando died without an heir, the throne was claimed by his illegitimate half brother, João of Avis, who defeated Juan of Castile, in 1385 at the famous Battle of Ajubarrota.

Statue of Manuel I and St Jerome on the Mosteiro dos Jerónimos

Musicians at the court of King Dinis

THE DISCOVERIES

Periodic outbreaks of plague continued to destabilize the economy and led to riots in Lisbon over grain shortages. Prosperity returned during the Age of Discovery *(see pp20–21)* when Vasco da Gama, setting out from Belém in 1497, successfully navigated a sea route to India. The resulting wealth from the spice trade made Lisbon the mercantile centre of Europe. In gratitude for this new-found prosperity, Manuel I ordered the building of the Torre de Belém *(see p70)* and the magnificent Mosteiro dos Jerónimos in Belém *(see pp66–7)*; their ornate late-Gothic style, known as Manueline after the king,

reflects the Discoveries in the exotic and nautical nature of the detailed sculpture on the two monuments.

The 16th century saw major developments: a new square, the Terreiro do Paço (now the Praça do Comércio), was built on the waterfront, and a new district, the Bairro Alto, sprang up to house the many merchants drawn to Lisbon. The Inquisition, a Catholic movement which persecuted heretics and non-believers, began a reign of terror. Mass trials and executions of those that were condemned took place regularly in the Terreiro do Paço.

SPANISH CONTROL

The young King Sebastião I was killed at the battle of Alcácer-Quibir in a doomed attempt to invade Morocco in 1578. The lack of an heir led to conquest by Spain in 1580. Ignoring his advisers, Philip II of Spain refused to make Lisbon the capital of his extended kingdom and left the government of Portugal to a viceroy. The Spanish were ousted in 1640 and the Duke of Bragança crowned João IV.

With the discovery of Brazilian gold in 1697, Lisbon enjoyed a new wave of prosperity. From 1706, João V began an ambitious building programme in the city. The most valuable addition to Lisbon at this time was the Águas Livres aqueduct *(see p84)*,

The battle of Alcácer-Quibir in Morocco, where 8,000 men were killed and 15,000 captured

which was carrying water across the Alcântara valley just a few years before the devastating earthquake struck the city in 1755 *(see pp22–3)*.

POMBAL'S VISION

Responsibility for rebuilding the ruined city fell to José I's chief minister, the Marquês de Pombal. Engineers drew up a plan that realigned Lisbon on a north–south axis and created a grid of streets with the Baixa at its heart. Pombal's vision was not continued by his successors; when the royal family fled to Brazil in 1807, ahead of Napoleon's invading army, Rio de Janeiro temporarily became the capital of the Portuguese empire, and Lisbon began to decline.

The Águas Livres aqueduct, completed in the 19th century

A suspension bridge across the Tagus was completed in 1966. Initially called the Ponte Salazar, it was later renamed Ponte 25 de Abril in commemoration of the peaceful Carnation Revolution in 1974 which finally ended the totalitarian regime instituted by Salazar.

MODERN LISBON

The years following the Revolution were a period of both euphoria and political chaos. Then, in 1986, Portugal joined the European Community and foreign companies began to set up in Lisbon. Under the leadership of the Social Democratic prime minister, Aníbal Cavaco Silva, Lisbon's economy recovered. Even the disastrous fire which swept through the Chiado district in 1988 failed to dampen the general optimism. To mastermind the rebuilding of this historic district, the city appointed Portugal's most prestigious architect, Álvaro Siza Vieira. Since then, Lisbon has enjoyed much prestige, and was voted European City of Culture in 1994. In 1998 the city hosted a World Exposition on the theme of the Oceans, in celebration of its maritime history. Today, Lisbon is a cosmopolitan city where the influence of its previous African and South American colonies is still widely evident.

The Marquês de Pombal pointing to the new Lisbon

REGENERATION

In the second half of the 19th century a period of economic revival and industrialization commenced. Railways and new roads were built, trams were introduced, modern drains and sewers were constructed and work began on the embankment of the Tagus. In 1908 the king was assassinated, and two years later the monarchy was overturned. Under António Salazar's lengthy dictatorship (1926–68), Lisbon's modernization continued at the expense of the rest of the country.

Soldiers in the Carnation Revolution of 1974 which ended the dictatorship

The Rulers of Portugal

Afonso Henriques declared himself Portugal's first king in 1139, but his descendants' ties of marriage to various Spanish kingdoms led to dynastic disputes. João I's defeat of the Castilians in 1385 established the House of Avis which presided over the golden age of Portuguese imperialism. Then in 1580, in the absence of a direct heir, Portugal was ruled by Spanish kings for 60 years before the Duke of Bragança became João IV. A Republican uprising ended the monarchy in 1910. However, in the first 16 years of the Republic there were 40 different governments, and in 1926 Portugal became a dictatorship under the eventual leadership of Salazar. Democracy was restored by the Carnation Revolution of 1974.

1557–78 Sebastião

1521–57 João III

1481–95 João II

1211–23 Afonso II

1185–1211 Sancho I

1248–79 Afonso III

1279–1325 Dinis

1100	1200	1300	1400	1500	
HOUSE OF BURGUNDY			AVIS		H
1100	1200	1300	1400	1500	

1325–57 Afonso IV

1357–67 Pedro I

1367–83 Fernando I

1223–48 Sancho II

1438–81 Afonso V

1139–85 Afonso Henriques (Afonso I)

1433–8 Duarte

1578–80 Henrique

1580–98 Felipe I (Philip II of Spain)

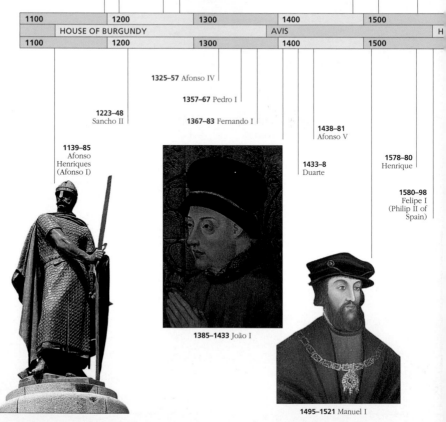

1385–1433 João I

1495–1521 Manuel I

1828–53 Maria II

2002–4
José Manuel
Durão Barroso
(prime minister)

1750–77 José I

1621–40 Felipe III
(Philip IV of Spain)

1640–56 João IV

1656–83 Afonso VI

1683–1706
Pedro II (regent
from 1668)

1816–26
João VI
(regent from
1792)

1853–61
Pedro V

1861–89
Luís I

1932–68
António Salazar
(prime minister)

**1976–8 &
1983–5**
Mário
Soares
(prime
minister)

2005–2011
José Sócrates
Carvalho Pinto
de Sousa (prime
minister)

1700	1800	1900	2000

BRAGANÇA | | REPUBLIC

1700	1800	1900	2000

1598–1621 Felipe II
(Philip III of Spain)

1777–1816
Maria I and Pedro III

1985–95 Aníbal
Cavaco Silva
(prime minister)

2011–
Pedro Manuel
Mamede Passos
Coelho (prime
minister)

2006–
Aníbal Cavaco
Silva (president)

2004–5
Pedro Miguel de
Santana Lopes
(prime minister)

1995–2001
António Guterres
(prime minister)

1908–10
Manuel II

1826–8 Pedro IV

1706–50 João V

1889–1908 Carlos I

The Age of Discovery

Portugal's astonishing period of conquest and exploration began in 1415 with the capture of the North African city of Ceuta. Maritime expeditions into the Atlantic and along the West African coast followed, motivated by conflict between Christianity and Islam and the desire for commercial gain. Great riches were earned from the gold and slaves taken from the Guinea coast in 1415, but the real breakthrough for Portuguese imperialism occurred in

Portuguese padrão

1498 when Vasco da Gama *(see p68)* reached India. Portugal soon controlled the Indian Ocean and the spice trade, and established an eastern capital at Goa. With Pedro Álvares Cabral's "discovery" of Brazil, Portugal became a mercantile super-power rivalled only by her neighbour Spain.

Armillary Sphere
This celestial globe with the earth in its centre was used by navigators for measuring the positions of the stars. It became the personal emblem of Manuel I.

Magellan (c.1480–1521)
With Spanish funding, Portuguese sailor Fernão de Magalhães, known as Magellan, led the first circumnavigation of the globe (1519–22). He was killed in the Philippines before the voyage's end.

1500–1501 Gaspar Corte Real reaches Newfoundland.

1427 Diogo de Silves discovers the Azores.

1434 Gil Eanes rounds Cape Bojador (Western Sahara).

1460 Diogo Gomes discovers the Cape Verde archipelago.

1470s Discovery of island of São Tomé.

1500 Pedro Álvares Cabral reaches Brazil.

1482 Diogo Cão reaches the mouth of the Congo.

1485 On his third voyage Diogo Cão reaches Cape Cross (Namibia).

1488 Bartolomeu Dias rounds Cape of Good Hope.

The Adoration of the Magi
Painted for Viseu Cathedral shortly after Cabral returned from Brazil in 1500, this panel is attributed to the artist Grão Vasco (c.1475–1540). King Baltazar is depicted as a Tupi Indian.

African Ivory Salt Cellar
This 16th-century ivory carving shows Portuguese warriors supporting a globe and a ship. A sailor peers out from the crow's nest at the top.

Japanese Screen (c.1600)
This screen shows traders unloading a nau, *or great ship. Between 1575 and their expulsion in 1638, the Portuguese monopolized the carrying trade between China and Japan.*

HENRY THE NAVIGATOR

Although he did not sail himself, Henry (1394–1460), the third son of João I, laid the foundations for Portugal's maritime expansion that were later built upon by João II and consolidated by Manuel I. As Master of the wealthy Order of Christ and Governor of the Algarve, Henry was able to finance expeditions along the African coast. By the time he died he had a monopoly on all trade south of Cape Bojador. Legend tells that he founded a school of navigation in the Algarve, at either Sagres or Lagos.

KEY

‒ ‒ ‒ Discoverers' route

1543 Portuguese arrive in Japan.

1513 Trading posts set up in China at Macau and Canton.

1510 Capture of Goa.

1498 Vasco da Gama reaches Calicut in India.

1518 Fortress built in Colombo (Sri Lanka).

1512 Portuguese reach Ternate in the Moluccas (Spice Islands).

Cloves

Pepper

Nutmeg

Cinnamon

The Spice Trade
Exotic spices were a great source of wealth for Portugal. The much-disputed Moluccas, or Spice Islands, were purchased from Spain in 1528.

PORTUGUESE DISCOVERIES

The systematic attempt to find a sea route to India, which led to a monopoly of the spice trade, began in 1482 with the first voyage of Diogo Cão, who planted a *padrão* (stone cross) on the shores where he landed.

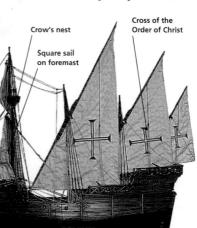

Crow's nest

Square sail on foremast

Cross of the Order of Christ

Lateen-rigged Caravel
These ships with three triangular sails were favoured by the first Portuguese explorers who sailed close to the African coast. For later journeys across the open ocean, square sails were found more effective.

The 1755 Lisbon Earthquake

Votive tile panel offered by survivors

The first tremor of the devastating earthquake was felt at 9:30am on 1 November. A few minutes later there was a second, far more violent shock, reducing over half the city to rubble. Although the epicentre was close to the Algarve, Lisbon, as the most populated area, bore the worst. Over 20 churches collapsed, crushing the crowds who had assembled for All Saints' Day. A third shock was followed by fires which quickly spread. An hour later, huge waves came rolling in from the Tagus and flooded the lower part of the city. Most of Portugal suffered damage and the shock was felt as far away as Italy. Perhaps 15,000 people lost their lives in Lisbon alone.

This anonymous painting *of the arrival of a papal ambassador at court in 1693 shows how Terreiro do Paço looked before the earthquake.*

Some buildings that might have survived an earthquake alone were destroyed by the fire that followed.

The old royal palace, the 16th-century Paço da Ribeira, was utterly ruined by the earthquake and ensuing flood.

The royal family *was staying at the palace in Belém, a place far less affected than Lisbon, and survived the disaster unscathed. Here the king surveys the city's devastation.*

Ships crammed full of people fleeing the fire were wrecked and anchors thrown up to water level.

This detail is *from a votive painting dedicated to Nossa Senhora da Estrela, given by a grateful father in thanks for the sparing of his daughter's life in the earthquake. The girl was found miraculously alive after being buried under rubble for seven hours.*

THE RECONSTRUCTION OF LISBON

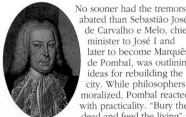

Marquês de Pombal (1699–1782)

No sooner had the tremors abated than Sebastião José de Carvalho e Melo, chief minister to José I and later to become Marquês de Pombal, was outlining ideas for rebuilding the city. While philosophers moralized, Pombal reacted with practicality. "Bury the dead and feed the living" is said to have been his initial response. He then began a progressive town-planning scheme. His efficient handling of the crisis won him almost total political control.

REACTIONS TO THE DISASTER

French author, Voltaire

The earthquake had a profound effect on European thought. Eyewitness accounts appeared in the papers, many written by foreigners living in Lisbon. A heated debate developed over whether the earthquake was a natural phenomenon or divine wrath. Pre-earthquake Lisbon had been a flourishing city, famed for its wealth – also for its Inquisition and idolatry. Interpreting the quake as punishment, preachers prophesied further catastrophes. Famous literary figures debated the significance of the event, among them the French writer Voltaire, who wrote a poem about the disaster, propounding his views that evil exists and man is weak and powerless, doomed to an unhappy fate on earth.

The ancient castle walls succumbed to the reverberating shock waves.

Flames erupted as the candles lit for All Saints' Day ignited the city's churches. The fire raged for seven days.

Some of Lisbon's finest buildings were destroyed, along with gold, jewellery, priceless furniture, archives, books and paintings.

At 11am, tidal waves rolled into Terreiro do Paço. The Alcântara docks, to the west, bore the brunt of the impact.

Churches, homes *and public buildings all suffered in the disaster. The Royal Opera House, here shown in ruins, was only completed in March the same year.*

A CONTEMPORARY VIEW OF THE EARTHQUAKE

This anonymous German engraving of 1775 gives a vivid picture of the scale of the disaster. Many who fled the flames made for the Tagus, but were washed away in the huge waves which struck the Terreiro do Paço. The human and material losses were incalculable.

The reconstruction *of the centre of Lisbon took place rapidly. By the end of November the Marquês de Pombal had devised a strikingly modern scheme for a grid of parallel streets running from the waterfront to Rossio. The new buildings are shown in yellow.*

Modern-day Lisbon *holds many reminders of the earthquake. Pombal's innovative grid system is clearly visible in this aerial view of the Baixa (see pp40–47). The scheme took many years to complete, and the triumphal arch that spans Rua Augusta was not finished until over a century later, in 1873.*

LISBON THROUGH THE YEAR

While the summer months are the most popular for visiting Lisbon and have many events on the calendar – the Festas dos Santos Populares, in June, are one of the highlights of the year – spring and autumn can also be rewarding if you want to tour the Lisbon Coast. In late winter, the colourful Carnaval celebrations attract many visitors to Lisbon. Other events during the year include music festivals, sporting fixtures and the many religious *festas*, which are great times of celebration for the Portuguese people.

SPRING

With the arrival of springtime in Lisbon, the café and restaurant terraces begin to fill with people. Many events, such as concerts, start to take place in the open air again as the weather improves. At the weekends the coastal resorts of Cascais and Estoril become livelier when on warm, bright days local people take day trips there to enjoy the seaside.

João Moura, one of Portugal's top bullfighters (cavaleiros)

MARCH

Moda Lisboa *(mid-Mar)*. The first of two annual editions of Portugal's main fashion show *(see p26)*.
World Poetry Day *(3rd Sat)*. Several literary events are held at the Centro Cultural de Belém, including debates, poetry workshops and music performances. Poets from all over the world present their latest works, and members of the public are encouraged to read their favourite poems.
Procissão dos Terceiros Franciscanos *(4th Sun before Easter)*. This colourful procession through the streets of Mafra *(see p96)* starts at the convent. The ceremonial robes worn in the procession were given to the church by João V, in the 18th century.
Lisbon's Half Marathon *(Mar or Apr – date varies)*. One of the city's most popular sporting events, the race draws international runners.

APRIL

Festa dos Merendeiros *(Apr – Sun after Easter)*. This traditional festival and procession takes place in Santo Isidoro, near Mafra *(see p96)*. There is a ceremony to bless the bread and the fields in the hope of a successful harvest later on in the year.

Formal military parades are held in Lisbon in celebration of Liberty Day

Liberty Day *(25 Apr)*. A public holiday throughout Portugal, the annual celebration of the Carnation Revolution that ended 48 years of dictatorship in 1974 *(see p17)* is also known as the Dia da Revoluçaõ. Commemorations include a military parade and political speeches at the Praça do Império. The unions organize festivities that take place all over the city.
Estoril Open Tennis Championship *(Apr/May)*. International players compete in Portugal's top tennis competition, which is held at the Jamor Tennis Courts.
Feira do Livro *(Apr–Jun – date varies)*. One of the main literary events in Lisbon, this book fair offers numerous bargains, such as second-hand books and signed copies. The event takes place at the Parque Eduardo VII, the city's largest park *(see p75)*.
Beginning of the bull-fighting season *(Apr–Sep)*. The Campo Pequeno bullring in Lisbon is the usual venue for this traditional entertainment. Bullfights may also be seen in Montijo.

MAY

Dia do Trabalhador *(1 May)*. Among the events organized by the unions on Labour Day are marches and political speeches throughout Lisbon.
Festival Estoril Jazz *(11–20 May)*. A series of jazz concerts in and around Lisbon.
Exhibition of Horse Riding at the Palácio de Queluz *(May–Oct)*. Every Wednesday at 11am riders from the Portuguese Equestrian School put on displays of their skills in the gardens of the Palácio de Queluz *(see pp108–9)*.

AVERAGE DAILY HOURS OF SUNSHINE

Hours

Jan Feb Mar Apr May Jun Jul Aug Sep Oct Nov Dec

Sunshine Chart
Although Lisbon enjoys a moderate amount of sunshine all year, the days are particularly hot and sunny in the summer months. Care should be taken to protect the skin against the sun, both when walking around Lisbon itself and when sunbathing along the coast on the beaches of Estoril or Cascais.

SUMMER

The summer months are a major holiday time in Lisbon, especially August when many Lisboetas retire to the coastal resorts, in particular Costa da Caparica and Cascais.

JUNE

Festas da Cidade *(throughout Jun).* A celebration of the city of Lisbon itself, which includes a variety of events from rock concerts to drive-in films. A major highlight is the lively parade along Lisbon's Avenida da Liberdade on the evening of 12 June, which is followed by a party. The festa is in addition to the three saints' festivals listed below.
Santo António *(12–13 Jun).*
São João *(23–24 Jun).*
São Pedro *(28–29 Jun).* Santo António is the major festival in Lisbon, marking the beginning of the Festas dos Santos Populares (Feasts of the

Celebrating Santo António, one of Lisbon's most important festivals

The beach at Estoril, just one of the many popular bays along the Lisbon Coast

People's Saints). Locals decorate the Alfama and bring out chairs for the hundreds who come to enjoy the celebrations. The festivities continue throughout June with the *festas* of São João and São Pedro.
Arraial Gay e Lésbico *(mid-to late Jun – date varies).* Events and celebrations are held in one of Lisbon's parks or squares.
Feira Grande de São Pedro *(29 Jun).* A market of crafts, antiques and local delicacies, in Sintra *(see pp100–3).*
Sintra Festival *(Jun–Jul).* A series of classical music concerts held in the parks and palaces of Sintra and Queluz *(see pp100–3).*
FIA-Lisbon International Handicraft Exhibition *(Jun–Jul).* This huge display of arts and crafts is held in the Parque de Nações.

JULY

Noites de Bailado em Seteais *(Jul).* Part of the Sintra Festival, these ballet performances are held in the gardens of the Tivoli Palácio de Seteais *(see p117).*
Feira de Artesanato *(Jul–early Sep).* This craft fair is held in

Estoril *(see p106),* and features both folk music and dance performances.
Feira dos Alhos *(3rd Sun in Jul).* Annual market of crafts, delicacies and wine- and cheese-tasting, near the Convent of Mafra *(see p96).*
Capuchos Summer Concerts *(Jul–Aug).* A series of musical events throughout the summer months, centred on the Capuchos Monastery on the south side of the Tagus.
BaixAnima *(Jul–Sep).* Street performances, music, dance and circus acts take place at weekends in the squares and streets of Baixa and Chiado.
Verão Em Sesimbra *(Jul–Sep).* Popular entertainment festival held in the town of Sesimbra *(see p110).*

AUGUST

Jazz em Agosto *(early Aug).* Jazz music is performed in the gardens of the Calouste Gulbenkian Cultural Centre.
Festival dos Oceanos *(first two weeks of Aug).* This festival comprises street entertainment, exhibitions, live *fado,* late-night museum openings and concerts in the city's main riverside square (Praça do Comércio).
Romaria de São Mamede *(14–22 Aug).* Farmers lead their animals around the chapel of Janas, north of Colares *(see p97),* to be blessed. The tradition originates in the fact that the site of the church was once that of a Roman temple dedicated to the goddess Diana.

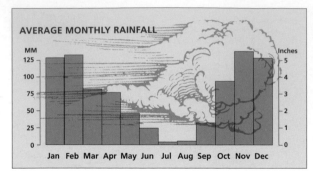

AVERAGE MONTHLY RAINFALL

Rainfall Chart
Rainfall is fairly heavy in the winter months in Lisbon, and then drops steadily until the height of summer, when there is almost no rain at all. The autumn, although still warm, can produce some wet days, the wettest month on average being November.

AUTUMN

In many ways, this is the best season for touring and sightseeing. The strong heat of the summer has passed but the weather is still pleasantly warm. The countryside around Sintra is particularly beautiful with the changing colours of the trees.

SEPTEMBER

Avante! *(1st weekend in Sep).* This lively *festa* in Seixal, south of the Tagus, attracts large crowds. It includes rock and folk music, exhibitions and cultural events and an array of delicious food.
Nossa Senhora da Luz *(2nd weekend of Sep).* A religious *festa* held in honour of Our Lady of the Light in Sampaio, near Sesimbra *(see p110).*
Festa das Vindimas *(early Sep).* At the foot of Palmela's medieval castle *(see p110),* the first grape harvest is blessed, amid traditional entertainment, wine- and cheese-tasting and fireworks.

Nossa Senhora do Cabo Espichel *(last Sun of Sep).* This event is held by local fishermen to honour the Virgin Mary with a procession up to the church at Cabo Espichel *(see p107).*
Feira da Luz *(throughout Sep).* This lively market focuses on arts and crafts, especially pottery and ceramics. It takes place in the Carnide district of Lisbon.
Festa de Senhora da Consolação *(throughout Sep).* This festival, which is held in the Assafora area of Sintra *(see p101–5),* celebrates Portugal's patron saint with a month of street parties, music, food and colourful events.

OCTOBER

Moda Lisboa *(Oct).* This biannual fashion show attracts important designers from all over the world and is Portugal's main fashion event.

Some catwalk shows take place at the Páteo da Galé, in Praça do Comércio. The autumn/winter collections are shown in March *(see p24).*
Republic Day *(5 Oct).* The revolution that brought the monarchy to an end in 1910 *(see p17),* is commemorated annually in Lisbon with military parades.

An old lady laying flowers at a cemetery in Lisbon in honour of All Saints' Day

NOVEMBER

All Saints' Day *(1 Nov).* An important festival in the Portuguese religious calendar, many families light candles and lay flowers in local cemeteries throughout the area, in honour of their dead relatives.
Feira de Todos os Santos *(1 Nov).* Also known as the Dried Fruits' Market, this is a lively fair held in Azureira, near Mafra *(see p96).*
Dia do Magusto e de São Martinho *(11 Nov).* The celebration of Roast Chestnut Day is based on the tradition of preparing for winter.
Circus *(late Nov–early Jan).* Before Christmas, circuses arrive in Lisbon. Check venues and dates with tourist offices.
Lisbon Marathon *(Nov/Dec).* Festive celebrations in the city as the runners compete.

Blessing the grape harvest at the Festa das Vindimas in Palmela

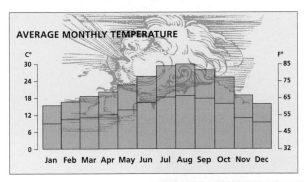

AVERAGE MONTHLY TEMPERATURE

Jan Feb Mar Apr May Jun Jul Aug Sep Oct Nov Dec

Temperature Chart
Lisbon is rarely very cold, and maintains a pleasantly mild climate, even during the winter months, making it a good city to visit in any season. However, the summer months bring days of consistent heat, and although the city is quiet in high summer, it can become humid and stifling.

WINTER

Those seeking mild, sunny climes and an escape from the winter cold, will find this a good time of year to visit Lisbon. The nightlife is very lively and continues until the early hours, especially at weekends. Christmas is a time of great celebration and an important occasion for families to reunite and enjoy long meals together.

Colourful parades during the annual Carnaval celebrations in Lisbon

DECEMBER

Festa de Imaculada Conceição *(8 Dec)*. This festival of the Immaculate Conception is a national holiday throughout Portugal. There are special church services and Lisbon's population celebrate with their usual festive spirit.
Christmas *(24–25 Dec)*. Throughout the Lisbon area, churches and shops display nativity scenes and cribs. The main celebrations take place on Christmas Eve, when families get together and go to midnight mass. They then return home for a large traditional meal of *bacalhau* (salted dried cod) and *sonhos* (small fried cakes similar to doughnuts, usually flavoured with pumpkin or orange).
Nossa Senhora da Conceição *(26 Dec)*. A traditional religious procession held in honour of Our Lady of the Immaculate Conception, the saint protector of Alfarim, near Sesimbra *(see p110)*.

The celebratory cake, *bolo rei*

JANUARY

New Year *(31 Dec–1 Jan)*. In Lisbon, a spectacular firework display is held in Praça do Comércio to welcome the New Year.
Epiphany *(6 Jan)*. The traditional cake baked for the Epiphany is *bolo rei* (king's cake), a small fruit cake made with a lucky charm and a bean inside. Crown-shaped, it is topped with crystallized fruit, resembling gems. The person who gets the bean must then buy the next cake. *Bolo rei* is also made at Christmas time.
Opera season *(Jan–Nov)*. The opera season starts at the Teatro Nacional de São Carlos *(see p53)*.

FEBRUARY

Carnaval *(date varies)*. This is celebrated throughout Portugal with spectacular costumes and floats; there is an especially colourful parade in Sesimbra *(see p110)*.

Procissão do Senhor dos Passos da Graça *(second Sun in Lent)*. The figure of Christ *(Senhor dos Passos)* is taken out of the Igreja da Graça *(see p37)* and carried through the streets of Graça, in Lisbon. The procession dates back to the 16th century.

PUBLIC HOLIDAYS

New Year's Day (1 Jan)
Carnaval (Feb)
Good Friday (Mar or Apr)
Dia 25 de Abril, *commemorating 1974 revolution* (25 Apr)
Dia do Trabalhador, *Labour Day* (1 May)
Corpus Christi (date varies)
Camões Day (10 Jun)
Santo António (13 Jun)
Assumption Day (15 Aug)
Republic Day (5 Oct)
All Saints' Day (1 Nov)
Dia da Restauração, *commemorating Independence from Spain, 1640* (1 Dec)
Immaculate Conception (8 Dec)
Christmas Day (25 Dec)

LISBON AREA BY AREA

ALFAMA

It is difficult to believe that this humble neighbourhood was once the most desirable quarter of Lisbon. For the Moors, the tightly packed alleyways around the fortified castle comprised the whole city. The seeds of decline were sown in the Middle Ages when wealthy residents moved west for fear of earthquakes, leaving the quarter to fishermen and paupers. The buildings survived the 1755 earthquake *(see pp22–3)* and, although there are no Moorish houses still standing, the quarter retains its kasbah-like layout. Compact houses line steep streets and stairways, their façades strung with washing.

Portugal's coat of arms in the treasury of the Sé

Long overdue restoration is under way in the most dilapidated areas, but daily life still revolves around local grocery stores and small, cellar-like tavernas.

Above the Alfama, the imposing Castelo de São Jorge crowns Lisbon's eastern hill. This natural vantage point, a defensive stronghold and royal palace until the 16th century, is today a popular promenade, with spectacular views from its reconstructed ramparts.

West of the Alfama stand the proud twin towers of the Sé. To the northeast, the domed church of Santa Engrácia and the white façade of São Vicente de Fora dominate the skyline.

SIGHTS AT A GLANCE

Museums and Galleries
Museu de Artes Decorativas ❷
Museu Militar ❻

Historic Buildings
Casa dos Bicos ❼
Castelo de São Jorge pp38–9 ❿

Churches
Santa Engrácia ❺

Santo António à Sé ❾
São Vicente de Fora ❸
Sé ❽

Belvederes
Miradouro da Graça ⓫
Miradouro de Santa Luzia ❶

Markets
Feira da Ladra ❹

GETTING THERE
Trams 12 and 28 run through the Alfama from the Baixa. Bus 737 runs from the Castle to Rossio. Many buses go east along Avenida Dom Infante Henrique to Santa Apolónia (which now has a Metro station), and west to Belém.

KEY

▨	Street-by-Street: Alfama *pp32–3*
🚉	Railway station
ℹ	Tourist Information
▬	Castle walls
Ⓜ	Metro station

0 metres   250
0 yards   250

◁ **Ironwork balconies on a house in Rua dos Bacalhoeiros, beside the Casa dos Bicos**

Street-by-Street: Alfama

A fascinating quarter at any time of day, the
Alfama comes to life in the late afternoon and
early evening when the locals emerge at their
doorways and the small tavernas start to fill.
A new generation of younger residents has
resulted in a small number of trendy shops and
bars. Given the steep streets and steps of the
quarter, the least strenuous approach is to start
at the top and work your way down.
A walk around the maze of winding
alleyways will reveal picturesque
corners and crumbling churches
as well as panoramic views from
the shady terraces, such as the
Miradouro de Santa Luzia.

Largo das Portas do Sol
*Café tables look out over the Alfama
towards the Tagus estuary. Portas
do Sol was one of the entrance
gates to the old city.*

Statue of St. Vincent

Largo das Portas do Sol has its
own terrace viewpoint on a
converted rooftop on the east
side of the Santa Luzia church.

The church of Santa Luzia
has 18th-century blue and
white *azulejo* panels
on its south wall.

L. DAS PORTAS DO SOL

BECO DE SANTA HELENA

RUA N. DE ARAÚJO

DO CAST

Castelo
de São
Jorge

★ **Museu de Artes Decorativas**
*Set up as a museum by the banker
Ricardo do Espírito Santo Silva, the
17th-century Palácio Azurara houses
fine 17th- and 18th-century Portuguese furniture and decorative arts* ❷

KEY

– – –   Suggested route

0 metres	25
0 yards	25

★ **Miradouro
de Santa Luzia**
*The view from this
bougainvillea-clad
terrace spans the tiled
roofs of the Alfama
toward the Tagus.
This is a pleasant
place to rest after
a walk around the
area's steep streets* ❶

STAR SIGHTS

★ Miradouro de
   Santa Luzia

★ Museu de Artes
   Decorativas

Beco dos Cruzes
*Like most of the alleyways
(becos) that snake their way
through the Alfama, is a steep
cobbled street. Locals often hang
washing between the tightly
packed houses.*

LOCATOR MAP
See Lisbon Street Finder map 8

Rua de São Pedro
*This street is the scene of a
lively early-morning fish
market where the varinas
sell the catch of the day.*
Peixe espada *(scabbard fish)
is one of the fish sold here.*

Largo do Chafariz de Dentro is
named after the 17th-century fountain
(chafariz) that was originally placed
within *(dentro)* rather than outside
the 14th-century walls.

The church of Nossa Senhora dos Remédios
*Rebuilt after the
1755 earthquake
(see pp22–3), the
pinnacled Manueline
portal is all that
remains of the
original building.*

São Miguel
was rebuilt after
it was damaged in
the 1755 earthquake.
It retains a few earlier
features, including a
fine ceiling of Brazilian
jacaranda wood.

Popular restaurants
*hidden in the labyrinth
of alleyways spill out
onto open-air patios.
The Lautasco (see p130),
in Beco do Azinhal,
serves excellent
Portuguese food.*

Tile panel showing pre-earthquake Praça do Comércio, Santa Luzia

Miradouro de Santa Luzia ❶

Rua do Limoeiro. **Map** 8 D4. 🚋 *28.*

The terrace by the church of Santa Luzia provides a sweeping view over the Alfama and the River Tagus. Distinctive landmarks, from left to right, are the cupola of Santa Engrácia, the church of Santo Estêvão and the two startling white towers of São Miguel. While tourists admire the views, old men play cards under the bougainvillea-clad pergola. The south wall of Santa Luzia has two modern tiled panels, one of Praça do Comércio before it was flattened by the earthquake, the other showing the Christians attacking the Castelo de São Jorge (*see pp38–9*) in 1147.

Museu de Artes Decorativas ❷

Largo das Portas do Sol 2. **Map** 8 D3. **Tel** *218 881 991 or 218 814 600.* 🚌 *37.* 🚋 *12, 28.* 🕐 *10am–5pm Wed–Mon.* ⬤ *1 Jan, Easter, 1 May, 25 Dec.* 📷 ♿ **www.fress.pt**

Also known as the Ricardo do Espírito Santo Silva Foundation, the museum was set up in 1953 to preserve the traditions and increase public awareness of the Portuguese decorative arts. The foundation was named after a banker who bought the 17th-century Palácio Azurara in 1947 to house his fine collection of

furniture, textiles, silver and ceramics. Among the 17th- and 18th-century antiques displayed in this handsome four-storey mansion are many fine pieces in exotic woods, including an 18th-century rosewood backgammon and chess table. Also of note are the collections of 18th-century silver and Chinese porcelain, and the Arraiolos carpets. The spacious rooms still retain some original ceilings and *azulejo* panels.

In the adjoining building are workshops where artisans preserve the techniques of cabinet-making, gilding, bookbinding and other traditional crafts. Temporary exhibitions, lectures and concerts are also held in the palace.

18th-century china cutlery case, Museu de Artes Decorativas

São Vicente de Fora ❸

Largo de São Vicente. **Map** 8 E3. **Tel** *218 824 400.* 🚌 *12, 34.* 🚋 *28.* 🕐 *9am–1pm, 2:30–5pm Tue–Sat, 9am–noon Sun.* **Monastery** ⬤ *10am–6pm Tue–Sun.* ⬤ *public hols.* 🚻 📷 📹 *to cloisters.*

St Vincent was proclaimed Lisbon's patron saint in 1173, when his relics were transferred from the Algarve, in southern Portugal, to a church on this site outside (*fora*) the city walls. Designed by the Italian architect Filippo Terzi, and completed in 1627, the off-white façade is sober and symmetrical, in Italian Renaissance style, with towers either side and three arches leading to the entrance hall. Statues of saints Augustine, Sebastian and Vincent can be seen over the entrance.

The adjoining former Augustinian monastery, reached via the nave, retains its 16th-century cistern and vestiges of the former cloister, but it is visited mainly for its 18th-century *azulejos*. Among the panels in the entrance hall off the first cloister there are lively, though historically inaccurate, tile scenes of Afonso Henriques attacking Lisbon and Santarém. Around the cloisters, the tiled rural scenes are surrounded by floral designs and cherubs, illustrating the fables of La Fontaine. A passageway leads behind the church to the old refectory, transformed into the Bragança Pantheon in 1885. The stone sarcophagi of almost every king and queen are here, from João IV, who died in 1656, to Manuel II, last king of Portugal. Only Maria I and Pedro IV are not buried here. A stone mourner kneels at the tomb of Carlos I and his son Luís Felipe, assassinated in Praça do Comércio in 1908.

Cloister of São Vicente de Fora, with tiled decorative panels

Feira da Ladra ❹

Campo de Santa Clara. **Map** 8 F2. ○
7:30am–1pm Tue & Sat. 🚌 *12.* 🚊 *28.*

The stalls of the so-called "Thieves' Market" have occupied this site on the edge of the Alfama for over a century, laid out under the shade of trees or canopies. As the fame of this flea market has grown, bargains are increasingly hard to find among the mass of bric-à-brac, but a few of the vendors have interesting wrought-iron work, prints and tiles as well as second-hand clothes. Evidence of Portugal's colonial past is reflected in the stalls selling African statuary, masks and jewellery. Fish, vegetables and herbs are sold in the central wrought-iron marketplace.

Bric-à-brac for sale in the Feira da Ladra

Santa Engrácia ❺

Campo de Santa Clara. **Map** 8 F2.
Tel 218 854 820. 🚌 *12.* 🚊 *28.*
○ *10am–5pm Tue–Sun.* ● *1 Jan,
25 Apr, Easter Sun, 25 Dec.* 🎟 🚶

One of Lisbon's most striking landmarks, the soaring dome of Santa Engrácia punctuates the skyline in the east of the city. The original church collapsed in a storm in 1681. The first stone of the new Baroque monument, laid in 1682, marked the beginning of a 284-year saga which led to the invention of a saying that a Santa Engrácia job was never done. The church was not completed until 1966.

The interior is paved with coloured marble and crowned by a giant cupola. As the National Pantheon, it houses cenotaphs of Portuguese heroes, such as Vasco da Gama *(see p68)* and Afonso de Albuquerque, Viceroy of India (1502–15) on the left, and on the right Henry the Navigator *(see p21)*. More contemporary tombs include that of the fadista, Amália Rodrigues *(see p145)*. A lift up to the dome offers a 360-degree panorama of the city.

Museu Militar ❻

Largo do Museu de Artilharia.
Map 8 D3. *Tel 218 842 569.*
🚌 *28, 735, 759.* 🚊 *28.*
○ *10am–5pm Tue–Fri, 10am–noon,
1–5pm Sat & Sun.* ● *public hols.*
🖥 *www.geira.pt/mmilitar*

Located on the site of a 16th-century cannon foundry and arms depot, the military museum contains an extensive collection. Visits begin in the Vasco da Gama Room with a collection of old cannons and modern murals depicting the discovery of the sea route to India. The Salas da Grande Guerra, on the first floor, display exhibits related to World War I. Other rooms focus on the evolution of weapons in Portugal, from primitive flints through spears to rifles. The large courtyard, flanked by cannons, tells the story of Portugal in tiled panels, from the Christian Reconquest to World War I. The Portuguese artillery section in the oldest part of the museum displays the wagon used to transport the triumphal arch to Rua Augusta *(see p46)*.

The multi-coloured marble interior beneath Santa Engrácia's dome

Casa dos Bicos ❼

Rua dos Bacalhoeiros.
Map 8 D4. 🚌 *28, 746, 759.*
🚊 *18, 25.* ● *to the public.*

Faced with diamond-shaped stones *(bicos)*, this house looks rather conspicuous among the other buildings in this area. It was built in 1523 for Brás de Albuquerque, illegitimate son of Afonso, Viceroy of India and conqueror of Goa and Malacca. The façade is an adaptation of a style that was popular in Europe during the 16th century. The two top storeys, ruined in the earthquake of 1755 *(see pp22–3)*, were restored in the 1980s, recreating the original from old views of Lisbon in tile panels and engravings. In the interim the building was used for salting fish (Rua dos Bacalhoeiros means "street of the cod fishermen").

The curiously faceted Casa dos Bicos, and surrounding buildings

The façade of the Sé, the city's cathedral

Sé **8**

Largo da Sé. **Map** 8 D4. **Tel** *218 866 752.* 737. 12, 28. 9am–7pm daily; cloister: 10am–6pm daily. to Gothic cloister & treasury.

In 1150, three years after Afonso Henriques recaptured Lisbon from the Moors, he built a cathedral for the first bishop of Lisbon, the English crusader Gilbert of Hastings, on the site of the old mosque. Sé is short for Sedes Episcopalis, the seat (or see) of a bishop. Devasted by three earth tremors in the 14th century as well as the earthquake of 1755 and renovated over the centuries, the cathedral you see today blends a variety of architectural styles. The façade, with twin castellated belltowers and a splendid rose window, retains its solid Romanesque aspect. The gloomy interior, for the most part, is simple and austere, and hardly anything remains of the embellishment lavished upon it by King João V in the first half of the 18th century. Beyond the Romanesque nave, the ambulatory has nine Gothic chapels. The Capela de Santo Ildefonso contains the 14th-century sarcophagi of Lopo Fernandes Pacheco, companion in arms to King Afonso IV and his wife, Maria Vilalobos. The bearded figure of the nobleman, who is holding a sword in his hand,

Detail of the Baroque nativity scene by Joaquim Machado de Castro

and his wife, clutching a prayer book, are carved onto the tombs with their dogs sitting faithfully at their feet. In the adjacent chancel are the tombs of Afonso IV and his wife Dona Beatriz.

The Gothic **cloister**, reached via the third chapel in the ambulatory, has elegant double arches with some finely carved capitals. One of the chapels is still fitted with its 13th-century wrought-iron gate. Archaeological excavations in the cloister have unearthed various Roman and other remains.

To the left of the cathedral entrance the Franciscan chapel contains the font where the saint was baptized in 1195 and is decorated with a charming tiled scene of St Antony preaching to the fishes. The adjacent chapel contains a Baroque

Tomb of the 14th-century nobleman Lopo Fernandes Pacheco in the ambulatory

nativity scene made of cork, wood and terracotta by Machado de Castro (1766).

The **treasury** is at the top of the staircase on the right. It houses silver, ecclesiastical robes, statuary, illustrated manuscripts and a few relics associated with St Vincent which were transferred to Lisbon from Cape St Vincent in southern Portugal in 1173. Legend has it that two sacred ravens kept a vigil over the boat that transported the relics. The ravens and the boat became a symbol of the city of Lisbon, still very much in use today. It is also said that the ravens' descendants used to dwell in the cloisters of the cathedral.

SANTO ANTONIO (C.1195–1231)

To the chagrin of the Lisboetas, their best-loved saint is known as St Antony of Padua. Although born and brought up in Lisbon, he spent the last months of his life in Padua, Italy.

St Antony joined the Franciscan Order in 1220, impressed by some crusading friars he had met at Coimbra where he was studying. The Franciscan friar was a learned and passionate preacher, renowned for his devotion to the poor and his ability to convert heretics. Many statues and paintings of St Antony depict him carrying the Infant Jesus on a book, while others show him preaching to the fishes, as St Francis preached to the birds.

In 1934 Pope Pius XI declared St Antony a patron saint of Portugal. On 13 June, the anniversary of his death, there are celebrations in the Alfama district and a costumed procession along Avenida da Liberdade.

Santo António à Sé ❾

Largo Santo António à Sé, 24.
Map 7 C4. *Tel* 218 869 145.
🚌 *737.* 🚋 *12, 28.* ⭕ *8am–12:30pm, 2–7pm daily.* 🏛 **Museu Antoniano** *Tel* 218 860 447.
⭕ *10am–1pm, 2–6pm Tue–Sun.* 📷

The popular little church of Santo António allegedly stands on the site of the house in which St Antony was born. The crypt, reached via the tiled sacristy on the left of the church, is all that remains of the original church destroyed by the earthquake of 1755. Work began on the new church in 1757 headed by Mateus Vicente, architect of the Basílica da Estrela *(see p55)* and was partially funded by donations collected by local children with the cry "a small coin for St Antony". Even today the floor of the tiny chapel in the crypt is strewn with escudos and the walls are scrawled with devotional messages from worshippers.

The church's façade blends the undulating curves of the Baroque style with Neo-Classical Ionic columns on either side of the main portal. Inside, on the way down to the crypt, a modern *azulejo* panel commemorates the visit of Pope John Paul II in 1982. In 1995 the church was given a facelift for the saint's eighth centenary. It is traditional for young couples to visit the church on their wedding day and leave flowers for St Antony who is believed to bring good luck to new marriages.

Next door the small **Museu Antoniano** houses artifacts relating to St Antony as well as gold and silverware which used to decorate the church. The most charming exhibit is a 17th-century tiled panel of St Antony preaching to the fishes.

The Miradouro and Igreja da Graça seen from the Castelo de São Jorge

Castelo de São Jorge ❿

See pp38–9.

Tiled panel recording Pope John Paul II's visit to Santo António à Sé

Miradouro da Graça ⓫

Map 8 D2. 🚌 *737.* 🚋 *12, 28.*

The working-class quarter of Graça developed at the end of the 19th century. Today, it is visited chiefly for the views from its *miradouro* (belvedere). The panorama of rooftops and skyscrapers is less spectacular than the view from the castle, but it is a popular spot, particularly in the early evenings when couples sit at café tables under the pines. Behind the *miradouro* stands an Augustinian monastery, founded in 1271 and rebuilt after the earthquake. Once a flourishing complex, the huge building is nowadays used as barracks but the church, the **Igreja da Graça**, can still be visited. Inside, in the right transept, is the *Senhor dos Passos*, a representation of Christ carrying the cross on the way to Calvary. This figure, clad in brilliant purple clothes, is carried on a procession through Graça on the second Sunday in Lent. The *azulejos* on the altar front, dating from the 17th century, imitate the brocaded textiles usually draped over the altar.

Castelo de São Jorge ⑩

Stone head of Martim Moniz

Following the recapture of Lisbon from the Moors in 1147, King Afonso Henriques transformed their hilltop citadel into the residence of the Portuguese kings. In 1511 Manuel I built a more lavish palace in what is now the Praça do Comércio and the castle was used variously as a theatre, prison and arms depot. After the 1755 earthquake the ramparts remained in ruins until 1938 when Salazar *(see p17)* began a complete renovation, rebuilding the "medieval" walls and adding gardens and wildfowl. The castle may not be authentic but the gardens and the narrow streets of the Santa Cruz district within the walls make a pleasant stroll and the views are the finest in Lisbon.

Torre de Ulisses has a camera obscura that projects views of Lisbon onto the inside walls of the tower.

RUA DAS COZINHAS

★ Battlements
Visitors can climb the towers and walk along the reconstructed ramparts of the castle walls.

Casa do Leão Restaurant
Part of the former royal residence can be booked for evening meals and parties.

The Museu do Castelo charts the history of the city and its inhabitants.

★ Observation Terrace
This large shaded square affords spectacular views over Lisbon and the Tagus. Local men play backgammon and cards under the trees.

KEY

– – – Suggested route

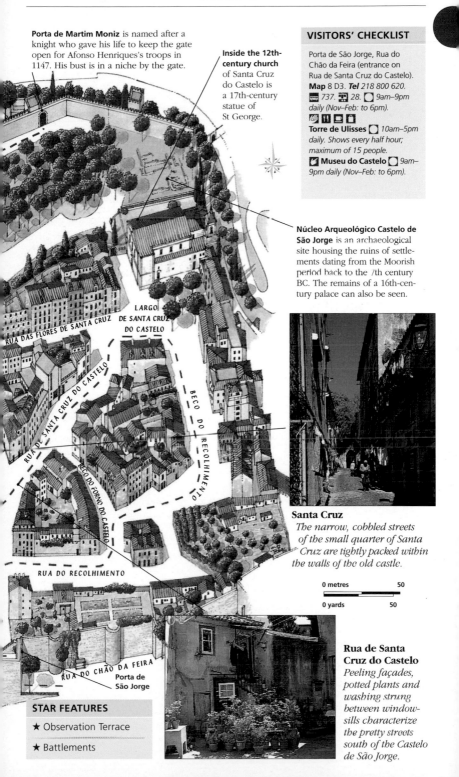

Porta de Martim Moniz is named after a knight who gave his life to keep the gate open for Afonso Henriques's troops in 1147. His bust is in a niche by the gate.

Inside the 12th-century church of Santa Cruz do Castelo is a 17th-century statue of St George.

VISITORS' CHECKLIST

Porta de São Jorge, Rua do Chão da Feira (entrance on Rua de Santa Cruz do Castelo). **Map** 8 D3. *Tel* 218 800 620. 737. 28. ☐ 9am–9pm daily (Nov–Feb: to 6pm).
Torre de Ulisses ☐ 10am–5pm daily. Shows every half hour; maximum of 15 people.
🎧 **Museu do Castelo** ☐ 9am–9pm daily (Nov–Feb: to 6pm).

Núcleo Arqueológico Castelo de São Jorge is an archaeological site housing the ruins of settlements dating from the Moorish period back to the 7th century BC. The remains of a 16th-century palace can also be seen.

LARGO DE SANTA CRUZ DO CASTELO

RUA DAS FLORES DE SANTA CRUZ

RUA DE SANTA CRUZ DO CASTELO

BECO DO RECOLHIMENTO

BECO DO FORNO DO CASTELO

RUA DO RECOLHIMENTO

RUA DO CHÃO DA FEIRA

Porta de São Jorge

Santa Cruz
The narrow, cobbled streets of the small quarter of Santa Cruz are tightly packed within the walls of the old castle.

0 metres	50
0 yards	50

Rua de Santa Cruz do Castelo
Peeling façades, potted plants and washing strung between window-sills characterize the pretty streets south of the Castelo de São Jorge.

STAR FEATURES

★ Observation Terrace

★ Battlements

BAIXA AND AVENIDA

rom the ruins of Lisbon, devastated by the earthquake of 1755 *(see pp22–3)*, the Marquês de Pombal created an entirely new centre. Using a grid layout of streets, he linked Praça do Comércio with the busy central square of Rossio. The streets were flanked by uniform, Neo-Classical buildings and named according to the shopkeepers and craftsmen who traded there. The Arco Triunfal was built 80 years later.

Detail on statue of José I in Praça do Comércio

The Baixa (lower town) is still the commercial hub of the capital, housing banks, offices and shops. At its centre, Rossio is a popular meeting point with cafés, theatres and restaurants. The geometric layout of the area has been retained, but most buildings constructed since the mid-18th century have not adhered to Pombaline formality. The streets are crowded by day, particularly the lively Rua Augusta, but after dark the quarter is almost deserted.

SIGHTS AT A GLANCE

Museums and Galleries
Museu da Sociedade de Geografia ❹

Churches
Nossa Senhora da Conceição Velha ❾

Parks and Gardens
Jardim Botânico ❶

Lifts
Elevador de Santa Justa ❼

Historic Streets and Squares
Avenida da Liberdade ❷
Praça do Comércio ❿
Praça da Figueira ❻
Praça dos Restauradores ❸
Rossio ❺
Rua Augusta ❽

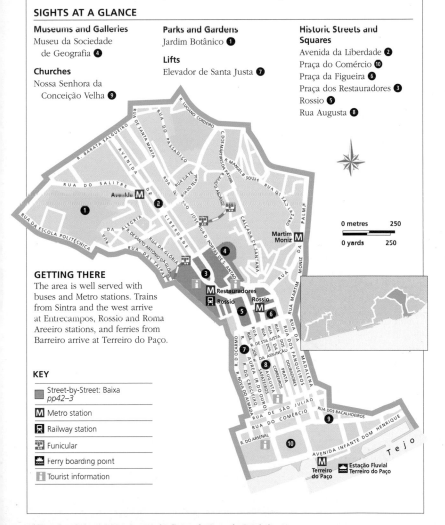

GETTING THERE

The area is well served with buses and Metro stations. Trains from Sintra and the west arrive at Entrecampos, Rossio and Roma Areeiro stations, and ferries from Barreiro arrive at Terreiro do Paço.

KEY

■	Street-by-Street: Baixa *pp42–3*
Ⓜ	Metro station
🚉	Railway station
🚡	Funicular
⛴	Ferry boarding point
ℹ	Tourist information

0 metres 250
0 yards 250

◁ **The triumphal arch in Rua Augusta leading to the Praça do Comércio**

Street-by-Street: Restauradores

This is the busiest part of the city, especially
the central squares of Rossio and Praça da
Figueira. Totally rebuilt after the
earthquake of 1755 *(see pp22–3)*,
the area was one of Europe's
first examples of town planning.
Today, the large Neo-Classical
buildings on the wide streets
and squares house business
offices. The atmosphere
and surroundings are best
absorbed from one of the
busy pavement cafés. Rua
das Portas de Santo Antão,
a pedestrianized street
where restaurants
display tanks of live
lobsters, is more
relaxing for a stroll.

**Tiled panel
on façade
of the
Tabacaria
Monaco**

Palácio Foz
*This magnificent 18th-century
palace built by the Italian
architect Francesco Fabri
now houses a tourist office.*

**The Elevador
da Glória** is
a funicular
that goes
up the hill to
the Bairro Alto
as far as the
Miradouro de São
Pedro de Alcântara
(see p54).

**Praça dos
Restauradores**
*This large tree-lined
square, named after
the men who gave their
lives during the War of
Restoration, is a busy
through road with café
terraces on the pat-
terned pavements* ❸

Restauradores

Rossio station,
*designed by
José Luís
Monteiro, is an
eye-catching
late 19th-century
Neo-Manueline
building with
two Moorish-
style horse-
shoe arches.*

KEY

− − − Suggested route

STAR SIGHT

★ Rossio

Museu da Sociedade de Geografia
This fascinating collection features items brought back from Portugal's former colonies ❹

LOCATOR MAP
See Lisbon Street Finder map 7

Rua das Portas de Santo Antão
Recalling a 15th-century gate that once stood here, this lively street is now full of excellent seafood restaurants.

PORTAS DE SANTO ANTÃO

Casa do Alentejo
This house, restored in 1919, has a tranquil interior with a Neo-Moorish patio and fountain. It is a restaurant and a meeting place for local Alentejans.

LARGO DO REGEDOR

LARGO DE SÃO DOMINGOS

PRAÇA MUN(...) CÂAMARA

Church of São Domingos

Teatro Nacional Dona Maria II
(see p45)

ROSSIO (PRAÇA DOM PEDRO IV)

Rossio

RUA 1º DE DEZEMBRO

PRAÇA DA FIGUEIRA

Café Nicola

Tabacaria Monaco

Rossio

Pastelaria Suiça

★ Rossio
This attractively paved square is a social focal point with cafés, pastelarias and the National Theatre on the north side ❺

Praça da Figueira
Designed as the city's main marketplace in Pombal's reconstruction of the area, this square is now presided over by a 20th-century statue of João I ❻

0 metres   50

0 yards   50

Bridge and pond shaded by trees in the Jardim Botânico

Jardim Botânico ❶

Rua da Escola Politécnica 58. **Map** 4 F1. *Tel* 213 921 893. 🚌 758. 🅜 *Rato*. **Gardens** ⬜ 9am–8pm daily (Oct–Mar: to 6pm). ● 1 Jan, 25 Dec. 📷 ♿ www.jb.ul.pt **Museu de História Natural** *Tel* 213 921 800. ⬜ 10am–5pm Tue–Fri, 11am–6pm Sat & Sun. 📷 **Museu de Ciência** *Tel* 213 921 808. ⬜ 10am–5pm Tue–Fri, 11am–6pm Sat & Sun. ● public hols. 📷 www.mc.ul.pt

This complex comprises two museums and four hectares (10 acres) of gardens. The botanical gardens have a distinct air of neglect. However, it is worth paying the entrance fee to wander among the exotic trees and dense paths as the gardens descend from the main entrance towards Rua da Alegria. A magnificent avenue of lofty palms connects the two levels.

The **Museu de História Natural** (Natural History Museum) charts human development across the Iberian peninsula as well as hosting temporary exhibitions on themes such as dinosaurs and local minerals. The **Museu de Ciência** (Science Museum), whose exhibits demonstrate basic scientific principles, is popular with school children.

Avenida da Liberdade ❷

Map 7 A2. 🚌 36, 702, 709 & many other routes. 🅜 *Restauradores, Avenida*.

After the earthquake of 1755 *(see pp22–3)*, the Marquês de Pombal created the Passeio Público (public promenade) in the area now occupied by the lower part of Avenida da Liberdade and Praça dos Restauradores. Despite its name, enjoyment of the park was restricted to Lisbon's high society and walls and gates ensured the exclusion of the lower classes. In 1821, when the Liberals came to power, the barriers were pulled down and the Avenida and square became open to all.

The boulevard you see today was built in 1879–82 in the style of the Champs-Elysées in Paris. The wide tree-lined avenue became a focus for pageants, festivities and demonstrations. A war memorial stands as a tribute to those who died in World War I. The avenue still retains a certain elegance with fountains and café tables shaded by trees; however, it no longer makes for a peaceful stroll. The once majestic thoroughfare, 90 m (295 ft) wide and decorated with abstract pavement patterns, is now divided by seven lanes of traffic linking Praça dos Restauradores and Praça Marquês de Pombal to the north. Some of the original mansions have been preserved, including the Neo-Classical Tivoli cinema at No. 188, with an original 1920s kiosk outside, and Casa Lambertini with its colourful mosaic decoration at No. 166. However, many of the Art Nouveau façades have given way to modern ones occupied by offices, hotels or shopping complexes.

19th-century monument in honour of the Restoration in Praça dos Restauradores

Praça dos Restauradores ❸

Map 7 A2. 🚌 36, 702, 709, 745 & many other routes. 🅜 *Restauradores*.

The square, distinguished by its soaring obelisk, erected in 1886, commemorates Portugal's liberation from the Spanish yoke in 1640. The bronze figures on the pedestal depict Victory, holding a palm and a crown, and Freedom. The names and dates that are inscribed on the sides of the obelisk are those of the battles of the War of Restoration.

On the west side the Palácio Foz now houses a small tourist and other offices. It was built by Francesco Savario Fabri in 1755–77 for the Marquês de Castelo-Melhor and renamed after the Marquês de Foz, who lived here in the 19th century. The smart Avenida Palace Hotel, on the southwest side of the square, was designed by José Lúis Monteiro (1849–1942), who also built Rossio railway station *(see p42)*.

Detail from the memorial to the dead of World War I in Avenida da Liberdade

Museu da Sociedade de Geografia ❹

Rua das Portas de Santo Antão 100. **Map** 7 A2. **Tel** 213 425 401.
🚌 709, 711, 790. Ⓜ Restauradores.
🗝 compulsory, 3pm Tue & by appointment. 🖥 ♿

Located in the Geographical Society building, the museum houses an idiosyncratic ethnographical collection brought back from Portugal's former colonies. On display are circumcision masks from Guinea Bissau, musical instruments and snake spears. From Angola there are neckrests to sustain coiffures and the original *padrão* – the stone pillar erected by the Portuguese in 1482 to mark their sovereignty over the colony. Most of the exhibits are arranged along the splendid Sala Portugal.

Rossio ❺

Map 6 B3. 🚌 36, 44, 745 & many other routes. Ⓜ Rossio.

Formally called Praça de Dom Pedro IV, this large square has been Lisbon's nerve centre for six centuries. During its history it has been the stage of bullfights, festivals, military parades and the burning of heretics during the Inquisition *(see p16)*. Today there is little more than an occasional political rally, and the sober

Teatro Nacional Dona Maria II in Rossio illuminated by night

Pombaline buildings, disfigured on the upper level by neon signs, are occupied at street level by souvenir shops and cafés. Centre stage is a statue of Dom Pedro IV, the first emperor of independent Brazil. At the foot of the statue, the four female figures are allegories of Justice, Wisdom, Strength and Moderation.

In the mid-19th century the square was paved with wave-patterned mosaics which gave it the nickname of "Rolling Motion Square". The hand-cut grey and white stone cubes were the first such designs to decorate the city's pavements. Today, only a small central section of the design survives.

On the north side of Rossio is the Teatro Nacional Dona Maria II, named after Dom

Pedro's daughter. The Neo-Classical structure was built in the 1840s by the Italian architect Fortunato Lodi. The interior was destroyed by fire in 1964 and reconstructed in the 1970s. On top of the pediment is Gil Vicente (1465–1536), the founder of Portuguese theatre.

Café Nicola on the west side of the square was a favourite meeting place among writers, including the poet Manuel du Bocage (1765–1805), who was notorious for his satires. Café Suíça, on the opposite side, is popular with tourists for its sunlit terrace.

Praça da Figueira ❻

Map 6 B3. 🚌 714, 759, 760 & many other routes. 🚊 12, 15. Ⓜ Rossio.

Before the 1755 earthquake *(see pp22–3)* the square next to Rossio was the site of the Hospital de Todos-os-Santos (All Saints). In Pombal's new design for the Baixa, the square took on the role of the city's central marketplace. In 1885 a covered market was introduced, but this was pulled down in the 1950s. Today, the four-storey buildings are given over to hotels, shops and cafés and the square is no longer a marketplace. Perhaps its most eye-catching feature is the multitude of pigeons that perch on the pedestal supporting Leopoldo de Almcida's bronze equestrian statue of João I, erected in 1971.

Bronze statue of King João I in Praça da Figueira

Elevador de Santa Justa ⑦

Rua de Santa Justa & Largo do Carmo. **Map** 7 B3. *Tel 213 613 000.* ○ *7am–9pm daily (May–Sep: to 11pm).* 🖩

Also known as the Elevador do Carmo, this Neo-Gothic lift was built at the turn of the 20th century by the French architect Raoul Mesnier du Ponsard, an apprentice of Alexandre Gustave Eiffel. Made of iron and embellished with filigree, it is one of the more eccentric features of the Baixa. The ticket office is located at the foot of the elevator.

Passengers can travel up and down inside the tower in one of two smart wood-panelled cabins with brass fittings; at the top of the elevator is a walkway, linking it to the Largo do Carmo in the Bairro Alto, 32 m (105 ft) above.

View of the Elevador de Santa Justa

The very top of the tower, which is reached via an extremely tight spiral stairway, is given over to a viewing gallery. This high vantage point commands splendid views of Rossio, the grid pattern of the Baixa, the castle on the opposite hill, the river and the nearby ruins of the Carmo church. The fire that gutted the Chiado district in 1988 *(see p52)* was extinguished very close to the lift.

Rua Augusta ⑧

Map 7 B4. Ⓜ *Rossio.* 🚌 *36, 714, 745 & many other routes.*

A lively pedestrianized street decorated with mosaic pavements and lined with boutiques and open-air cafés, Rua Augusta is the main tourist thoroughfare and the smartest in the Baixa. Street performers provide entertainment, while vendors sell lottery tickets, street art, books and souvenirs. The triumphal Arco da Rua Augusta frames the equestrian statue of José I in Praça do Comércio. Designed by the architect Santos de Carvalho to commemorate the city's recovery from the earthquake *(see pp22–3)*, the arch was completed only in 1873.

The other main thorough-fares of the Baixa are Rua da Prata (silversmiths' street) and Rua do Ouro or Rua Aurea (goldsmiths' street). Cutting across these two main streets full of shops and banks are smaller streets that give glimpses up to the Bairro Alto to the west and the Castelo de São Jorge *(see pp38–9)* to the east. Many of the streets retain shops that gave them their name: there are jewellers in Rua da Prata and Rua do Ouro and banks in Rua do Comércio.

The most incongruous sight in the heart of the Baixa is a small section of the Roman baths, located within the Banco Comercial Português in Rua dos Correeiros. The ruins and mosaics can be seen from the street window at the rear side of the bank; alternatively you can book ahead to visit the "museum" on 211 131 000.

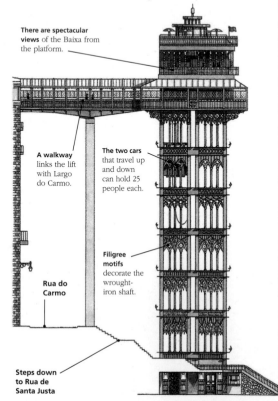

There are spectacular views of the Baixa from the platform.

A walkway links the lift with Largo do Carmo.

The two cars that travel up and down can hold 25 people each.

Filigree motifs decorate the wrought-iron shaft.

Rua do Carmo

Steps down to Rua de Santa Justa

Nossa Senhora da Conceição Velha ⑨

Rua da Alfândega. **Map** 7 C4.
Tel 218 870 202. 🚌 709, 745, 790.
🚊 18. ⬜ 9am–5pm Mon–Fri,
10am–2pm Sun. ✝ 📷 ♿

The elaborate Manueline doorway of the church is the only feature that survived from the original 16th-century Nossa Senhora da Misericórdia, which stood here until the 1755 earthquake. The portal is decorated with a profusion of Manueline detail including angels, beasts, flowers, armillary spheres and the cross of the Order of Christ. In the tympanum, the Virgin Mary spreads her protective mantle over various contemporary figures. These include Pope Leo X, Manuel I and his sister, Queen Leonor, widow of João II. It was Leonor who founded the original Misericórdia (alms-house) on the site of a former synagogue.

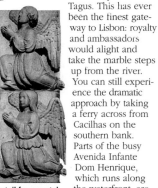

Detail from portal of Conceição Velha

Enjoyment of the portal is hampered by the constant stream of traffic along Rua da Alfândega and the cars parked right in front of the church. The interior has an unusual stucco ceiling; in the second chapel on the right is a statue of Our Lady of Restelo. This came from the Belém chapel where navigators prayed before embarking on their historic voyages east.

Praça do Comércio ⑩

Map 7 C5. 🚌 709, 711, 714, 745 & many other routes. 🚊 15, 18, 25.

More commonly known by the locals as *Terreiro do Paço* (Palace Square), this huge open space was the site of the royal palace for 400 years. Manuel I transferred the royal residence from Castelo de São Jorge to this more convenient location by the river in 1511. The first palace, along with its library and 70,000 books, was destroyed in the 1755 earthquake. In rebuilding the city, the square became the *pièce de résistance* of Pombal's Baixa design. The new palace occupied spacious arcaded buildings extending around three sides of the square. After the 1910 revolution (*see p17*), these were converted into government administrative offices and painted Republican pink. They have since been re-painted royal yellow, however.

The south side, graced by two square towers, looks across the wide expanse of the Tagus. This has ever been the finest gateway to Lisbon: royalty and ambassadors would alight and take the marble steps up from the river. You can still experience the dramatic approach by taking a ferry across from Cacilhas on the southern bank. Parts of the busy Avenida Infante Dom Henrique, which runs along the waterfront, are lined with restaurants and bars. In the centre of Praça do Comércio is the equestrian statue of King José I erected in 1775 by Machado de Castro, the leading Portuguese sculptor of the 18th century. The bronze horse, depicted trampling on serpents, earned the statue its third name of "Black Horse Square", used by English travellers and merchants. Over the years, however, the horse has acquired a green patina.

Shaded arcades along the north side of Praça do Comércio

The impressive triumphal arch on the north side of the square leads to Rua Augusta and is the gateway to the Baixa. Opened in 2001, in the northwest of the square, the Lisboa Welcome Centre has a tourist information service, gallery, restaurants and shops. In the opposite corner is Lisbon's oldest café, the Martinho da Arcada, formerly a haunt of the city's literati.

On 1 February 1908, King Carlos and his son, Luís Felipe, were assassinated as they were passing through the square. In 1974 the square saw the first uprising of the Armed Forces Movement which overthrew the Caetano regime in a bloodless revolution (*see p17*). For many years the area was requisitioned as a car park, but today this is a vast open space used for cultural events and festivals.

Statue of King José I in Praça do Comércio

BAIRRO ALTO AND ESTRELA

Tile panel in Largo Rafael Bordalo Pinheiro, Bairro Alto

Laid out in a grid pattern in the late 16th century, the hilltop Bairro Alto is one of the most picturesque districts of the city. First settled by rich citizens who moved out of the disreputable Alfama, by the 19th century it had become a run-down area frequented by prostitutes. Today, its small workshops and family-run *tascas* (cheap restaurants) exist alongside a thriving nightlife.

Very different in character to the heart of the Bairro Alto is the elegant commercial district known as the Chiado, where affluent Lisboetas do their shopping. To the northwest, the Estrela quarter is centred on the huge domed basilica and popular gardens. The mid-18th century district of Lapa, to the southwest, is home to foreign embassies and large, smart residences.

SIGHTS AT A GLANCE

Museums and Galleries
Museu da Marioneta ❻
Museu do Chiado ❺
*Museu Nacional de Arte
   Antiga pp56–9* ⓫

Churches
Basílica da Estrela ⓭
Igreja do Carmo ❷
São Roque ❶

Historic Buildings and Districts
Chiado ❸
Palácio de São Bento ❿
Solar do Vinho
   do Porto ❼
Teatro
   Nacional
   de São
   Carlos
   (Opera) ❹

Gardens and Belvederes
Jardim da Estrela ⓬
Miradouro de São Pedro
   de Alcântara ❽
Praça do Príncipe Real ❾

GETTING THERE
This area is reached via the Elevador da Glória from Praça dos Restauradores, the Elevador de Santa Justa from the Baixa, or by a steep walk. There is a metro station on Largo do Chiado. Tram 28 passes Bairro Alto on its way between Graça and Estrela.

KEY
	Street-by-Street: Bairro Alto and Chiado *pp50–51*
M	Metro station
▣	Railway station
⛟	Funicular
⛴	Ferry boarding point
≈	Railway line

Map showing streets of Bairro Alto and Estrela district with numbered sights, including Tejo river, Santos, Cais do Sodré, Baixa-Chiado, Estação Fluvial

0 metres   250
0 yards   250

◁ Art Nouveau decoration in the Chiado's Café Brasileira, once popular with writers and intellectuals

Street-by-Street: Bairro Alto and Chiado

The Bairro Alto (high quarter) is a fascinating area of cobbled streets adjacent to the Carmo and Chiado areas. Since the 1980s, this has been Lisbon's best-known nightlife zone, with countless small bars and restaurants alongside the older *casas de fado*. Much restoration work has taken place over the last few years, and many modern buildings now stand alongside old, peeling houses and tiny grocery shops. In contrast, the Chiado is an area of elegant shops and old-style cafés that extends down from Praça Luís de Camões towards Rua do Carmo and the Baixa. Major renovation work has taken place since a fire in 1988 *(see p52)* destroyed many of the buildings.

Baroque cherub, Igreja do Carmo

Once a haunt *of writers and intellectuals, Chiado is now an elegant shopping district. The Brasileira café, on Largo do Chiado, is adorned with gilded mirrors.*

Praça Luís de Camões

RUA DO NORTE

RUA DAS GÁVEAS

RUA DO ALECRIM

L. DO CHIADO

RUA GARRE

The statue of Eça de Queirós (1845–1900), *by Teixeira Lopes, was erected in 1903. The great novelist takes inspiration from a scantily veiled muse.*

Largo do Chiado is flanked by the churches of Loreto and Nossa Senhora da Encarnação.

Baixa/Chiado

Rua Garrett is the main shopping street of the Chiado.

Ⓜ

Chiado

0 metres	50
0 yards	50

KEY

– – – Suggested route

Tavares, *at No. 37 Rua da Misericórdia, first opened as a café in 1784. Today it is an elegant restaurant* (see p131) *decorated at the turn of the century with mirrors and elaborate stucco designs.*

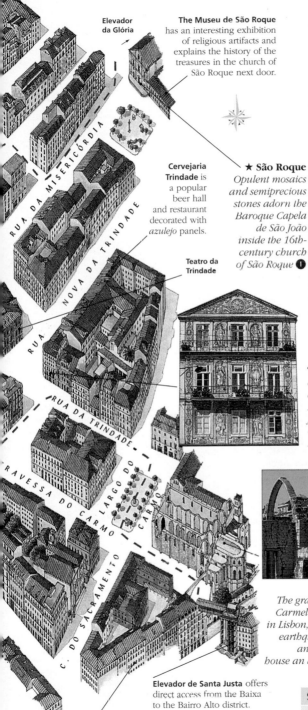

Elevador da Glória

The Museu de São Roque has an interesting exhibition of religious artifacts and explains the history of the treasures in the church of São Roque next door.

Cervejaria Trindade is a popular beer hall and restaurant decorated with *azulejo* panels.

Teatro da Trindade

LOCATOR MAP
See Lisbon Street Finder map 7

★ **São Roque**
Opulent mosaics and semiprecious stones adorn the Baroque Capela de São João inside the 16th-century church of São Roque ❶

The tile decoration
on the façade of this house, erected in 1864 on Largo Rafael Bordalo Pinheiro, features allegorical figures of Science, Agriculture, Industry and Commerce.

★ **Igreja do Carmo**
The graceful skeletal arches of this Carmelite church, once the largest in Lisbon, stand as a reminder of the earthquake of 1755. The chancel, and main body of the church house an archaeological museum ❷

Elevador de Santa Justa offers direct access from the Baixa to the Bairro Alto district.

The shops in Rua do Carmo have been restored and renewed after the devastating fire in 1988 (*see p52*).

STAR SIGHTS

★ São Roque

★ Igreja do Carmo

Ruins of the 14th-century Igreja do Carmo seen from the Baixa

São Roque ❶

Largo Trindade Coelho. **Map** 7 A3.
Tel 213 235 247. ▦ 758. ⬤ 9am–
6pm daily (from 2pm Mon, to 9pm
Thu). ⬤ public holidays. 🏛 **Museu
de São Roque** *Tel* 213 235 380.
⬤ 10am–6pm Tue, Wed & Fri–Sun,
2–9pm Thu. ⬤ public hols. 📷 📷

São Roque's plain façade
belies a remarkably rich
interior. The church
was founded at
the end of the 16th
century by the Jesuit
Order, then at the
peak of its power. In
1742 the Chapel of
St John the Baptist
(last on the left) was
commissioned by
the prodigal João V
from the Italian
architects Luigi
Vanvitelli and Nicola

Tile detail, Chapel
of São Roque

Salvi. Constructed in
Rome and embellished with
lapis lazuli, agate, alabaster,
amethyst, precious marbles,
gold, silver and mosaics, the
chapel was given the Pope's
blessing in the church of
Sant'Antonio dei Portoghesi
in Rome, dismantled and sent
to Lisbon in three ships.

Among the many tiles in the
church, the oldest and most
interesting are those in the
third chapel on the right,
dating from the mid-16th
century and dedicated to São
Roque (St Roch), protector
against the plague. Other
features of the church are
the scenes of the Apocalypse
painted on the ceiling, and
the sacristy with its coffered
ceiling, as well as painted
panels of the life of St Francis
Xavier, the 16th-century

missionary. Treasures from the
Chapel of St John, including
the silver and lapis lazuli altar
front, are in the adjoining
Museu de Arte Sacra.

Igreja do Carmo ❷

Largo do Carmo. **Map** 7 B3.
Tel 213 421 790. ▦ 758. 🚋 28.
Ⓜ Baixa-Chiado. ⬤ 8:30am–noon
Tue–Sun. 🏛 **Museu do
Carmo** ⬤ 10am–6pm Mon–
Sat (to 7pm Jun–Sep). 📷

The Gothic ruins
of this Carmelite
church, built on a
slope overlooking
the Baixa, are
evocative reminders
of the devastation left
by the earthquake of
1755. As the congrega-
tion was attending
mass the shockwaves
caused the church to collapse,
depositing tons of masonry
on to the people below.

Founded in the late 14th century by Nuno Álvares Pereira,
the commander who became
a member of the Carmelite
Order, the church was at one
time the biggest in Lisbon.

Nowadays the main body
of the church and the chancel, whose roof withstood
the earthquake, houses the
Museu do Carmo with a small,
heterogeneous collection of
sarcophagi, statuary, ceramics
and mosaics.

Among the more ancient
finds from Europe are a
remnant from a Visigothic
pillar and a Roman tomb
carved with reliefs depicting
the Muses. There are also
impressive finds from Mexico
and South America, including
ancient mummies.

Outside the ruins, in the
Largo do Carmo, stands the
Chafariz do Carmo, an 18th-
century fountain designed by
Ângelo Belasco, elaborately
decorated with four dolphins.

Chiado ❸

Map 7 A4. ▦ 758. 🚋 28.
Ⓜ Baixa-Chiado.

Hypotheses abound for the
origin of the word Chiado, in
use since 1567. One of the
most interesting recalls the
creak *(chiar)* of the wheels of
the carts as they negotiated the
area's steep slopes. A second
theory refers to the nickname
given to the 16th-century poet
António Ribeiro, "O Chiado".
An area traditionally known

THE CHIADO FIRE

On 25 August 1988 a disastrous fire began in a store in
Rua do Carmo, the street that
links the Baixa with the Bairro
Alto. Fire engines were unable
to enter this pedestrianized
street and the fire spread into
Rua Garrett. Along with shops
and offices, many important
18th-century buildings were
destroyed, the worst damage
being in Rua do Carmo. The
renovation project, which is
now complete, has preserved
many original façades, and
was headed by the Portuguese
architect Álvaro Siza Vieira.

Firemen attending the raging
fire in Rua do Carmo

Stalls and circle of the 18th-century Teatro Nacional de São Carlos

for its intellectual associations, various statues of literary figures can be found here. Fernando Pessoa, Portugal's most famous 20th-century poet, is seated at a table outside the Café Brasileira. Established in the 1920s, this was a favourite rendezvous of intellectuals.

The name Chiado is often used to mean just Rua Garrett, the main shopping street of the area, named after the author and poet João Almeida Garrett (1799–1854). This elegant street, which descends from Largo do Chiado towards the Baixa, is known for its clothes shops, cafés and bookshops. Devastated by fire in 1988, the former elegance of this quarter has now been restored.

On Largo do Chiado stand two Baroque churches: the Italian church, Igreja do Loreto, on the north side and opposite, Nossa Senhora da Encarnação, whose exterior walls are partly decorated with *azulejos*.

Teatro Nacional de São Carlos ❹

Rua Serpa Pinto 9. **Map** 7 A4.
Tel 213 253 000. 🚍 758, 790.
🚋 28. Ⓜ *Baixa-Chiado.* ⬭ *for performances.* **www**.saocarlos.pt

Replacing a former opera house which was ruined by the earthquake of 1755, the Teatro de São Carlos was built in 1792–5 by José da Costa e Silva. Designed on the lines of La Scala in Milan, the building has a beautifully proportioned façade and an enchanting Rococo interior. Views of the exterior, however, are spoiled by the car park, invariably crammed, which occupies the square in front. The opera season lasts from September to June, but concerts and ballets are also staged here at other times of the year.

Museu do Chiado ❺

Rua Serpa Pinto 4–6. **Map** 7 A5.
Tel 213 432 148. 🚍 758, 790.
🚋 28. Ⓜ *Baixa-Chiado.*
⬭ 10am–6pm Tue–Sun.
⬤ 1 Jan, Easter, 1 May, 25 Dec. 🏛
www.museudochiado-ipmuseus.pt

The National Museum of Contemporary Art, whose collection of 1850–1950 paintings could no longer be described as contemporary, changed its name in 1994 and moved to a stylishly restored warehouse. The paintings and sculpture are arranged over three floors in 12 rooms. Each room has a different theme illustrating the development

from Romanticism to Modernism. The majority are Portuguese works, often showing the marked influence from other European countries. This is particularly noticeable in the 19th-century landscape painters who had contact with artists from the French Barbizon School. The few international works of art on display include a collection of drawings by Rodin (1840–1917) and some French sculpture from the late 19th century. There are also temporary exhibitions which are held for "very new artists, preferably inspired by the permanent collection".

Grotesque puppet in Museu da Marioneta

Museu da Marioneta ❻

Convento das Bernardas,
Rua da Esperança 146. **Map** 4 D3.
Tel 213 942 810. 🚍 60, 713, 727.
🚋 15, 25. Ⓜ *Cais do Sodré.*
🚆 Santos. ⬭ 10am–1pm, 2–5:30pm
Tue–Sun. ⬤ 1 Jan, 1 May, 25 Dec. 🏛
www.museudamarioneta.pt

This small puppet museum, housed in an elegantly refurbished convent building, includes characters from 17th- and 18th-century theatre and opera, including jesters, devils, knights and satirical figures. Many of the puppets possess gruesome, contorted features that are unlikely to appeal to small children. The museum explains the history of the art form and runs videos of puppet shows. Phone ahead to see if a live performance is being held on the small stage. There is also a space for pedagogical activities.

Art Nouveau façade of the popular Café Brasileira in the Chiado

The wide selection of port at the Solar do Vinho do Porto

Solar do Vinho do Porto ❼

Rua de São Pedro de Alcântara 45.
Map 4 F2. *Tel* 213 475 707. 🚌 758.
🚋 28, Elevador da Glória. ◯ 11am–
midnight Mon–Fri, 2pm–midnight
Sat. ◉ public hols.

The Portuguese word *solar* means mansion or manor house and the Solar do Vinho do Porto occupies the ground floor of an 18th-century mansion. The building was once owned by the German architect, Johann Friedrich Ludwig (Ludovice), who built the monastery at Mafra *(see p96)*. The port wine institute of Oporto runs a pleasant if dated bar here for the promotion of port. Nearly 200 types of port are listed in the lengthy drinks menu, with every producer represented and including some rarities. Unfortunately, many of the listed wines are often unavailable. All but the vintage ports are sold by the glass, with prices ranging from one euro for the simplest ruby to €70 for a glass of 40-year-old tawny.

Miradouro de São Pedro de Alcântara ❽

Rua de São Pedro de Alcântara.
Map 7 A2. 🚌 758. 🚋 28.

The belvedere *(miradouro)* commands a sweeping view of eastern Lisbon, seen across the Baixa. A tiled map, conveniently placed against the balustrade, helps you locate the landmarks in the city below. The panorama extends from the battlements of the Castelo de São Jorge *(see pp38–9)*, clearly seen surrounded by trees on the hill to the southeast, to the 18th-century church of Penha da França in the northwest. The large monastery complex of the Igreja da Graça *(see p37)* is also visible on the hill, and in the distance São Vicente de Fora *(see p35)* is recognizable by the symmetrical towers that flank its white façade.

Benches and ample shade from the trees make this terrace a pleasant stop after the steep walk up Calçada da Glória from the Baixa. Alternatively, the yellow funicular, Elevador da Glória, will drop you off nearby.

The memorial in the garden, erected in 1904, depicts Eduardo Coelho (1835–89), founder of the newspaper *Diário de Notícias*, and below him a ragged paper boy running with copies of the famous

daily. This area was once the centre of the newspaper industry, however the modern printing presses have now moved to more spacious premises west of the city.

The view is most attractive at sunset and by night when the castle is floodlit and the terrace becomes a popular meeting point for young Lisboetas.

Praça do Príncipe Real ❾

Map 4 F1. 🚌 758, 790.

Playing cards in Praça do Príncipe Real

Laid out in 1860 as a prime residential quarter, the square still retains an air of affluence. Smartly painted mansions surround a particularly pleasant park with an open-air café, statuary and some splendid robinia, magnolia and Judas trees. The branches of a huge cedar tree have been trained on a trellis, creating a wide shady spot for the locals who play cards beneath it. On the large square, at No. 26, the eye-catching pink and white Neo-Moorish building with domes and pinnacles is part of Lisbon university.

View across the city to Castelo de São Jorge from Miradouro de São Pedro de Alcântara

Attractive wrought-iron music pavilion in Jardim da Estrela

Palácio de São Bento ⑩

Largo das Cortes, Rua de São Bento. **Map** 4 E2. **Tel** *213 919 000.*
🚌 *790.* 🚊 *28.* ⭕ *by appt only.*
📋 *call 213 919 446 or 213 919 625.*
www.*parlamento.pt*

Also known as the Assembleia República, this massive white Neo-Classical building started life in the late 1500s as the Benedictine monastery of São Bento. After the dissolution of the religious orders in 1834, the building became the seat of the Portuguese Parliament, known as the Palácio das Cortes. The interior is suitably grandiose with marble pillars and Neo-Classical statues.

Museu Nacional de Arte Antiga ⑪

See pp56–9.

Jardim da Estrela ⑫

Praça da Estrela. **Map** 4 D2.
🚌 *720, 738.* 🚊 *25, 28.* Ⓜ *Rato.*
⭕ *7am–midnight daily.*

Laid out in the middle of the 19th century, opposite the Basílica da Estrela, the popular gardens are a focal part of the Estrela quarter. Local families congregate here at weekends to feed the ducks and carp in the lake, sit at the waterside café or wander among the flower beds, plants and trees. The formal gardens are planted with herbaceous borders and shrubs surrounding plane trees and elms. The central feature of the park is a green wrought-iron bandstand, decorated with elegant filigree, where musicians strike up in the summer months. This was built in 1884 and originally stood on the Passeio Público, before the creation of Avenida da Liberdade *(see p44).*

The English Cemetery to the north of the gardens is best known as the burial place of Henry Fielding (1707–54), the English novelist and playwright who died in Lisbon at the age of 47. The *Journal of a Voyage to Lisbon,* published posthumously in 1775, recounts his last voyage to Portugal made in a fruitless attempt to recover his failing health.

Basílica da Estrela ⑬

Praça da Estrela. **Map** 4 D2. **Tel** *213 960 915.* 🚌 *720, 738.* 🚊 *25, 28.*
⭕ *7:45am–8pm daily (large groups by appointment).* 🚹 📷

The tomb of the pious Maria I in the Basílica da Estrela

In the second half of the 18th century Maria I *(see p109),* daughter of José I, vowed she would build a church if she bore a son and heir to the throne. Her wish was granted and construction of the basilica began in 1779. Her son José, however, died of smallpox two years before the completion of the church in 1790. The huge domed basilica, set on a hill in the west of the city, is one of Lisbon's great landmarks. A simpler version of the basilica at Mafra *(see p96),* this church was built by architects from the Mafra School in late Baroque and Neo-Classical style. The façade is flanked by twin belltowers and decorated with an array of statues of saints and allegorical figures.

The spacious, somewhat awe-inspiring interior, where light streams down from the pierced dome, is clad in grey, pink and yellow marble. The elaborate Empire-style tomb of Queen Maria I, who died in Brazil, lies in the right transept. Locked in a room nearby is Machado de Castro's extraordinary Nativity scene, composed of over 500 cork and terracotta figures. (To see it, ask the sacristan.)

Neo-Classical façade and stairway of Palácio de São Bento

Museu Nacional de Arte Antiga ⑪

Portugal's national art collection is housed in a 17th-century palace that was built for the counts of Alvor. In 1770 it was acquired by the Marquês de Pombal and remained in the possession of his family for over a century. Inaugurated in 1884, the museum is known to locals as the Museu das Janelas Verdes, referring to the former green windows of the palace. In 1940 a modern annexe (including the main façade) was added. This was built on the site of the St Albert Carmelite monastery, which was partially demolished between 1910 and 1920. The only surviving feature was the chapel, now integrated into the museum.

15th-century wood carving of St George

★ **St Jerome**
This masterly portrayal of old age by Albrecht Dürer expresses one of the central dilemmas of Renaissance humanism: the ephemeral nature of man (1521).

GALLERY GUIDE
The ground floor contains 14th–19th-century European paintings as well as some decorative arts and furniture. Oriental and African art, Chinese and Portuguese ceramics, and silver, gold and jewellery are on display on the first floor. The top floor is dedicated to Portuguese art and sculpture.

The Temptations of St Antony by **Hieronymus Bosch**

St Augustine by **Piero della Francesca**

Stairs down to 🖥 🍴 ♿

St Leonard
This statue is by the renowned Florentine Renaissance sculptor Andrea della Robbia (1435–1525), nephew of Luca della Robbia (1400–82).

60 61 62 59 63 58 64 57 65 56 55 66 54 67 68 53 69 52 70 51 49 50

KEY
- ☐ European art
- ☐ Portuguese painting and sculpture
- ☐ Portuguese and Chinese ceramics
- ☐ Oriental and African art
- ☐ Silver, gold and jewellery
- ☐ Decorative arts
- ☐ Chapel of St Albert
- ☐ Furniture
- ☐ Temporary exhibitions
- ☐ Non-exhibition space

STAR EXHIBITS
★ St Jerome by Dürer

★ Namban Screens

★ Panels of St Vincent by Gonçalves

The Mystic Marriage of St Catherine
Hans Holbein the Elder's balanced composition of a Sacra Conversazione *(1519) is set among majestic Renaissance architecture with saints clothed in detailed contemporary costumes sewing or reading.*

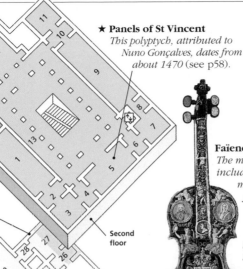

★ **Panels of St Vincent**
This polyptych, attributed to Nuno Gonçalves, dates from about 1470 (see p58).

VISITORS' CHECKLIST

Rua das Janelas Verdes. **Map** 4 D4. *Tel* 213 912 800. 🚌 713, 727, 760. 🚋 15, 18. ⏰ 2–6pm Tue, 10am–6pm Wed–Sun. ⬤ public hols. 🎟 (free 10am–2pm Sun). 📷 ♿ 🖥 🍴
http://mnaa.imc-ip.pt

Faïence Violin
The museum's ceramics collection includes many decorative items made in Portugal for the royal family. This 19th-century objet d'art by Wenceslau Cifka is decorated with the royal coat of arms and portraits of the Italian Baroque composers, Scarlatti and Corelli.

First floor

Second floor

★ **Namban Screens**
This detail from one of the museum's 16th-century Japanese screens illustrates a contemporary trading scene and the Portuguese fashion at the time.

Entrance

Ground floor

The Chapel of St Albert, dating from the 16th century, has a sumptuous Baroque interior decorated with blue and white *azulejos*.

Ivory Salt Cellar
Portuguese knights and dignitaries are carved on this 16th-century ivory salt cellar from Benin, West Africa.

Exploring the Collections of the Museu Nacional de Arte Antiga

The museum has the largest collection of paintings in Portugal and is particularly strong on early religious works by Portuguese artists. The majority of exhibits came from convents and monasteries following the suppression of religious orders in 1834. There are also extensive displays of sculpture, silverware, porcelain and applied arts giving an overview of Portuguese art from the Middle Ages to the 19th century, complemented by many fine European and Oriental pieces. The theme of the discoveries is ever-present, illustrating Portugal's links with Brazil, Africa, India, China and Japan.

EUROPEAN ART

Paintings by European artists, dating from the 14th to the 19th century, are arranged chronologically on the ground floor. Unlike the Portuguese art, which is located on the second floor, most of the works in this section were donated from private collections, contributing to the great diversity of works on display. The first rooms, dedicated to the 14th and 15th centuries, trace the transition from medieval Gothic taste to the aesthetic of the Renaissance.

Among the painters best represented in the European Art section are the 16th-century German and Flemish artists. Notable works are *St Jerome* by Albrecht Dürer (1471–1528), *Salomé* by Lucas Cranach the Elder (1472–1553), *Virgin and Child* by Hans Memling (c.1430–94) and *The Temptations of St Anthony* by the great Dutch master of fantasy, Hieronymus

Bosch (1450–1516). Of the small number of Italian works, the finest include *St Augustine* by the Renaissance painter Piero della Francesca (c.1420–92) and a graceful early altar panel representing *The Miracle of St Eusebius of Cremona* by Raphael (1483–1520).

PORTUGUESE PAINTING AND SCULPTURE

Many of the earliest works of art are by the Portuguese primitive painters who were influenced by the realistic detail of Flemish artists. There had always been strong trading links between Portugal and Flanders and in the 15th and 16th centuries several painters of Flemish origin, for example Frey Carlos of Évora, set up workshops in Portugal.

Pride of place, however, goes to the São Vicente de Fora polyptych, the most important painting of 15th-century Portuguese art and

Central panel of *The Temptations of St Anthony* by Hieronymus Bosch

Cistercian monks from Alcobaça in central Portugal

Friar

Fisherman

one that has become a symbol of national pride in the Age of Discovery. Painted around 1470–80, and generally believed to be by Nuno Gonçalves, the altarpiece shows St Vincent, patron saint of Lisbon, surrounded by dignitaries, knights and monks as well as beggars and fishermen. The accurate portrayal of contemporary figures makes the painting an invaluable historical and social document.

Later works include a 16th-century portrait of the young Dom Sebastião (1557–78) by Cristóvão de Morais and paintings by Neo-Classical artist Domingos António de Sequeira.

The museum's sculpture collection has many Gothic polychrome stone and wood statues of Christ, the Virgin and saints. There are also statues from the 17th century and a late 18th-century nativity scene by Barros Laborão in the Chapel of St Albert.

PORTUGUESE AND CHINESE CERAMICS

The extensive collection of ceramics enables visitors to trace the evolution of Chinese porcelain and Portuguese faïence and to see the influence of oriental designs on

Nuno Gonçalves, self-portrait of the artist

Queen Eleanor of Aragon, the Queen mother

Henry the Navigator *(see p49)*

Archbishop of Lisbon, Jorge da Costa

Queen Isabel

King Afonso V

Infante João (King João II)

Infante Fernão, the king's brother

Knight

St Vincent

Moorish knight

Jewish scholar

Beggar

Duke of Bragança

Member of city council holding a fragment of St Vincent's skull

---

Portuguese pieces, and vice versa. From the 16th century Portuguese ceramics show a marked influence of Ming, and conversely the Chinese pieces bear Portuguese motifs such as coats of arms. By the mid-18th century individual potters had begun to develop an increasingly personalized, European style, with popular, rustic designs. The collection also includes ceramics from Italy, Spain and the Netherlands.

Chinese porcelain vase, 18th century

ORIENTAL AND AFRICAN ART

The collection of ivories and furniture, with their European motifs, further illustrates the reciprocal influences of Portugal and her colonies. The 16th-century predilection for the exotic gave rise to a huge demand for items such as carved ivory hunting horns from Africa. The 16th- and 17th-century Japanese Namban screens show the Portuguese trading in Japan. *Namban-jin* (barbarians from the south) is the name the Japanese gave to the Portuguese.

SILVER, GOLD AND JEWELLERY

Among the museum's fine collection of ecclesiastical treasures are King Sancho I's gold cross (1214) and the Belém monstrance (1506). Also on display is the 16th-century Madre de Deus reliquary, allegedly containing a thorn from the crown of Christ. Highlight of the foreign collection is a sumptuous set of rare 18th-century silver tableware. Commissioned by José I from the Paris workshop of François Thomas Germain, the 1,200 pieces include intricately decorated tureens, sauce boats and salt cellars. The rich collection of jewels came from the convents, originally donated by members of the nobility and wealthy bourgeoisie on entering the religious orders.

APPLIED ARTS

Furniture, tapestries and textiles, liturgical vestments and bishops' mitres are among the wide range of objects on display. The furniture collection includes many Medieval and Renaissance pieces as well as Baroque and Neo-Classical items from the reigns of King João V, King José and Queen Maria I. Of the foreign furniture, French pieces from the 18th century are prominent.

The textiles include 17th-century bedspreads, tapestries, many of Flemish origin, such as the *Baptism of Christ* (16th century), embroidered rugs and Arraiolos carpets.

Gold Madre de Deus reliquary inlaid with precious stones (c.1510–25)

BELÉM

At the mouth of the River Tagus, where the caravels set sail on their voyages of discovery, Belém is inextricably linked with Portugal's golden age of discovery. When Manuel I came to power in 1495 he reaped the profits of those heady days of expansion, building grandiose monuments and churches that mirrored the spirit of the time. Two of the finest examples of the exuberant and exotic Manueline style of architecture are the Mosteiro dos Jerónimos and the Torre de Belém. Today Belém is a spacious, relatively green suburb with many museums, parks and gardens, as well as an attractive riverside setting with cafés and a promenade. On sunny days there is a distinct seaside feel to the river embankment.

Before the Tagus receded, the monks in the monastery used to look out onto the river and watch the boats set forth. In contrast today several lanes of traffic along the busy Avenida da Índia cut central Belém off from the picturesque waterfront, and silver and yellow trains rattle regularly past.

Generosity, **statue at entrance to Palácio da Ajuda**

SIGHTS AT A GLANCE

Museums and Galleries
Museu Colecção Berardo Arte
 Moderna e Contemporânea ❿
Museu de Marinha ❼
Museu Nacional
 de Arqueologia ❺
Museu Nacional
 dos Coches ❷
Planetário Calouste
 Gulbenkian ❻

Parks and Gardens
Jardim Agrícola Tropical ❸
Jardim Botânico da Ajuda ⓰

Churches and Monasteries
Ermida de São Jerónimo ⓬
Igreja da Memória ⓭
Mosteiro dos Jerónimos
 pp66–7 ❹

Historic Buildings
Palácio de Belém ❶
Palácio Nacional da Ajuda ⓯
Torre de Belém p70 ⓫

Monuments
Monument to the
 Discoveries ❾

Cultural Centres
Centro Cultural
 de Belém ❽

KEY

▨	Street-by-Street: Belém *pp62–3*
🚉	Railway station
⛴	Ferry boarding point
═	Railway line
ℹ	Tourist information

GETTING THERE

The best way to reach Belém is to take tram 15 from Praça do Comércio along the busy waterfront. Buses 28, 727, 729 and 751 also go to Belém. Slow trains from Cais do Sodré to Oeiras stop at Belém.

◁ **Nave of Santa Maria de Belém, the church of the Jerónimos monastery**

Street-by-Street: Belém

Stone caravel, Jerónimos monastery

Portugal's former maritime glory, expressed in the imposing, exuberant buildings such as the Jerónimos monastery, is evident all around Belém. In Salazar's *(see p17)* attempted revival of awareness of Portugal's Golden Age, the area along the waterfront, which had silted up since the days of the caravels, was restructured to celebrate the former greatness of the nation. Praça do Império was laid out for the Exhibition of the Portuguese World in 1940 and Praça Afonso de Albuquerque was dedicated to Portugal's first viceroy of India. The royal Palácio de Belém, restored with gardens and a riding school by João V in the 18th century, briefly housed the royal family after the 1755 earthquake.

★ **Mosteiro dos Jerónimos**
Vaulted arcades and richly carved columns adorned with foliage, exotic animals and navigational instruments decorate the Manueline cloister of the Jerónimos monastery ④

| 0 metres | 50 |
| 0 yards | 50 |

LARGO

DOS

JERÓNIMOS

PRAÇA DO IMPÉRIO

Torre de Belém *(see p70)*

Museu Nacional de Arqueologia
Archaeological finds ranging from an Iron Age gold bracelet to Moorish artifacts are among the interesting exhibits on display ⑤

STAR SIGHTS

★ Mosteiro dos Jerónimos

★ Jardím Botânico Tropical

KEY

– – – Suggested route

Praça do Império
is the great square in front of the monastery. The central fountain is lit up on special occasions.

★ Jardím Botânico Tropical

Exotic plants and trees gathered from Portugal's former colonies fill these peaceful gardens that were once part of the Palácio de Belém ❸

LOCATOR MAP
See Lisbon Street Finder maps 1 & 2

Antiga Confeitaria de Belém, a 19th-century café, sells pastéis de Belém, rich custard in a flaky pastry cup.

TRAVESSA DOS FERREIROS

T. MARTA PINTO

RUA DE BELÉM

Central Lisbon

RUA VIEIRA PORTUENSE

Palácio de Belém

Also known as the Palácio Cor de Rosa (pink palace) because of its faded pink façade, the former royal palace is the residence of the Portuguese president. It also houses the Museu da Presidência ❶

Museu Nacional dos Coches (see p64) ❷

Rua Vieira Portuense *runs along a small park. Its colourful 16th- and 17th-century houses contrast with the typically imposing buildings in Belém.*

Praça Afonso de Albuquerque

is named after the first Portuguese viceroy of India. A Neo-Manueline column in the centre bears his statue, with scenes from his life carved on the base.

Palácio de Belém ❶

Praça Afonso de Albuquerque.
Map 1 C4. **Tel** 213 614 600. 🚌 28,
714, 727, 729, 751. 🚊 15. 🚇 Belém.
⬜ 10am–6pm Sat, 2:30–4:30pm Sun.
📷 compulsory (213 414 660). 📷
Museu da Presidência ⬜ 10am–
6pm Tue–Sun. ● Easter, 1 May,
25 Dec. **www**.museu.presidencia.pt

Built by the Conde de Aveiras
in 1559, before the Tagus had
receded, this palace once had
gardens bordering the river.
In the 1700s it was bought by
João V, who made it suitably
lavish for his amorous liaisons.

When the 1755 earthquake
struck (see pp22–3), the king,
José I, and his family were
staying here and thus survived
the devastation of central
Lisbon. Fearing another tremor,
the royal family temporarily set
up camp in tents in the palace
grounds; the interior was used
as a hospital. Today the elegant
pink building is the residence
of the President of Portugal.

The Museu da Presidência,
located within the palace,
uses multimedia systems to
illustrate Portugal's political
history.

Pink façade of the Palácio de Belém, home of the President of Portugal

Museu Nacional dos Coches ❷

Praça Afonso de Albuquerque.
Map 2 D4. **Tel** 213 610 850.
🚌 28, 714, 727, 729, 751. 🚊 15.
🚇 Belém. ⬜ 10am–6pm Tue–Sun.
● 1 Jan, Easter, 1 May, 25 Dec.
📷 (free until 2pm Sun). 📷 for
groups by appt. 📷 ♿ ground floor
only. **www**.museudoscoches.pt

The museum's collection of
coaches is arguably the finest
in Europe. Occupying the east
wing of the Palácio de Belém,
this was formerly the riding
school built

by the Italian architect
Giacomo Azzolini in 1726.
Seated in the upper gallery,
the royal family used to watch
their beautiful Lusitanian horses
performing in the arena. In
1905 the riding school was
turned into a museum by King
Carlos's wife, Dona Amélia,
whose riding cloak is on show.

Made in Portugal, Italy,
France, Austria and Spain, the
coaches span three centuries
and range from the plain to
the preposterous. The main
gallery, in Louis XVI style
with splendid painted ceiling,
is the setting for two straight,
regimented rows of coaches
created for Portuguese royalty.
The collection starts with
the comparatively plain
17th-century red leather
and wood coach of Philip
II of Spain. The coaches
become more sumptuous,
the interiors are lined with
red velvet and gold, the
exteriors are carved and
decorated with allegories
and royal coats of arms. The
rows end with three huge
Baroque coaches made in
Rome for the Portuguese
ambassador to the Vatican,
Dom Rodrigo Almeida e
Menezes, the Marquês de
Abrantes. The epitome of
pomp and extravagance,
these 5-tonne carriages
are embellished with
life-size gilded statues.
The neighbouring gallery
has further examples of
royal carriages, including
two-wheeled cabriolets,
landaus and pony-drawn
chaises used by young
members of the royal
family. There is also a 19th-
century Lisbon cab, painted
black and green, the colours of

Rear view of a coach built in 1716 for the Marquês de
Abrantes, the Portuguese ambassador to Pope Clement XI

taxis right up to the 1990s. The 18th-century Eyeglass Chaise, whose black leather hood is pierced by sinister eye-like windows, was made during the era of Pombal *(see p17)* when lavish decoration was discouraged. The upper gallery has a collection of harnesses, court costumes and portraits of members of the royal family.

Jardim Botânico Tropical ❸

Rua da Junqueira 86 (entrance on Largo do Jerónimos). **Map** 1 C4. **Tel** *213 609 665.* 🚌 *28, 49, 112, 727, 751.* 🚋 *15.* ⭘ *9am–6pm Mon–Fri (Oct–Mar: to 5pm), 11am–7pm Sat & Sun (Oct–Mar: 10am–5pm).* ⬤ *1 Jan, Easter, 25 Dec.* 🎫 ♿

Also known as the Jardim do Ultramar, this peaceful park with ponds, waterfowl and peacocks, attracts surprisingly few visitors. Designed at the beginning of the 20th century as the research centre of the Institute for Tropical Sciences, it is more of an arboretum than a flower garden. The emphasis is on rare and endangered tropical and plants. Among the most striking are dragon trees, native to the Canary Islands and Madeira, monkey puzzle trees from South America and an avenue of Washington palms. The oriental garden with its streams and bridges is heralded by a large Chinese-style gateway that represented Macau in the Exhibition of the Portuguese World in 1940 *(see p62)*.

The research buildings are housed in the Palácio dos Condes da Calheta, whose interior walls are covered with *azulejos* spanning three centuries. Temporary exhibitions are held in the palace (closed 12:30–2pm).

Mosteiro dos Jerónimos ❹

See pp66–7.

Washington palms in the Jardim Botânico Tropical

Museu Nacional de Arqueologia ❺

Praça do Império. **Map** 1 B4. **Tel** *213 620 000.* 🚌 *28, 714, 727, 729, 751.* 🚋 *15.* ⭘ *10am–6pm Tue–Sun.* ⬤ *1 Jan, Easter, 1 May, 25 Dec.* 🎫 *(free until 2pm Sun & hols).* 📷 ♿ **www.**mnarqueologia-ipmuseus.pt

The long west wing of the Mosteiro dos Jerónimos *(see pp66–7),* formerly the monks' dormitory, has been a museum since 1893. Reconstructed in the middle of the 19th century, the building is a poor imitation of the Manueline original. The museum houses Portugal's main archaeological research centre and the exhibits, from sites all over the country, include a gold Iron Age bracelet, Visigothic jewellery found in the Alentejo in southern Portugal, Roman ornaments and early 8th-century Moorish artifacts. The main Greco-Roman and Egyptian section is strong on funerary art, featuring figurines, tombstones, masks, terracotta amulets and funeral cones inscribed with hieroglyphics alluding to the solar system. The dimly lit Room of Treasures has a fine collection of coins, necklaces, bracelets

Visigothic buckle, Museu Nacional de Arqueologia

and other jewellery dating from 1800–500 BC. This room has been refurbished to allow more of the magnificent jewellery, unseen by the public for decades, to be shown.

Planetário Calouste Gulbenkian ❻

Praça do Império. **Map** 1 B4. **Tel** *213 620 002.* 🚌 *28, 714, 727, 751.* 🚋 *15.* ⭘ *4pm Thu, 3pm & 4pm Sat, 11:30am, 3pm & 4pm Sun. Jul & Aug: 11am & 2:30pm Tue & Wed.* 🎫 📷 ♿ **www.**planetario.online.pt

Financed by the Gulbenkian Foundation *(see p79)* and built in 1965, this modern building sits incongruously beside the Jerónimos monastery. Inside, the Planetarium reveals the mysteries of the cosmos. There are shows in Portuguese, English and French explaining the movement of the stars and our solar system, as well as presentations on more specialist themes, such as the constellations or the Star of Bethlehem (Belém).

The dome of the Planetário Calouste Gulbenkian

Mosteiro dos Jerónimos ●

Armillary sphere in the cloister

A monument to the wealth of the Age of Discovery *(see pp20–21)*, this monastery is the culmination of Manueline architecture in this period. Commissioned by Manuel I in around 1501, after Vasco de Gama's return from his historic voyage, it was financed largely by "pepper money", a tax levied on spices, precious stones and gold. Various masterbuilders worked on the building, the most notable of whom was Diogo Boitac, replaced by João de Castilho in 1517. The monastery was cared for by the Order of St Jerome (Hieronymites) until 1834, when all religious orders were disbanded.

Tomb of Vasco da Gama
The 19th-century tomb of the navigator (see p68) *is carved with armillary spheres and other seafaring symbols.*

Refectory
The walls of the refectory are tiled with 18th-century azulejos. *The panel at the northern end depicts the Feeding of the Five Thousand.*

The fountain is in the shape of a lion, the heraldic animal of St Jerome.

The modern wing, built in 1850 in Neo-Manueline style, houses the Museu Nacional de Arqueologia *(see p65).*

The west portal was designed by the French sculptor Nicolau Chanterène.

Entrance to church and cloister

Gallery

View of the Monastery
This 17th-century scene by Felipe Lobo shows women at a fountain in front of the Mosteiro dos Jerónimos.

STAR FEATURES

★ South Portal

★ Cloister

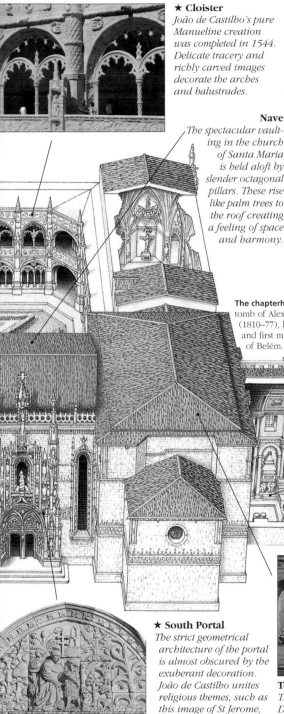

★ Cloister
João de Castilho's pure Manueline creation was completed in 1544. Delicate tracery and richly carved images decorate the arches and balustrades.

Nave
The spectacular vaulting in the church of Santa Maria is held aloft by slender octagonal pillars. These rise like palm trees to the roof creating a feeling of space and harmony.

The chapterhouse holds the tomb of Alexandre Herculano (1810–77), historian and first mayor of Belém.

The chancel was commissioned in 1572 by Dona Catarina, wife of João III.

The tombs of Manuel I, his wife Dona Maria, João III and Catarina are supported by elephants.

★ South Portal
The strict geometrical architecture of the portal is almost obscured by the exuberant decoration. João de Castilho unites religious themes, such as this image of St Jerome, with the secular, exalting the kings of Portugal.

Tomb of King Sebastião
The tomb of the "longed for" Dom Sebastião stands empty. The young king never returned from battle in 1578.

Façade of the Museu de Marinha

Museu de Marinha 🕖

Praça do Império. **Map** 1 B4.
Tel 213 620 019. 🚌 28, 727,
729, 751. 🚊 15. ⬜ 10am–6pm
Tue–Sun (Oct–Apr: to 5pm). ⬤ 1 Jan,
Easter, 1 May, 25 Dec. 🎫 (213 620
010). 📷 (free 10am–2pm Sun). 📷
📱 http://museu.marinha.pt

The Maritime Museum was
inaugurated in 1962 in the
west wing of the Jerónimos
monastery (see p66–7). It was
here, in the chapel built by
Henry the Navigator (see p21),
that mariners took mass before
embarking on their voyages.

A hall devoted to the
Discoveries illustrates
the progress in ship-
building from the
mid-15th century,
capitalizing on the
experience of long-
distance explorers.
Small replicas show
the transition from
the bark to the
lateen-rigged caravel,
through the faster
square-rigged caravel,
to the Portuguese
nau. Also here are
navigational instru-
ments, astrolabes and
replicas of 16th-cen-
tury maps showing
the world as it was
known then. The
stone pillars, carved
with the Cross of the
Knights of Christ, are
replicas of the types
of *padrão* set up as
monuments to Portu-
guese sovereignty
on the lands discovered.

A series of rooms displaying
models of modern Portuguese
ships leads on to the Royal
Quarters, where you can see
the exquisitely furnished
wood-panelled cabin of King
Carlos and Queen Amélia
from the royal yacht *Amélia*,
built in Scotland in 1900.

The modern, incongruous
pavilion opposite houses original royal barges, the most
extravagant of which is the
royal brig built in 1780 for
Maria I. The collection ends
with a display of seaplanes,
including the *Santa Clara*
which made the first crossing
of the South Atlantic in 1922.

Centro Cultural de Belém 🕗

Praça do Império. **Map** 1 B5.
Tel 213 612 400. 🚌 28, 727, 729,
751. 🚊 15. 🚊 Belém. ⬜ 8am–
8pm Mon–Fri, 10am–10pm Sat,
10am–7pm Sun. 📷 📱 www.ccb.pt

The construction of a stark
modern building between the
Manueline splendour of the
Jéronimos monastery and the
Tagus proved controversial.
Built as the headquarters of
the Portuguese presidency
of the European Community,
the Centro Cultural de Belém
opened as a cultural and
conference centre in 1993. It
stresses music, performing arts
and films. An exhibition centre
houses the Museu Colecção
Berardo (see opposite).

Both the café and restaurant
spill out onto the ramparts of
the building whose peaceful
gardens of olive trees and
geometric lawns look out
over the quay and the river.

**The modern complex of the
Centro Cultural de Belém**

Monument to the Discoveries 🕘

Padrão dos Descobrimentos, Avda de
Brasília. **Map** 1 C5. **Tel** 213 031 950.
🚌 28, 727, 729, 751. 🚊 15.
🚊 Belém. ⬜ May–Sep: 10am–7pm
daily; Oct–Apr: 10am–6pm Tue–Sun.
⬤ 1 Jan, 1 May, 25 Dec. 📷 for lift.
📷 www.padraodosdescobrimentos.
egeac.pt

Standing prominently on the
Belém waterfront, this massive angular monument, the
Padrão dos Descobrimentos,
was built in 1960 to mark the
500th anniversary of the death
of Henry the Navigator (see
p21). The 52-m- (170-ft-) high
monument, commissioned by
the Salazar regime, commemorates the mariners, royal

VASCO DA GAMA (C.1460–1524)

In 1498 Vasco da Gama sailed
around the Cape of Good Hope
and opened the sea route to India
(see pp20–21). Although the Hindu
ruler of Calicut, who received him
wearing diamond and ruby rings,
was not impressed by his humble
offerings of cloth and wash basins,
da Gama returned to Portugal
with a cargo of spices. In 1502 he
sailed again to India, establishing
Portuguese trade routes in the
Indian Ocean. João III nominated
him Viceroy of India in 1524, but
he died of a fever soon after.

**16th-century painting of
Vasco da Gama in Goa**

The huge pavement compass in front of the Monument to the Discoveries

Museu Colecção Berardo Arte Moderna e Contemporânea ⑩

Praça do Império. **Map** 1 B5.
Tel *213 612 878.* 🚌 *28, 727, 729, 751.* 🚊 *15.* 🚋 *Belém.*
⏰ *10am–7pm daily.* ♿
www.museuberardo.pt

patrons and all those who took part in the development of the Portuguese Age of Discovery. The monument is designed in the shape of a caravel, with Portugal's coat of arms on the sides and the sword of the Royal House of Avis rising above the entrance. Henry the Navigator stands at the prow with a caravel in hand. In two sloping lines either side of the monument are stone statues of Portuguese heroes linked with the Age of Discovery. On the western face these include Dom Manuel I holding an armillary sphere, the poet Camões with a copy of *Os Lusíadas* and the painter Nuno Gonçalves with a paint pallet.

On the monument's north side, the huge mariner's compass cut into the paving stone was a present from the Republic of South Africa in 1960. The central map, dotted with galleons and mermaids, shows the routes of the discoverers in the 15th and 16th centuries. Inside the monument a lift whisks you up to the sixth floor where steps then lead to the top for a splendid panorama of the river and Belém. The basement level is used for temporary exhibitions. The monument also functions as an educational centre where children can learn about Portugal's golden age of discovery and Lisbon's chequered history.

The Padrão is not to everyone's taste but the setting is undeniably splendid and the caravel design is imaginative. The monument looks particularly dramatic when viewed from the west in the light of the late afternoon sun.

The brainchild of business mogul and art collector José Manuel Rodrigues Berardo, this fascinating gallery boasts around 1,000 works by more than 500 artists. The Museu Berardo provides a rich compendium of a century of modern and contemporary art through a variety of media, from canvas to sculpture and from photography to video installations.

Among the highlights are Pablo Picasso's *Tête de Femme* (1909), a good example of the Spanish artist's Cubist style; several variants of Andy Warhol's famous *Brillo Box* (1964–8); Jeff Koons's *Poodle* (1991) and Balthus's *Portrait de Femme en Robe Bleue* (1935). Other artists on show include Piet Mondrian, Francis Bacon, Willem de Kooning, Richard Long and Henry Moore. There is also much Portuguese art on display, including Alberto Carneiro's sculptures, etchings by Paula Rego and dramatic black-and-white photographs by Fernando Lemos.

EASTERN FACE OF THE MONUMENT TO THE DISCOVERIES

Afonso V (1432–81), patron of the first explorers

Henry the Navigator (1394–1460)

Pedro Álvares Cabral (1467–1520), discoverer of Brazil

Vasco da Gama (1460–1524)

Fernão Magalhães (Magellan), who crossed the Pacific in 1520–21

Padrão erected by Diogo Cão in the Congo in 1482

Torre de Belém ⑪

Arms of Manuel I

Commissioned by Manuel I, the tower was built as a fortress in the middle of the Tagus in 1514–20. The starting point for the navigators who set out to discover the trade routes, this Manueline gem became a symbol of Portugal's great era of expansion. The real beauty of the tower lies in the decoration of the exterior. Adorned with rope carved in stone, it has openwork balconies, Moorish-style watchtowers and distinctive battlements in the shape of shields. The Gothic interior below the terrace, which served as a storeroom for arms and a prison, is very austere but the private quarters in the tower are worth visiting for the loggia and the panorama.

VISITORS' CHECKLIST

Avenida de Brasilia. **Map** 1 A5. **Tel** 213 620 034. 📧 28, 727, 729, 751. 🚊 15. 🚋 Belém. ⏰ 10am–6:30pm Tue–Sun (Oct–Apr: to 5:30pm). 🎫 (free Sun & pub hols until 2pm). 📷 ♿ partial.

Renaissance Loggia
The elegant arcaded loggia, inspired by Italian archi-tecture, gives a light touch to the defensive battlements.

Armillary spheres and nautical rope are symbols of Portugal's seafaring prowess.

Chapel

Royal coat of arms of Manuel I

Battlements are decorated with the cross of the Order of Christ.

Virgin and Child
A statue of Our Lady of Safe Homecoming faces the sea, a symbol of protection for sailors.

Governor's room

Entrance

Gangway to shore

Sentry posts

The vaulted dungeon was used as a prison until the 19th century.

The Torre de Belém in 1811
This painting of a British ship navigating the Tagus, by JT Serres, shows the tower further from the shore than it is today. Land on the north bank was reclaimed in the 19th century.

The simple Manueline chapel, Ermida de São Jerónimo

Ermida de São Jerónimo ⑫

Rua Pero de Covilhã. **Map** 1 A3. **Tel** 213 018 648. 28, 49, 73, 714, 729, 751. Mon–Sat (by appt only).

Also known as the Capela de São Jerónimo, this elegant little chapel was constructed in 1514 when Diogo Boitac was working on the Jerónimos monastery (see pp66–7). Although a far simpler building, it is also Manueline in style and may have been built to a design by Boitac. The only decorative elements on the monolithic chapel are the four pinnacles, corner gargoyles and Manueline portal. Perched on a quiet hill above Belém, the chapel has fine views down to the River Tagus and a path from the terrace winds down the hill towards the Torre de Belém.

Igreja da Memória ⑬

Calçada do Galvão, Ajuda. **Map** 1 C3. **Tel** 213 635 295. 28, 732. 18. for mass 6pm Mon–Sat, 10am Sun.

Built in 1760, the church was founded by King José I in gratitude for his escape from an assassination plot on this site in 1758. The king was returning from a secret liaison with a lady of the noble Távora family when his carriage was attacked and a bullet hit him in the arm. Pombal (see p17) used this as an excuse to get rid of his enemies in the Távora family, accusing them of conspiracy. In 1759 they were savagely tortured and executed. Their deaths are commemorated by a pillar in Beco do Chão Salgado, off Rua de Belém.

The Neo-Classical domed church has a marble-clad interior and a small chapel, on the right, containing the tomb of Pombal. He died at the age of 83, a year after he had been banished from Lisbon.

Jardim Botânico da Ajuda ⑭

Calçada da Ajuda. **Map** 1 C2. **Tel** 213 622 503. 28, 73, 714, 727, 729, 732. 18. 9am–6pm daily (Apr: to 7pm; May–Sep: to 8pm). 1 Jan, 25 Dec.

Laid out on two levels by Pombal (see p17) in 1768, these Italian-style gardens provide a pleasant respite from the noisy suburbs of Belém. The entrance (wrought-iron gates in a pink wall) is easy to miss. The park comprises 5,000 plant species from Africa, Asia and America. Notable features are the 400-year-old dragon tree, native of Madeira, and the 18th-century fountain decorated with serpents, winged fish, sea horses and mythical creatures. A terrace looks out over the lower level of the gardens.

Palácio Nacional da Ajuda ⑮

Calçada da Ajuda. **Map** 2 D2. **Tel** 213 620 264. 60, 732, 742. 18. 10am–5:30pm Thu–Tue. 1 Jan, Easter, 1 May, 25 Dec. (free until 2pm Sun & pub hols). www.pnajuda.imc-ip.pt

The royal palace, destroyed by fire in 1795, was replaced in the early 19th century by this Neo-Classical building. It was left incomplete when the royal family was forced into exile in Brazil in 1807.

The palace only became a permanent residence of the royal family when Luís I became king in 1861 and married an Italian Princess, Maria Pia di Savoia. No expense was spared in furnishing the apartments, which feature silk wallpaper, Sèvres porcelain and crystal chandeliers.

A prime example of regal excess is the extraordinary Saxe Room, a wedding present to Maria Pia from the King of Saxony, in which every piece of furniture is decorated with Meissen porcelain. On the first floor the huge Banqueting Hall, with crystal chandeliers, silk-covered chairs and an allegory of the birth of João VI on the frescoed ceiling, is truly impressive. At the other end of the palace, Luís I's Neo-Gothic painting studio is a more intimate display of intricately carved furniture.

19th-century throne from the Palácio Nacional da Ajuda

Manicured formal gardens of the Jardim Botânico da Ajuda

FURTHER AFIELD

The majority of the outlying sights, which include some of Lisbon's finest museums, are easily accessible by bus or metro from the city centre. A ten-minute walk north from the gardens of the Parque Eduardo VII brings you to Portugal's great cultural complex, the Calouste Gulbenkian Foundation, set in a pleasant park. Few tourists go further north than the Gulbenkian, but the Museu da Cidade on Campo Grande is worth a detour for its fascinating overview of Lisbon's history.

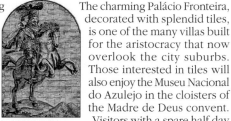

Azulejo **panel from Palácio Fronteira**

The charming Palácio Fronteira, decorated with splendid tiles, is one of the many villas built for the aristocracy that now overlook the city suburbs. Those interested in tiles will also enjoy the Museu Nacional do Azulejo in the cloisters of the Madre de Deus convent. Visitors with a spare half day can cross the Tagus to the Cristo Rei monument. Northeast of Lisbon is the vast oceanarium, Oceanário de Lisboa, in the Parque das Nações, which includes other family-oriented attractions, hotels and shops.

SIGHTS AT A GLANCE

Museums and Galleries
Centro de Arte Moderna **7**
Museu da Água **9**
Museu Calouste Gulbenkian pp76–9 **6**
Museu da Cidade **13**
Museu Nacional do Azulejo pp82–3 **10**

Modern Architecture
Colombo Shopping Centre **3**
Cristo Rei **1**
Parque das Nações **11**
Ponte 25 de Abril **2**

Historic Architecture
Aqueduto das Águas Livres **15**
Campo Pequeno **8**
Palácio Fronteira **16**
Praça Marquês de Pombal **4**

Parks and Gardens
Parque Eduardo VII **5**
Parque do Monteiro-Mor **17**

Zoos
Jardim Zoológico **14**
Oceanário de Lisboa **12**

KEY
Main sightseeing areas
Airport
Ferry boarding point
Motorway
Major road
Minor road

0 kilometres   4

0 miles   2

SIGHTS BEYOND THE CITY CENTRE

Vila Franca de Xira

17 Pontinha
A9
IC17
Amadora
IC19
Benfica
3 IC17
13 Campo Grande
IP1 – A1 (E1)
Olivais
11
12
IC2
14
16
PARQUE FLORESTAL **15** **5** Estefânia
DE MONSANTO **4**
Carnaxide
IC15 – A5
8
6
7
Xabregas
10
9
Graça
Cascais
N6
Alcântara
N6
Montijo
A9
IP7 – A2 (E1)
Tejo
2
Cacilhas
Almada
Burretro
Porto Brandão
Setúbal
1
Seixal

◁ **Nymph fountain among tropical vegetation inside the Estufa Fria, Parque Eduardo VII**

The towering monument of Cristo Rei overlooking the Tagus

Cristo Rei 1

Santuário Nacional do Cristo Rei, Alto do Pragal, Almada. *Tel 212 751 000*. 🚢 *from Cais do Sodré to Cacilhas then* 🚌 *101*. ⏰ *9:30am– 6:15pm daily (Jul–Sep: to 6:30pm Mon–Fri, to 7pm Sat & Sun)*. 🕳

Modelled on the more famous Cristo Redentor in Rio de Janeiro, this giant-sized statue stands with arms outstretched on the south bank of the Tagus. The 28-m- (92-ft-) tall figure of Christ, mounted on

a huge pedestal, was built by Francisco Franco in 1949–59 at the instigation of Prime Minister Salazar.

You can see the monument from various viewpoints in the city, but it is fun to take a ferry to the Outra Banda (the other bank), then a bus or taxi to the monument. A lift, plus some steps, takes you up 82 m (269 ft) to the top of the pedestal, affording fine views of the city and river.

Ponte 25 de Abril 2

Map 3 A5. 🚌 *753*.

Originally called the Ponte Salazar after the dictator who had it built in 1966, Lisbon's suspension bridge was renamed (like many other monuments) to commemorate the revolution of 25 April 1974 which restored democracy to Portugal *(see p17)*.

Inspired by San Francisco's Golden Gate Bridge in the United States, this steel construction stretches for 1 km (half a mile). The lower tier was modified in 1999 to accommodate the Fertagus, a much-needed railway across the Tagus.

The bridge's notorious traffic congestion has been partly resolved by the open- ing of the 17-km (11-mile) Vasco da Gama bridge.

Spanning the River Tagus from Montijo to Sacavém, north of the Parque das Nações, this bridge was completed in 1998.

Colombo Shopping Centre 3

Avenida Lusíada. *Tel 217 113 600*. Ⓜ *Colégio Militar/Luz*. 🚌 *729, 764*. ⏰ *10am–midnight daily*. 🌑 *1 Jan, 25 Dec*. ♿ **www**.colombo.pt

Colombo is the largest shopping centre in the Iberian Peninsula. This vast complex houses more than 420 shops, including fashion stores such as Mango, Zara, H&M and Timberland, a Disney Store and a branch of FNAC. It also offers ten cinema screens, a health club, an indoor amusement park, a bowling alley and over 60 restaurants, from American fast-food joints to traditional and typically Portuguese establishments.

Praça Marquês de Pombal 4

Map 5 C5. Ⓜ *Marquês de Pombal*. 🚌 *12, 22, 36, 702, 711, 720, 723, 727, 732, 738 & many other routes*.

At the top of the Avenida da Liberdade *(see p44)*, traffic thunders round the "Rotunda" (roundabout), as the praça is

Ponte 25 de Abril linking central Lisbon with the Outra Banda, the south bank of the Tagus

Detail on the base of the monument in Praça Marquês de Pombal

also known. At the centre is the lofty monument to Pombal. The despotic statesman, who virtually ruled Portugal from 1750–77, stands on the top of the column, his hand on a lion (symbol of power) and his eyes directed down to the Baixa, whose creation he masterminded *(see p17)*. Allegorical images depicting Pombal's political, educational and agricultural reforms decorate the base of the monument. Standing figures represent Coimbra University where he introduced a Faculty of Science. Although greatly feared, this dynamic politician propelled the country into the Age of Enlightenment. Broken blocks of stone at the foot of the monument and tidal waves flooding the city are an allegory of the destruction caused by the 1755 earthquake.

An underpass, which is not always open, leads to the centre of the square where the sculptures on the pedestal and the inscriptions relating to Pombal's achievements can be seen. Nearby, the well-tended Parque Eduardo VII extends northwards behind the square. The paving stones around the Rotunda are decorated with a mosaic of Lisbon's coat of arms. Similar patterns in small black and white cobbles decorate many of the city's streets and squares.

Many of the city's sightseeing operators have their main pick-up located at the bottom of Parque Eduardo VII. There is also a multi-lingual booth where visitors can buy tickets and plan excursions.

Parque Eduardo VII ❺

Praça Marquês de Pombal. **Map** 5 B4. *Tel* 213 882 278. Ⓜ *Marquès de Pombal.* 🚌 *12, 22, 711, 738.* **Estufa Fria** *Tel* 213 882 278. ⬤ *9am–5pm daily (Apr–Oct: to 6pm).* 🚫

Central Lisbon's largest park was named after King Edward VII of England, who came here in 1902 to reaffirm the Anglo-Portuguese alliance. The wide grassy slope, which extends for 25 hectares (62 acres), was laid out as Parque da Liberdade, a continuation of Avenida da Liberdade *(see p44)*, in the late 19th century.

Neatly clipped box hedging, flanked by mosaic patterned walkways, stretches uphill from the Praça Marquês de Pombal to a belvedere at the top. Here are a flower-filled garden dedicated to the memory of Amália Rodrigues and a pleasant café. From here there are fine views of the city. On clear days it is possible to see as far as the Serra da Arrábida *(see p111)*.

Located at the northwest corner, the most inspiring feature of this rather monotonous park is the jungle-like **Estufa Fria**, or greenhouse, where exotic plants, streams and waterfalls provide an oasis from the city streets. There are in fact two greenhouses: in the Estufa Fria (cold greenhouse), palms push through the slatted bamboo roof and paths wind through a forest of ferns, fuchsias, flowering shrubs and banana trees; the warmer Estufa Quente, or hot-house, is a glassed-over garden with lush plants, water-lily ponds and cacti.

Near the estufas a pond with carp and a galleon-shaped play area are popular with children. On the east side the **Pavilhão Carlos Lopes**, named after the 1984 Olympic marathon winner, is now used for concerts and conferences.

Tropical plants in the Estufa Quente glasshouse, Parque Eduardo VII

Museu Calouste Gulbenkian ⑥

Thanks to a wealthy Armenian oil magnate, Calouste Gulbenkian *(see p79)*, with wide-ranging tastes and an eye for a masterpiece, the museum has one of the finest collections of art in Europe. Inaugurated in 1969, the purpose-built museum was created as part of the charitable institution bequeathed to Portugal by the multimillionaire. The design of the building, set in a spacious park allowing natural light to fill some of the rooms, was devised to create the best layout for the founder's varied collection.

Mustard Barrel
This 18th-century silver mustard barrel was made in France by Antoine Sébastien Durant.

Lalique Corsage Ornament
The sinuous curves of the gold and enamel snakes are typical of René Lalique's Art Nouveau jewellery.

★ Diana
This fine marble statue (1780) by the French sculptor Jean-Antoine Houdon, was once owned by Catherine the Great of Russia but was considered too obscene to exhibit. The graceful Diana, goddess of the hunt, stands with a bow and arrow in hand.

Entrance

Stairs to

★ St Catherine
This serene bust of St Catherine was painted by the Flemish artist Rogier Van der Weyden (1400–64). The thin strip of landscape on the left of the wooden panel brings light and depth to the still portrait.

STAR EXHIBITS

★ Portrait of an Old Man by Rembrandt

★ Diana by Houdon

★ St Catherine by Van der Weyden

★ Portrait of an Old Man

Rembrandt was a master of light and shade. In this expressive portrait, dated 1645, the fragile countenance of the old man is contrasted with the strong and dramatic lighting.

VISITORS' CHECKLIST

Avenida de Berna 45.
Map 5 B2. **Tel** *217 823 000.*
Ⓜ *Praça de Espanha or São Sebastião.* 🚌 *16, 56, 718, 726, 742, 746.* ⏰ *10am–6pm Tue–Sun.* ⏺ *1 Jan, Easter Sun, 1 May, 25 Dec.*
🎫 *(free Sun).* ♿ ▯ 🍴
www.museu.gulbenkian.pt

Vase of a Hundred Birds

The enamel decoration that adorns this Chinese porcelain vase is known as Famille Verte. *This type of elaborate design is characteristic of the Ch'ing dynasty during the reign of the Emperor K'ang Hsi (1662–1722)*

Renaissance art

GALLERY GUIDE

The galleries are laid out both chronologically and geographically, the first section (rooms 1–6) dedicated to Classical and Oriental art, the second section (rooms 7–17) housing the European collection of paintings, sculpture, furniture, silverware and jewellery.

Armenian art

Statue of Bes

Dating from 660–610 BC, this statue depicts the Egyptian god Bes. Other stunning Egyptian pieces include a gilded mask of a mummy.

Persian faïence

Turkish Faïence Plate

The factories at Iznik in Turkey produced some of the most beautiful jugs, plates and vases of the Islamic world, including this 17th-century deep plate decorated with stylized animal forms.

KEY TO FLOORPLAN

- ▢ Egyptian, Classical and Mesopotamian art
- ▢ Oriental Islamic art
- ▢ Far Eastern art
- ▢ European art (14th–17th centuries)
- ▢ French 18th-century decorative arts
- ▢ European art (18th–19th centuries)
- ▢ Lalique collection
- ▢ Non-exhibition space

Exploring the Gulbenkian Collection

Housing Calouste Gulbenkian's unique collection of art, the museum ranks with the Museu de Arte Antiga *(see pp56–9)* as the finest in Lisbon. The exhibits, which span over 4,000 years from ancient Egyptian statuettes, through translucent Islamic glassware, to Art Nouveau brooches, are displayed in spacious and well-lit galleries, many overlooking the gardens or courtyards. The museum is quite small, however each individual work of art, from the magnificent pieces that make up the rich display of Oriental and Islamic art, to the selection of European paintings and furniture, is worthy of attention.

Late 16th-century Persian faïence tile from the School of Isfahan

EGYPTIAN, CLASSICAL AND MESOPOTAMIAN ART

Priceless treasures chart the evolution of Egyptian art from the Old Kingdom (c.2700 BC) to the Roman Period (1st century BC). The exhibits range from an alabaster bowl of the 3rd Dynasty to a surprisingly modern-looking blue terracotta torso of a statuette of *Venus Anadyomene* from the Roman period.

Outstanding pieces in the Classical art section are a magnificent red-figure Greek vase and 11 Roman medallions, found in Egypt. These are believed to have been struck to commemorate the athletic games held in Macedonia in AD 242 in honour of Alexander the Great. In the Mesopotamian art section the large Assyrian

5th-century BC Greek vase

alabaster bas-relief represents the winged genius of Spring, carrying a container of sacred water (9th century BC).

ORIENTAL ISLAMIC ART

Being Armenian, Calouste Gulbenkian had a keen interest in art from the Near and Middle East. The Oriental Islamic gallery has a fine collection of Persian and Turkish carpets, textiles, costumes and ceramics. In the section overlooking the courtyard, the Syrian mosque lamps and bottles commissioned by princes and sultans, are beautifully decorated with coloured enamel on glass. The Armenian section has some exquisite illustrated manuscripts from the 16th to 18th centuries, produced by Armenian refugees in Istanbul, Persia and the Crimea.

FAR EASTERN ART

Calouste Gulbenkian acquired a large collection of Chinese porcelain between 1910 and 1930. One of the rarest pieces is the small blue-glazed bowl from the Yüan Dynasty (1279–1368), on the right as you go into the gallery. The majority of exhibits, however, are the later, more exuberantly decorated *famille verte* porcelain and the K'ang Hsi biscuitware of the 17th and 18th centuries. Further exhibits from the Far East are translucent Chinese jades and other semi-precious stones, Japanese prints, brocaded silk hangings and bound books, and lacquerwork.

EUROPEAN ART (14TH–17TH CENTURIES)

Illuminated manuscripts, rare-printed books and medieval ivories introduce the section on Western art. The delicately sculpted 14th-century ivory diptychs and triptychs, made in France, show scenes from the lives of Christ and the Virgin.

The collection of early European paintings starts with panels of *St Joseph and St Catherine* by Rogier van der Weyden, leading painter of the mid-15th century in Flanders. Italian Renaissance painting is represented by Cima da Conegliano's *Sacra Conversazione* from the late 15th century and Domenico Ghirlandaio's *Portrait of a Young Woman* (c.1490).

The collection progresses to Flemish and Dutch works of the 17th century, including two works by Rembrandt: *Portrait of an Old Man* (1645),

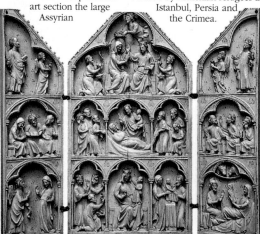

French ivory triptych of
Scenes from the Life of the Virgin **(14th century)**

a masterpiece of psychological penetration, and *Pallas Athena* (c.1660–61), said to have been modelled on Rembrandt's son, Titus, and previously thought to have portrayed the Greek goddess Pallas Athena. Rubens is represented by three paintings, the most remarkable of which is the *Portrait of Hélène Fourment* (1630), the artist's second wife.

The gallery beyond the Dutch and Flemish paintings has tapestries and textiles from Italy and Flanders, Italian ceramics, rare 15th-century medallions and sculpture.

View of the Molo with the Ducal Palace (1790) by Francesco Guardi

FRENCH 18TH-CENTURY DECORATIVE ARTS

Some remarkably elaborate Louis XV and Louis XVI pieces, many commissioned by royalty, feature in the collection of French 18th-century furniture. The exhibits, many of them embellished with laquer panels, ebony and bronze, are grouped together according to historical style with Beauvais and "chinoiserie" Aubusson tapestries decorating the walls.

The French silverware from the same period, much of which once adorned the dining tables of Russian palaces, includes lavishly decorated soup tureens, salt-cellars and platters.

Louis XV chest of drawers inlaid with ebony and bronze

EUROPEAN ART (18TH–19TH CENTURIES)

The art of the 18th century is dominated by French painters, including Watteau (1684–1721), Fragonard (1732–1806) and Boucher (1703–70). The most celebrated piece of sculpture is a statue of *Diana* by Jean-Antoine Houdon. Commissioned in 1780 by the Duke of Saxe-Gotha for his

gardens, it became one of the principal exhibits in the Hermitage in Russia during the 19th and early 20th centuries.

One whole room is devoted to views of Venice by the 18th-century Venetian painter Francesco Guardi, and a small collection of British art includes works by leading 18th-century portraitists, such as Gainsborough's *Portrait of Mrs Lowndes-Stone* (c.1775) and Romney's *Portrait of Mrs Constable* (1787). There are also two stormy seascapes by JMW Turner (1775–1851). French 19th-century landscape painting is well represented here, reflecting Gulbenkian's preference for naturalism, with works by the Barbizon school and the Impressionists. The best-known paintings in the section, however, are probably Manet's *Boy with Cherries*, painted in about 1858 at the beginning of the artist's career, and *Boy Blowing*

Bubbles, painted about 1867. Renoir's *Portrait of Madame Claude Monet* was painted in about 1872–4 when the artist was staying with Monet at his country home in Argenteuil, in the outskirts of Paris.

LALIQUE COLLECTION

The tour of the museum ends with an entire room filled with the flamboyant creations of French Art Nouveau jeweller, René Lalique (1860–1945). Gulbenkian was a close friend of Lalique's and he acquired many of the pieces of jewellery, glassware and ivory on display here directly from the artist. Inlaid with semi-precious stones and covered with enamel or gold leaf, the brooches, necklaces, vases and combs are decorated with the dragonfly, peacock or sensual female nude motifs characteristic of Art Nouveau.

CALOUSTE GULBENKIAN

Born in Scutari (Turkey) in 1869, Gulbenkian started his art collection at the age of 14 when he bought some ancient coins in a bazaar. In 1928 he was granted a 5 per cent stake in four major oil companies, including BP and Shell, in thanks for his part in the transfer of the assets of the Turkish Petroleum Company to those four companies. He thereby earned himself the nickname of "Mr Five Percent". With the wealth he accumulated, Gulbenkian was able to indulge his passion for fine works of art. During World War II, he went to live in neutral Portugal and, on his death in 1955, bequeathed his estate to the Portuguese in the form of a charitable trust. The Foundation supports many cultural activities and has its own orchestra, art library, concert halls and a modern art centre.

A light-filled gallery at the Centro de Arte Moderna

Centro de Arte Moderna ❼

Rua Dr Nicolau de Bettencourt. **Map** 5 B3. **Tel** 217 823 483. Ⓜ *São Sebastião.* 🚌 *716, 726, 742, 746, 756.* ◯ *10am–6pm Tue–Sun.* ● *1 Jan, Easter, 1 May, 25 Dec.* 🈺 *(free Sun).* ♿ www.gulbenkian.pt

The Modern Art Museum lies across the gardens from the Calouste Gulbenkian museum and is part of the same cultural foundation *(see p79).*

The permanent collection features paintings and sculpture by Portuguese artists from the turn of the 20th century to the present

day. The most famous painting is the striking portrait of poet Fernando Pessoa in the Café Irmãos Unidos (1964) by José de Almada Negreiros (1893–1970), a main exponent of Portuguese Modernism. Also of interest are paintings by Eduardo Viana (1881–1967), Amadeo de Sousa Cardoso (1887–1910) as well as contemporary artists such as Paula Rego, Rui Sanches, Graça Morais and Teresa Magalhães.

The museum is light and spacious, with pleasant gardens and a busy cafeteria.

Campo Pequeno ❽

Map 5 C1. Ⓜ *Campo Pequeno.* 🚌 *36, 745.* **Bullring Tel** *217 998 450.* ◯ *10am–11pm daily.* 🈺 ♿

This square is dominated by the red-brick Neo-Moorish bullring built in the late 19th century. The building has undergone major development, and an underground car park and leisure centre have been added. Much of the bullring's distinctive architecture, such as keyhole-shaped windows and double

cupolas, have been retained. Call the tourist office or the number listed above for information on this and other bullfight venues.

Renovated 19th-century steam pump in the Museu da Água

Museu da Água ❾

Rua do Alviela 12. **Tel** 218 100 215. 🚌 *35, 107.* ◯ *10am–6pm Mon–Sat.* ● *public hols.* 🈺 🅾 **Águas Livres aqueduct** ◯ *Mar–Nov.*

Dedicated to the history of Lisbon's water supply, this small but informative museum was imaginatively created around the city's first steam pumping station. It commemorates Manuel da Maia, the 18th-century engineer who masterminded the Águas Livres aqueduct *(see p84)*. The excellent layout of the museum earned it the Council of Europe Museum Prize in 1990.

Pride of place goes to four lovingly preserved steam engines, one of which still functions (by electricity) and can be switched on for visitors. The development of technology relating to the city's water supply is documented with photographs. Particularly interesting are the sections on the Águas Livres aqueduct and the Alfama's 17th-century Chafariz d'El Rei, one of Lisbon's first fountains. Locals used to queue at one of six founts, depending on their social status.

Museu Nacional do Azulejo ❿

See pp82–3.

Neo-Moorish façade of the bullring in Campo Pequeno

The impressive Oriente Station, located next to Parque das Nações

Parque das Nações ⑪

Avenida Dom João II. *Tel 218 919 898.*
M Oriente. 🚌 *25, 28, 44, 705, 750, 782.* 🚉 *Gare do Oriente.* ◯ *24 hours daily.* ♿ 🍴 🏪 **Pavilhão do Conhecimento – Ciencia Viva** *Tel 218 917 100.* ◯ *10am–6pm Tue–Fri, 11am–7pm Sat & Sun.* ● *1 Jan, 24, 25 & 31 Dec.* 📷 **Casino Lisboa** *Alameda dos Oceanos. Tel 218 929 000.* ◯ *3pm–3am Sun–Thu, 4pm–4am Fri & Sat.* ● *24 Dec.* **Cable car** *Tel 218 956 143.* ◯ *11am–8pm daily (Oct–May: to 7pm).* ● *in adverse weather.* 📷 *www.*portaldasnacoes.pt

Originally the site of Expo '98, Parque das Nações is now a Lisbon hub. With its contemporary architecture and family-oriented attractions, the park has renewed the eastern waterfront, which was once an industrial wasteland. The soaring geometry of the platform canopies over Santiago Calatrava's Oriente Station set the tone for the development. The **Portugal Pavilion**, designed by the Portuguese architect Álvaro Siza Vieira, has a large reinforced-concrete roof suspended like a sailcloth above its forecourt.

The **Pavilhão do Conhecimento – Ciencia Viva** (Knowledge and Science Pavilion) is a modern museum of science and technology that houses several interactive exhibitions. Also in the park is **Casino Lisboa**, with two floors of gaming tables, an auditorium hosting theatrical and musical performances and a range of restaurants. Spectacular views can be had from the **cable car** that links the Torre Vasco da Gama with the marina.

The promenade along the river also offers delightful views, including of the 17.5-km- (11-mile-) long **Vasco da Gama** bridge, the longest in Europe. Also in the area is the Pavilhão Atlântico.

Oceanário de Lisboa ⑫

Esplanada D. Carlos 1, Parque das Nações. *Tel 218 917 002.* M *Oriente.* 🚌 *5, 25, 28, 44, 750, 782.* 🚉 *Oriente.* ◯ *Apr–Oct: 10am–8pm daily; Nov–Mar: 10am–7pm daily.* 📷 ♿ *www.*oceanario.pt

Centrepiece of Expo '98 and now the main attraction at Parque das Nações, the somewhat futuristic oceanarium was designed by American architect Peter Chermayeff, and is perched at the end of a pier, surrounded by water. It is the second-largest aquarium in the world, and holds an impressive array of species – birds and some mammals as well as fish and other underwater dwellers.

Four separate sea- and landscapes represent the habitats of the Atlantic, Pacific, Indian and Antarctic oceans, with suitable fauna and flora. The main attraction for most visitors, though, is the vast central tank with a dazzling variety of fish, large and small, swimming round and round. Sharks co-exist peaceably with bream, barracudas with rays. The softly lit

waters can be viewed through any number of glass panes, on two levels.

Museu da Cidade ⑬

Campo Grande 245. *Tel 217 513 200.*
M *Campo Grande.* 🚌 *36, 47, 750.* ◯ *10am–1pm, 2–6pm Tue–Sun.* ● *public hols.* 📷 *(free Sun until 1pm).* ♿

Palácio Pimenta was allegedly commissioned by João V *(see p16)* for his mistress Madre Paula, a nun from the nearby convent at Odivelas. When the mansion was built, in the middle of the 18th century, it occupied a peaceful site outside the capital. Nowadays it has to contend with the traffic of Campo Grande. The house itself, however, retains its period charm and the city museum is one of the most interesting in Lisbon.

The displays follow the development of the city, from prehistoric times, through the Romans, Visigoths and Moors, traced by means of tiles, drawings, paintings, models and historical documents. Some of the most fascinating exhibits are those depicting the city before the earthquake of 1755, including a highly detailed model made in the 1950s and an impressive 17th-century oil painting by Dirk Stoop (1610–86) of *Terreiro do Paço*, as Praça do Comércio was known then *(see p47)*. One room is devoted to the Águas Livres aqueduct *(see p84)* with detailed

18th-century Indian toy, Museu da Cidade

architectural plans for its construction as well as prints and watercolours of the completed aqueduct.

The earthquake theme is resumed with pictures of the city amid the devastation and various plans for its reconstruction. The museum brings you into the 20th century with a large colour poster celebrating the Revolution of 1910 and the proclamation of the new republic *(see p17)*.

Museu Nacional do Azulejo ⑩

Pelican on the Manueline portal

Dona Leonor, widow of King João II, founded the Convento da Madre de Deus in 1509. Originally built in Manueline style, the church was restored under João III using simple Renaissance designs. The striking Baroque decoration was added by João V.

 The convent cloisters provide a stunning setting for the National Tile Museum. Decorative panels, individual tiles and photographs trace the evolution of tile-making from its introduction by the Moors, through Spanish influence and the development of Portugal's own style up to the present day.

Panorama of Lisbon
A striking 18th-century panel, located on the top floor, depicts Lisbon before the 1755 earthquake (see pp22–3). This detail shows the royal palace on Terreiro do Paço.

Hunting Scene
Artisans rather than artists began to decorate tiles in the 17th century. This detail shows a naive representation of a hunt.

Level 2

Level 1

KEY

- ☐ Moorish tiles
- ☐ 16th-century tiles
- ☐ 17th-century tiles
- ☐ 18th-century tiles
- ☐ 19th-century tiles
- ☐ 20th-century tiles
- ☐ Temporary exhibition space
- ☐ Non-exhibition space

STAR FEATURES

- ★ Madre de Deus
- ★ Manueline Cloister
- ★ Nossa Senhora da Vida

★ Nossa Senhora da Vida
This detail showing St John is part of a fine 16th-century maiolica altarpiece. The central panel of the huge work depicts The Adoration of the Shepherds.

Tiles from the 17th century with oriental influences are displayed here.

Kitchen Tiles
The walls of the restaurant are lined with 19th-century tiles showing hanging game, including wild boar and pheasant.

Level 3

VISITORS' CHECKLIST

Rua da Madre de Deus 4. *Tel 218 100 340.* 28, 718, 742, 759, 794. 10am–6pm Tue–Sun; last adm: 30 mins before closing. pub hols. (free 10am–2pm Sun). www.mnazulejo-imc-ip.pt

Moorish Tiles
Decorated with a stylized animal motif, this 15th-century tile is typical of Moorish azulejo patterns.

Entrance

The Renaissance cloister is the work of Diogo de Torralva (1500–66).

★ **Madre de Deus**
Completed in the mid-16th century, it was not until two centuries later, under João V, that the church of Madre de Deus acquired its ornate decoration. The sumptuous Rococo altarpiece was added after the earthquake of 1755.

GALLERY GUIDE
The rooms around the central cloister are arranged chronologically with the oldest tiles on the ground floor. Access to the Madre de Deus is via the ground floor. The front entrance of the church is used only during religious services.

The carved Manueline portal was recreated from a 16th-century painting.

★ **Manueline Cloister**
This cloister is an important surviving feature of the original convent. Fine geometrical patterned tiles dating from the 17th century were added to the walls in the 19th century.

Jardim Zoológico ⑭

Estrada de Benfica 158–60. *Tel 217 232 910.* Ⓜ *Jardim Zoológico.* 🚌 *16, 31, 755, 758 and other routes.* 🕐 *10am–6pm (Apr–Sep: 8pm) daily.* 🎫 ⍟ www.zoolisboa.pt

The gardens of the Jardim Zoológico are as much a feature as the actual zoo. Opened in 1905, the zoo has been revamped, and the majority of its aviaries and cages now provide more comfortable conditions for the specimens. It has an impressive collection of 2,000 animals comprising 400 different species. Current attractions of the zoo include a cable car touring the park, a reptile house, dolphin shows and an amusement park. The area is divided into four zones and the admission ticket provides access to all of the attractions.

A dolphin show at Dolphin's Bay in Lisbon's Jardim Zoológico

Aqueduto das Águas Livres ⑮

Best seen from Calçada da Quintinha. *Tel 218 100 215.* 🚌 *12, 702, 713, 742, 758.* 🕐 *Mar–Nov: 10am–6pm Mon–Sat.* ⬤ *public hols.*
Mãe d'Água das Amoreiras
Praça das Amoreiras. *Tel 213 251 646.* 🕐 *10am–6pm Mon–Sat.* ⬤ *public hols.* 🎫

Considered the most beautiful sight in Lisbon at the turn of the century, the Aqueduto das Águas Livres looms over the Alcântara valley northwest of the city. The construction of an aqueduct gave João V *(see p16)* the opportunity to indulge his passion for grandiose building schemes, as the only area of Lisbon with fresh drinking water was the Alfama. A tax on meat, wine, olive oil and other comestibles funded the project, and although not complete until the 19th century, it was already supplying the city with water by 1748. The main pipeline measures 19 km (12 miles), but the total length, including all the secondary channels, is 58 km (36 miles). The most visible part of this imposing structure, classified a National Monument in 2002, are the 35 arches crossing the Alcântara valley, the tallest of which rise to a spectacular 65 m (213 ft) above ground.

The public walkway along the aqueduct has been closed since 1853. This is partly due to Diogo Alves, the infamous robber who threw his victims over the edge. Today, it is possible to take lively guided tours over the Alcântara arches. There are also tours of the Mãe d'Água reservoir and trips to the Mãe d'Água springs, the source of the water supply. These tours can be irregular, so it is best to contact the Museu da Água *(see p80)* for details of the trips on offer.

At the end of the aqueduct, the **Mãe d'Água das Amoreiras** is a castle-like building which once served as a reservoir for the water supplied from the aqueduct. The original design of 1745 was by the Hungarian architect, Carlos Mardel, who worked under Pombal *(see pp22–3)* in the rebuilding of the Baixa. Completed in 1834, it became a popular meeting place and acquired a reputation as the rendezvous for kings and their mistresses. Today the space is used for art exhibitions, fashion shows and other events. There are great views from the roof.

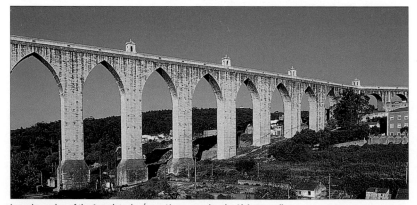

Imposing arches of the Aqueduto das Águas Livres spanning the Alcântara valley

Palácio Fronteira

Largo São Domingos de Benfica 1.
Tel 217 782 023. **M** *Jardim
Zoológico.* 🚌 *70.* 🚊 *Benfica.*
◯ *Mon–Sat:* 🎫 *Jun–Sep: 10:30,
11am, 11:30am, noon; Oct–May:
11am, noon.* ● *public hols.* 🖼

This delightful country manor
house was built as a hunting
pavilion for João de Mascar-
enhas, the first Marquês de
Fronteira, in 1640. Although
skyscrapers are visible in the
distance, it still occupies a
quiet spot, by the Parque
Florestal de Monsanto. Both
house and garden have *azulejo*
decoration whose subjects
include battle scenes and
trumpet-blowing monkeys.

Although the palace is still
occupied by the 12th Marquis,
some of the living rooms and
the library, as well
as the formal gar-
dens, are included
in the tour. The
Battles Room has
lively tiled panels
depicting scenes
of the War of
Restoration
(1640–1668), with
a detail of João de
Fronteira fighting
a Spanish general.
It was his loyalty
to Pedro II during
this war that earned him the
title of Marquis. Interesting
comparisons can be made between these naive 17th-century
Portuguese tiles and the Delft
ones from the same period in
the dining room, depicting
naturalistic scenes. The dining
room is also decorated with
frescoed panels and portraits
of Portuguese nobility by artists such as Domingos António
de Sequeira (1768–1837).

The late 16th-century chapel
is the oldest part of the house.
The façade is adorned with
stones, shells, broken glass and
bits of china. These fragments
of crockery are believed to
have been used at the feast
inaugurating the palace and
then smashed to ensure no one
else could sup off the same set.
Visits to the **garden** start at the
chapel terrace, where tiled
niches are decorated with
figures personifying the arts
and mythological creatures.

Tiled terrace leading to the chapel of the Palácio Fronteira

In the formal Italian garden the
immaculate box hedges are
cut into shapes to represent
the seasons of the year. To
one end, tiled
scenes of dashing
knights on horse-
back, representing
ancestors of the
Fronteira family,
are reflected in the
waters of a large
tank. On either
side of the water,
a grand staircase
leads to a terrace
above. Here,
decorative niches
contain the busts
of Portuguese kings and colourful majolica reliefs adorn
the arcades. More blue and
white tiled scenes, realistic and
allegorical, decorate the wall
at the far end of the garden.

**Bust of João I in gardens
of Palácio Fronteira**

**Entrance to the theatre museum
in Parque do Monteiro-Mor**

Parque do Monteiro-Mor ⑰

Largo Júlio Castilho. *Tel 217 567 620.*
🚌 *36, 108, 701, 703.* **M** *Lumiar.*
Park ◯ *2–6pm Tue, 10am–10pm
Wed–Sun.* ● *1 Jan, Easter, 1 May,
25 Dec.* **Museu Nacional do Traje**
Tel 217 567 620. ◯ *2–6pm Tue,
10am–10pm Wed–Sun.* 🖼 *(free
10am–2pm Sun).* **Museu Nacional
do Teatro** *Tel 217 567 418.*
◯ *2–6pm Tue, 10am–6pm
Wed–Sun.* 🖼 *(combined ticket
for park & museums.)* 📷 ♿

Monteiro Mor Park was sold
to the state in 1975 and the
18th-century palace buildings
were converted to museums.
The gardens are attractive and
rather more romantic than the
manicured box-hedge gardens
so typical of Lisbon. Much of
the land is wooded, though the
area around the museums has
gardens with flowering shrubs,
duck ponds and tropical trees.

The rather old-fashioned
Museu Nacional do Traje
(costume museum) has a vast
collection of textiles, accesso-
ries and costumes worn by
musicians, politicians, poets,
aristocrats and soldiers.

The **Museu Nacional do
Teatro** has two buildings, one
devoted to temporary exhibitions, the other containing a
small permanent collection.
Photos, posters and cartoons
feature famous 20th-century
Portuguese actors, and one
section is devoted to Amália
Rodrigues, the famous *fado*
singer *(see pp144–5).*

TWO GUIDED WALKS

The folds and creases of Lisbon's many hills demand to be explored on foot, yet they can also be quite demanding on the walker. It is possible to plan routes that avoid most steep inclines, but such routes often miss many of the hidden treasures of the city's *bairros*.

The two walks described here give a true taste of Lisbon's topography and of the rich mix of the city's lifestyles via some of the most charming neighbourhoods. The first walk takes you from lofty Estrela in northwest Lisbon

Tiled panel in central Lisbon

through picturesque *bairros*, passing the grandiose Palacio de São Bento (Portuguese parliament building), towards the historic centre. The second walk begins in the Baixa and leads walkers through one of the many narrow entrances into the labyrinthine alleyways of Alfama before climbing to Castelo de São Jorge for spectacular views. In addition to these walks, each of the four areas of Lisbon described in the *Area-by-Area* section of this book has a walk on its *Street-by-Street* map.

CHOOSING A WALK

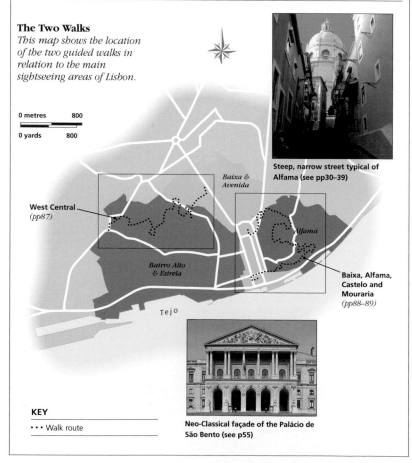

The Two Walks
This map shows the location of the two guided walks in relation to the main sightseeing areas of Lisbon.

0 metres   800
0 yards   800

West Central *(pp87)*

Baixa & Avenida

Bairro Alto & Estrela

Tejo

Alfama

Steep, narrow street typical of Alfama (see pp30–39)

Baixa, Alfama, Castelo and Mouraria *(pp88–89)*

KEY

• • • Walk route

Neo-Classical façade of the Palácio de São Bento (see p55)

A 45-Minute Walk Around West Central Lisbon

The mainly residential Estrela neighbourhood is typical of well-to-do west Lisbon. The Portuguese parliament lies to the east, then the terrain rises to Praça do Príncipe Real. This sloping neighbourhood with its small, bustling streets and energetic nightlife is typically Lisboetan. On the other side of the ridge, the Jardim Botânico descends steeply towards the city centre.

TIPS FOR WALKERS

Starting point: *Basílica de Estrela*
Length: *2.5 km (1.5 miles)*
Getting there: *Catch Tram 25 or 28 or Bus 709, 720 or 738.*
Stopping off points: *Pão de Canela in Praça das Flores is a pleasant café with outdoor seating. Another good spot is the café in Praça do Príncipe Real. Stop for a glass of wine at Enoteca ⑩.*

several appealing cafés. Cross the square to Rua do Monte Olivete, home of the British Council in its handsome palace ⑥. The grand polytechnic building, on Rua da Escola Politécnica, now houses the Museu de História Natural. Behind this is the Jardim Botânico ⑦ *(see p44)*. Turn right and head to Praça do Príncipe Real ⑧ *(see p54)*, with its delightful magnolia-shaded garden and

Inside Lisbon's 18th-century Basílica da Estrela ①

reservoir, now the excellent Enoteca wine bar ⑩. Continue down Rua da Mãe d'Água to Rua da

Alegria, passing the infamous jazz venue, Hot Clube ⑪ *(see pp142–3)*. From there, Travessa do Salitre will take you past atmospheric Parque Mayer ⑫, the city's old vaudeville park, before you reach the splendid, tree-lined Avenida da Liberdade *(see p44)*, where you can catch the metro.

Begin at Basílica da Estrela ① *(see p55)*, one of Lisbon's landmarks, then enjoy a stroll through the pleasant Jardim da Estrela ② *(see p55)*. On leaving the park, head down Rua de Santo Amaro which descends steeply to Rua de São Bento ③. Turn right past attractive tiled façades and a number of antique shops and head to the Palácio de São Bento ④ *(see p55)*, the seat of the Portuguese parliament. Retrace your steps and turn right down Rua da Piedade to Praça das Flores ⑤, a typical Lisbon square with

café. Opposite is the striking, Neo-Moorish Palácio Ribeiro da Cunha ⑨. Cross the street and walk down the narrow lane to a flight of steps. These lead down the side of a grand marble water

KEY

••• Walk route

Ⓜ Metro station

Peaceful Jardim da Estrela ②

A 90-Minute Walk Around Baixa, Alfama, Castelo and Mouraria

From the late 18th-century splendour of the Baixa, this walk takes you into the alleyways of Alfama, a much older and humbler neighbourhood. Castelo de São Jorge crowns the hill, standing on a site that has been fortified for thousands of years. Behind it, Mouraria was the quarter to which Lisbon's remaining Moors were relegated after Afonso Henriques conquered the city in 1147. Their legacy survives most notably in the cadences of *fado*, which is at its most authentic here.

Braga and then the steps on the left (Beco de Loureiro). These lead to a small square which opens on Rua da Regueira; turn right here and follow it to Rua do Castelo Picão, which takes you back into the heart of Alfama.

Equestrian statue of José I in Praça do Comércio ①

Begin the walk at Praça do Comércio ① *(see p47)*, which was once the grand maritime entrance to Lisbon. The statue at the centre of the vast square is of José I, king at the time of the great 1755 earthquake which destroyed the palace and most of lower-lying Lisbon *(see pp20–21)*. The grand arcades of the post-earthquake buildings surrounding the square ② faintly echo the palace, creating a somewhat ghostly atmosphere. Walk along Rua

TIPS FOR WALKERS

Starting point: *Praça do Comércio*
Length: *3 km (1.9 miles)*
Getting there: *Catch Tram 25 or Bus 709 or 711*
Stopping off points: *Pois, Café ⑤ is well worth a visit. Alfama has several cheerful eateries, including Santo António de Alfama ⑧ and Mesa de Fradesis on Rua dos Remédios. The café by the statue of São Vicente ⑪ is a popular drinking spot, as is Bar Cerca Moura across the street.*

da Alfândega and turn left on Rua da Madalena. The first street on your right is Rua dos Bacalhoeiros ③, named after the cod merchants who once dominated it. Continue along Rua da Alfândega to the unmistakable Casa dos Bicos ④ *(see p35)* and pass through the arch at Arco de Jesus, which leads via steps up to Rua de São João da Praça. Now you have entered Alfama proper, protected by the hulking Sé to the left and with a gradually winding web of small streets, steps and alleys to the right. Head left and enjoy a coffee at Pois, Café ⑤ *(see pp136–7)*. Then head back and follow Rua de São João da Praça until it becomes Rua de São Pedro ⑥. The stalls selling fresh fish along here are an Alfama institution. The narrow street empties into Largo do Chafariz de Dentro, with the Casa do Fado ⑦ *(see pp144–5)* across the street. To re-enter the small alleyways, cross the square and head up Rua dos Remédios. If lunch is needed, stop at Santo António de Alfama ⑧ *(see p130)*, in nearby Beco de São Miguel. Next, find Escadinhas de Santo Estêvão or Calcadinha de Santo Estêvão and climb up to Santo Estêvão church ⑨. Lisbon is a city of viewing points, and this is one of the best. From the square by the church, take Rua Guilherme

Fish market on Rua de São Pedro ⑥

Sweeping views over the rooftops of Alfama

0 metres   200

0 yards   200

São Lourenço tower and continue around the back of the castle. A small gate here ⑰ is said to have been the scene of a decisive event during Afonso Henriques' 1147 siege of the castle. According to legend, the knight Martim Moniz prevented the gate from closing with his own body, sacrificing his life to allow Afonso Henriques and his men to storm the castle.

Next, follow the path round into Largo Rodrigues Freitas on the left. Take this past Beco da Laje on the right and turn left into a small square, then left again out of it. Now you are at the top of Calçada de Santo André and the Mouraria quarter. Head down the *calçada* and take the first left, Rua da Amendoeira. Descend this street to a small square and bear left into Rua Marquês de Ponte do Lima. Turn right at the junction with Escadinhas da Saúde and then immediately left into Rua das Fontainhas de São Lourenço. This is the heart of Mouraria ⑱. Stay on the charming Rua de São Lourenço, which becomes Largo das Farinhas. Turn right down the steps to Largo dos Trigueiros and follow this down to Beco do Rosendo. Descend down the steps and cross Rua da Madalena to Rua dos Condes de Monsanto. From the warren of Mouraria you have arrived in the Baixa. Ahead is Praça da Figueira ⑲ *(see p45)*, with an impressive equestrian statue of João I. Take the metro from Rossio station or one of the many buses that run from the square.

Norberto Araújo. Turn right and follow the street up steps and around the corner to Largo das Portas do Sol and the statue of the city's patron saint, São Vicente ⑪.

Across the square is the Museu de Artes Decorativas ⑫ *(see p34)*. Find Beco do Maldonado on the far side of the square and climb its steps until you can turn left into Pátio de Dom Fradique ⑬. Walk down Rua do Chão da Feira, the main access to the Castelo de São Jorge *(see pp38–9)*. In a corner here is a single-booth urinal whose ornate iron sign makes it a much-photographed work of art ⑭. In a niche inside the gateway to the citadel is a statue of St George ⑮. The steep incline up to the castle entrance is lined with tourist shops ⑯ as well as the ticket office. This walk takes you around the castle perimeter with its stunning views. Pass under the long stairway that leads down to the outlying

Follow its 45-degree turn to the right at Beco das Cruzes and continue walking to Calçadinha de São Miguel ⑩. Pass through the narrow arch here and onto Escadinhas de São Miguel. Then turn right and climb up Beco da Corvinha, passing through another arch up to Rua

View from the battlements of Castelo de São Jorge

THE LISBON COAST

THE LISBON COAST

ithin an hour's drive northwest of Lisbon you can reach the rocky Atlantic coast, the wooded slopes of Sintra or countryside dotted with villas and royal palaces. South of Lisbon you can enjoy the sandy beaches and fishing towns along the coast or explore the lagoons of the Tagus and Sado river estuaries.

Traders and invaders, from the Phoenicians to the Spanish, have left their mark in this region, in particular the Moors whose forts and castles, rebuilt many times over the centuries, can be found all along this coast. After Lisbon became the capital in 1256, Portuguese kings and nobles built summer palaces and villas in the countryside west of the city, particularly on the cool, green heights of the Serra de Sintra.

Across the Tagus, the less fashionable southern shore (Outra Banda) could be reached only by ferry, until the suspension bridge was built in 1966. Now, the long sandy beaches of the Costa da Caparica, the coast around the fishing town of Sesimbra and even the remote Tróia peninsula have become popular resorts during the summer months. Fortunately, large stretches of coast and unspoilt countryside are being protected as conservation areas and nature reserves.

Despite the region's rapid urbanization, small fishing and farming communities still survive. Lively fish markets offer a huge variety of fresh fish and seafood; Palmela and the Sado region are noted for their wine; sheep still roam the unspoilt Serra da Arrábida, providing milk for Azeitão cheese; and rice is the main crop in the Sado estuary. Traditional industries also survive, such as salt panning near Alcochete and marble quarries at Pero Pinheiro.

Though the sea is cold and often rough, especially on west-facing coasts, the beaches are among the cleanest in Europe. As well as surfing, fishing and scuba diving, the region provides splendid golf courses, horse riding facilities and a motor-racing track. Arts and entertainment range from music and cinema festivals to bullfights and country fairs where regional crafts, such as hand-painted pottery, lace and baskets, are on display.

Tiled façades of houses in Alcochete, an attractive town on the Tagus estuary

◁ **Brightly painted fishing boats moored in the harbour at Sesimbra**

Exploring the Lisbon Coast

North of the Tagus, the beautiful hilltown of Sintra is dotted with historic palaces and surrounded by wooded hills, at times enveloped in an eerie sea mist. On the coast, cosmopolitan Cascais and the traditional fishing town of Ericeira are both excellent bases from which to explore the rocky coastline and surrounding countryside. South of the Tagus, the Serra da Arrábida and the rugged coast around Cabo Espichel can be visited from the small port of Sesimbra. Inland, the nature reserves of the Tagus and Sado estuaries offer a quiet retreat.

SIGHTS AT A GLANCE

0 kilometres   10

0 miles   5

Torres Vedras
Encarnação
Turcifal
Sobral de Monte Agraço
Ribamar
Santo Isidoro
N8
Vila Franca do Rosário
A8
Sobreiro
Murgeira
N116
ERICEIRA **2**
N116
A21
1
PALÁCIO DE MAFRA
Malveira
Milhar
Cheleiros
São João das Lampas
N247
N9
Lousa
Azenhas do Mar
Pero Pinheiro
LISBOA
Lour
Praia das Maçãs
MONSERRATE
Caneças
COLARES **3** **5** **6** SINTRA
N117
Odivelas
4
Belas
Cabo da Roca
SERRA DE SINTRA
9 PALÁCIO DE QUELUZ
A16
Malveira da Serra
Alcabideche
A9
Guincho
A5
LISBO
Caxias
Boca do Inferno
8 ESTORIL
Oeiras
Almada
7
Carcavelos
Trafaria
CASCAIS
Arieiro
COSTA DA CAPARICA **11**
ATLANTIC OCEAN
Lagoa de Albufeira
Alfarim
Nossa Senhora do Cabo
12
CABO ESPICHEL

KEY

- ═══ Motorway
- ─── Major road
- ═══ Minor road
- ─── Scenic route
- ─── Main railway
- ─── Minor railway
- ═══ Regional border

Cabo da Roca on the western edge of Serra de Sintra

For additional map symbols *see back flap*

**Convento da Arrábida in the hills
of the Serra da Arrábida**

GETTING AROUND

Motorways give quick access from
Lisbon to Sintra, Estoril, Palmela and
Setúbal. Main roads are generally
well signposted and surfaced, though
traffic congestion can be a problem.
Watch out for potholes on smaller
roads. Fast, frequent trains run west
from Lisbon's Cais do Sodré station to
Estoril and Cascais, and from Rossio,
Roma Areeiro and Entrecampos stations
to Queluz and Sintra. For trains south
to Setúbal, Alcácer do Sal and beyond,
use either the Fertagus service or
Barreiro station on the southern bank
of the Tagus. There are good bus services to all parts of the region, which
leave mainly from Praça de Espanha.

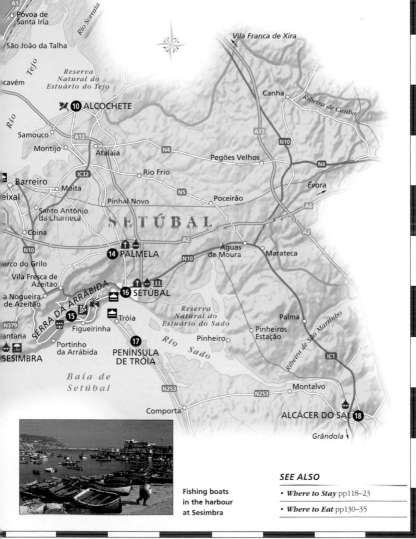

**Fishing boats
in the harbour
at Sesimbra**

SEE ALSO

- *Where to Stay* pp118–23

- *Where to Eat* pp130–35

The stunning library in the Palácio de Mafra, paved with chequered marble

Palácio de Mafra ●

Terreiro de Dom João V, Mafra.
Tel 261 817 550. 🚌 *from Lisbon.*
Ⓜ *Campo Grande, then* 🚌 *Ericeira.*
🕐 *10am–4:30pm Wed–Mon (last adm: 30 mins before closing).*
⦿ *1 Jan, Easter, 1 May, 25 Dec.*
🎫 🎟 *(free 10am–2pm Sun).*
📷 *compulsory.* **www**.ipmuseus.pt

This massive Baroque palace and monastery dwarfs the small town of Mafra. It was built during the reign of João V, and began with a vow by the young king to build a new monastery and basilica, supposedly in return for an heir (but more likely, to atone for his well-known sexual excesses). Work began in 1717 on a modest project to house 13 Franciscan friars but, as the wealth began to pour into the royal coffers from Brazil, the king and his Italian-trained architect, Johann Friedrich Ludwig (1670–1752), made

ever more extravagant plans. No expense was spared: 52,000 men were employed and the finished project eventually housed not 13, but 330 friars, a royal palace and one of the finest libraries in Europe, decorated with precious marble, exotic wood and countless works of art. The magnificent basilica was consecrated on the king's 41st birthday, 22 October 1730.

The palace was only popular with those members of the royal family who enjoyed hunting deer and wild boar. Today, a wolf conservation project runs here. Most of the finest furniture and art works were taken to Brazil when the royal family escaped the French invasion in 1807. The monastery was abandoned in 1834 following the dissolution of all religious orders, and the palace itself was finally abandoned in 1910, when the last Portuguese king, Manuel II, escaped from here to the Royal Yacht anchored off Ericeira.

Allow at least an hour for the lengthy tour which starts in the rooms of the monastery, through the pharmacy, with

fine old medicine jars and some alarming medical instruments, to the hospital, where 16 patients in private cubicles could see and hear mass in the adjoining chapel without leaving their beds.

Upstairs, the sumptuous palace state rooms extend across the whole of the monumental west façade, with the King's apartments at one end and the Queen's apartments at the other, a staggering 232 m (760 ft) apart. Halfway between the two, the long, imposing façade is relieved by the twin bell towers of the domed basilica. The interior of the church is decorated in contrasting colours of marble and furnished with six early 19th-century organs. Fine Baroque sculptures, executed by members of the Mafra School of Sculpture, adorn the atrium of the basilica. Begun by José I in 1754, many renowned Portuguese and foreign artists trained in the school under the directorship of the Italian sculptor Alessandro Giusti (1715–99). Further on, the Sala da Caça has a grotesque collection of hunting trophies and boars' heads.

Mafra's greatest treasure, however, is its magnificent library, which has a patterned marble floor, Rococo-style wooden bookcases and a collection of over 40,000 books in gold embossed leather bindings, including a prized first edition of *Os Lusíadas* (1572) by the celebrated Portuguese poet, Luís de Camões (1524–80).

Statue of St Bruno in the atrium of Mafra's basilica

Environs

Once a week, on Thursday mornings, the small country town of **Malveira**, 10 km (6 miles) east of Mafra, has the region's biggest market, selling clothes and household goods as well as food.

At the village of **Sobreiro**, 6 km (4 miles) west of Mafra, Zé Franco's model village is complete with houses, farms, a waterfall and a windmill.

The king's bedroom in the Royal Palace

Tractor pulling a fishing boat out of the sea at Ericeira

Ericeira ②

🏠 7,500. 🚌 🛈 Rua Dr. Eduardo Burnay 46 (261 863 122).
🚢 Jun–Oct daily.

Ericeira is an old fishing village which keeps its traditions despite an ever-increasing influx of summer visitors, from Lisbon and abroad, who enjoy the bracing climate, clean, sandy beaches and fresh seafood. In July and August, when the population leaps to 30,000, pavement cafés, restaurants and bars around the tree-lined Praça da República are buzzing late into the night. Red flags warn when swimming is dangerous: alternative attractions include a crazy golf course in Santa Marta park and a local history museum, the **Museu da Ericeira**, exhibiting model boats and traditional regional fishing equipment.

The unspoilt old town, a maze of whitewashed houses and narrow, cobbled streets, is perched high above the ocean. From Largo das Ribas, at the top of a 30-m (100-ft) stone-faced cliff, there is a bird's-eye view over the busy fishing harbour below, where tractors haul the boats out of reach of the tide. On 16 August, the annual fishermen's festival is celebrated with a candlelit procession to the harbour at the foot of the cliffs for the blessing of the boats.

On 5 October 1910, Manuel II, the last king of Portugal (see p19), finally sailed into exile from Ericeira as the Republic was declared in Lisbon; a tiled panel in the fishermen's chapel of Santo António above the harbour records the event. The banished king settled in Twickenham, southwest London, where he died in 1932.

> **🏛 Museu da Ericeira**
> Largo da Misericórdia. **Tel** 261 862 536. ⬜ 10am–noon, 1–6pm Sat & Sun (summer months only). 🖼

Colares ③

🏠 7,500. 🚌 🛈 Cabo da Roca, (219 280 081).

On the lower slopes of the Serra de Sintra, this lovely village faces towards the sea over a green valley, the Várzea de Colares. A leafy avenue winds its way up to the village, lined with pine and chestnut trees. Small quantities of the famous Colares wine are still made, but current vintages lack the character and ageing potential of classic Colares and growers face a financial struggle to survive. Their hardy old vines grow in sandy soil, with their roots set deep below in clay; these were among the few vines in Europe to survive the disastrous phylloxera epidemic brought from America in the late 19th century with the first viticultural exchanges. The insect, which destroyed vineyards all over Europe by eating the vines' roots, could not penetrate the dense sandy soil of the Atlantic coast. Wine can be sampled at the Adega Regional de Colares on Alameda de Coronel Linhares de Lima.

Environs

There are several popular beach resorts west of Colares. From the village of Banzão you can ride 3 km (2 miles) to **Praia das Maçãs** on the old tramway, which opened in 1910 and still runs from 1 July to 30 September. Just north of Praia das Maçãs is the picturesque village of **Azenhas do Mar**, clinging to the cliffs; to the south is the larger resort of **Praia Grande**. Both have natural pools in the rocks, which are filled by seawater at high tide and are now closed to swimmers. The unspoilt **Praia da Adraga**, 1 km (half a mile) further south, has a delightful beach café and restaurant. In the evenings and off-season, fishermen catch bass, bream and flat fish.

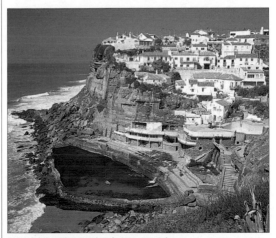

Natural rock pool at Azenhas do Mar, near Colares

Serra de Sintra Tour ❹

This round trip from Sintra follows a dramatic route over the top of the wooded Serra. The first part is a challenging drive with hazardous hairpin bends on steep, narrow roads that are at times poorly surfaced. It passes through dense forest and a surreal landscape of giant moss-covered boulders, with breathtaking views over the Atlantic coast, the Tagus estuary and beyond.

Tiled angels, Peninha chapel

After dropping down to the rugged, windswept coast, the route returns along small country roads passing through hill villages and large estates on the cool, green northern slopes of the Serra de Sintra.

Atlantic coastline seen from Peninha

Colares ⑥
The village of Colares rests on the lower slopes of the wooded Serra, surrounded by gardens and vineyards (see p97).

Peninha ④
This 490-m- (1,600-ft-) high peak affords stunning views towards the coast. A 17th-century chapel decorated with *azulejo* panels is perched high on the grey rocks.

Cabo da Roca ⑤
A lighthouse at the top of an impressive cliff, 140 m (459 ft) high, marks the most westerly point of the European mainland.

| 0 kilometres | 2 |
| 0 miles | 1 |

KEY

▬	Tour route
═	Other roads
☆	Viewpoint

Seteais ⑧
The elegant palace, now a luxury hotel and restaurant *(see p123 & p135)*, was built in the 18th century for the Dutch Consul, Daniel Gildemeester.

TIPS FOR WALKERS

Length: *36 km (22 miles).*
Stopping-off points: *There are cool springs of drinking water and fountains along the mountain roads. At Cabo da Roca you will find a café, restaurant and souvenir shops; at Colares there are several delightful restaurants and bars.*

Monserrate ⑦
The cool, overgrown forest park and elaborate 19th-century palace epitomize the romanticism of Sintra.

Sintra ②
From the centre of the old town the road winds steeply upwards past magnificent *quintas* (country estates) hidden among the trees.

ERICEIRA
MAFRA
N247

one way road →

⑧

②

● *Palácio da Pena*

①

CRUZ ALTA

SERRA DE SINTRA

ESTORIL CASCAIS

LISBOA

N249

Parque da Pena ①
This huge, exotic park can be explored on foot *(see p101)*. It is also possible to visit the beautiful Palácio da Pena *(see pp104–5)*.

Convento dos Capuchos ③
Two huge boulders guard the entrance to this remote Franciscan monastery, founded in 1560, where the monks lived in tiny rock-hewn cells lined with cork. There are stunning views of the coast from the hill above this austere, rocky hideaway.

Palace of Monserrate

Monserrate ❺

Rua Barbosa du Bocage. **Tel** *219 237 300.* to Sintra then taxi or bus 435. *daily; Apr–Sep: 9:30am–8pm; Oct–Mar: 10am–6pm (last adm: 1 hour before closing).* 25 Dec.
www.parquesdesintra.pt

The wild, romantic garden of this once magnificent estate is a jungle of exotic trees and flowering shrubs. Among the sub-tropical foliage and valley of tree ferns, the visitor will come across a waterfall, a small lake and a chapel, built as a ruin, tangled in the roots of a giant *Ficus* tree. Its history dates back to the Moors but it takes its name from a small 16th-century chapel dedicated to Our Lady of Montserrat in Catalonia, Spain. The gardens were landscaped in the late 1700s by a wealthy young Englishman, William Beckford. They were later immortalized by Lord Byron in *Childe Harold's Pilgrimage* (1812).

In 1856, the abandoned estate was bought by another Englishman, Sir Francis Cook, who built a fantastic Moorish-style palace (which is in the process of being restored) and transformed the gardens with a large sweeping lawn, camellias and sub-tropical trees from all over the world. These include the giant *Metrosideros* (Pacific Islands Christmas tree, covered in a blaze of red flowers in July), the native *Arbutus* (known as the strawberry tree because of its juicy red berries), from which the *medronho* firewater drink is distilled, and cork oak, with small ferns growing on its bark.

The Friends of Monserrate is an organization of volunteers who help restore and maintain the house and gardens.

Sintra ⑥

Sintra's stunning setting on the north slopes of the granite Serra, among wooded ravines and freshwater springs, made it a favourite summer retreat for the kings of Portugal. The tall, conical chimneys of the Palácio Nacional de Sintra *(see pp102–3)* and the fabulous Palácio da Pena *(see pp104–5)*, eerily impressive on its peak when the Serra is blanketed in mist, are unmistakable landmarks.

Today, the town (recognized as a UNESCO Cultural Landscape site in 1995) draws thousands of visitors all through the year. Even so, there are many quiet walks in the wooded hills around the town, especially beautiful in the long, cool evenings of the summer months.

Fonte Mourisca on Volta do Duche

Exploring Sintra
Present-day Sintra is in three parts, Sintra Vila, Estefânia and São Pedro, joined by a confusing maze of winding roads scattered over the surrounding hills. In the pretty cobbled streets of the old town, Sintra Vila, which is centred on the **Palácio Nacional de Sintra**, are the museums and beautifully tiled **post office**. The curving **Volta do Duche** leads from the old town, past the lush **Parque da Liberdade**, north to the Estefânia district and the striking Neo-Gothic **Câmara Municipal** (Town Hall). To the south and east, the hilly village of São Pedro spreads over the slopes of the Serra. The Sunday **market**, held on the second and fourth Sunday of every month, extends across the broad market square.

Exploring Sintra on foot involves a lot of walking and climbing up and down its steep hills. For a more leisurely tour, take one of the horse and carriage rides around the town. The **Miradouro da Vigia** in São Pedro offers impressive views, as does the cosy **Casa de Sapa** café, where you can sample *queijadas*, the local sweet speciality.

The many fountains dotted around the town are used by locals for their fresh spring drinking water. Two of the most striking are the tiled **Fonte Mourisca** (Arab Fountain), named for its Neo-Moorish decoration, and **Fonte da Sabuga**, where the water spouts from a pair of breasts.

🏛 Museu do Brinquedo
Rua Visconde de Monserrate.
Tel 219 242 171. ⏱ *10am–6pm Tue–Sun.* ● *1 Jan, 1 May, 25 Dec.* ♿ www.museu-do-brinquedo.pt
This small museum has a fine collection of toys, ranging from model planes, cars and trains, to dolls and dolls' houses, tin toys and clockwork models of cars and soldiers. There is also a restoration workshop and a playroom with puppets and story tellers.

Toy Alfa Romeo, Museu do Brinquedo

🏛 Museu de Arte Moderna
Avenidada Heliodoro Salgado.
Tel 219 248 170. ⏱ *10am–6pm Tue–Sun.* ● *1 Jan, 25 Dec.* 🎟 *(free 10am–2pm Sun).* ♿ 🍴 www.berardocollection.com
This museum was built to house José Berardo's modern and contemporary art collection. Now that this has moved to the Museu Colecção Berardo in Lisbon *(see p69)*, the building hosts temporary exhibitions of modern art movements such as Surrealism and Pop Art.

🏛 Quinta da Regaleira
Rua Barbosa du Bocage. *Tel 219 106 650.* 🚌 *435.* ⏱ *10am–6:30pm daily (to 8pm Apr–Sep, to 5:30pm Nov–Jan).* 🎟 🍴 🖼 www.regaleira.pt
Built in the 1890s, this palace and extensive gardens are a feast of historical and religious references, occult symbols and mystery. The obsession of the eccentric millionaire António Augusto Carvalho Monteiro, they are a must for anyone interested in esoterica.

Chimneys of the Palácio Nacional de Sintra above the old town

♣ Castelo dos Mouros

Estrada da Pena. *Tel* 219 237 300.
◯ daily; May–Oct: 9am–7pm;
Nov–Apr: 9:30am–6pm (last entrance
1 hour before closing). ● 25 Dec.
Standing above the old town,
the ramparts of the 8th-century
Moorish castle conquered by
Afonso Henriques in 1147,
snake over the top of the Serra.
On a fine day, there are great
views from the castle walls
over the old town to Palácio da
Pena, on a neighbouring peak,
and along the coast. Hidden
inside the walls are a ruined
chapel and an ancient Moorish cistern. A steep footpath
threads up through wooded
slopes from the 12th-century
church of **Santa Maria**. Follow
the signs to a dark green swing
gate where the footpath begins.
The monogram "DFII" carved
on the gateway is a reminder
that the castle walls were
restored by Fernando II *(see
p105)* in the 19th century.

Battlements of the Castelo dos Mouros perched on the slopes of the Serra

VISITORS' CHECKLIST

🏘 25,000. 🚉 🚌 *Avenida Dr
Miguel Bombarda.* 🛈 *Praça da
República 23 (219 231 157); Sintra
station (211 932 545).* 📅 *2nd &
4th Sun of month in São Pedro.*
🎭 *Sintra Festival (Jun–Jul).*

♣ Parque da Pena

Estrada da Pena. *Tel* 219 237 300.
◯ daily; May–Oct: 9:30am–7pm;
Nov–Apr: 10am–6pm (last entrance
1 hour before closing). ● 25 Dec.
♿ www.parquesdesintra.pt
A huge park surrounds the
Palácio da Pena and hidden
among the foliage are gazebos,
follies and fountains, and a
chalet built by Fernando II for
his mistress in 1869. Cruz Alta,
the highest point of the Serra
at 529 m (1,740 ft), commands
spectacular views of the Serra
and surrounding plain. On a
nearby crag is the statue of
Baron Von Eschwege, architect
of the palace and park.

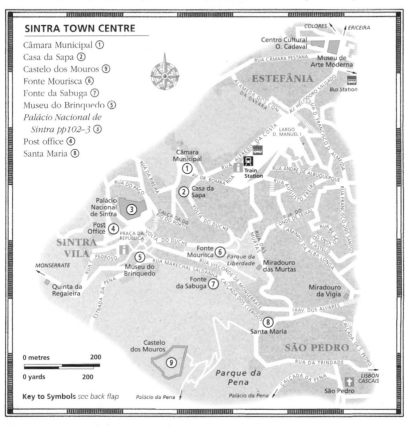

SINTRA TOWN CENTRE

Câmara Municipal ①
Casa da Sapa ②
Castelo dos Mouros ⑨
Fonte Mourisca ⑥
Fonte da Sabuga ⑦
Museu do Brinquedo ⑤
*Palácio Nacional de
Sintra pp102–3* ③
Post office ④
Santa Maria ⑧

COLORES · ERICEIRA

Centro Cultural
O. Cadaval

RUA CÂMARA PESTANA · Museu de
Arte Moderna

ESTEFÂNIA

ALAMEDA DOS · DA GUERRA

AV. HELIODORO SALGADO · VIA D FRANCISCO D ALMEIDA

Bus Station

LARGO
D. MANUEL I

Câmara
Municipal
①

RUA ALFREDO DA COSTA

RUA ANDRÉ DE ALBUQUERQUE

Train
Station

RUA DA RIBEIRA

AV. DR BOMBARDA

Casa da
Sapa ②

RUA DO PAÇO

Palácio
Nacional
de Sintra ③

CALÇA DA DO RIO DO PORTO

VOLTA DA DUCHA

RUA AUGUSTO FELIPE

RUA FRANCISCO DOS SANTOS

RUA DO
CONDE DE SEIXAL

Post
Office ④

PRAÇA DA
REPÚBLICA

VOLTA DO DUCHE

CAMINHO DA ALBA LONGA

SINTRA
VILA

RUA C PEDROSO

Fonte ⑥
Mourisca

RUA DAS MURTAS

DO OYO

MONSERRATE

Museu do
Brinquedo ⑤

RUA MARECHAL SALDANHA

Parque da
Liberdade

Miradouro
das Murtas

RUA DA PENA

Fonte ⑦
da Sabuga

RUA VISCONDE DE MONSERRATE

CALÇADA DOS CLÉRIGOS

Miradouro
da Vigia

Quinta da
Regaleira

ESTRADA DA PENA

CALÇADA DOS CLÉRIGOS

TRAV. DOS ÁLVARES

⑧
Santa Maria

CALÇADA DE S PEDRO

Castelo
dos Mouros
⑨

SÃO PEDRO

RUA DA TRINDADE

LISBOA
CASCAIS

Parque da
Pena

CALÇADA DA PENA

São Pedro

0 metres   200

0 yards   200

Palácio da Pena ↓ · *Palácio da Pena* ↓

Key to Symbols *see back flap*

Palácio Nacional de Sintra

Swan panel, Sala dos Cisnes

At the heart of the old town of Sintra (Sintra Vila), a pair of strange conical chimneys rises high above the Royal Palace. The main part of the palace, including the central block with its plain Gothic façade and the large kitchens beneath the chimneys, was built by João I in the late 14th century, on a site once occupied by the Moorish rulers. The Paço Real, as it is also known, became the favourite summer retreat for the court, and continued as a residence for Portuguese royalty until the 1880s. Additions to the building by the wealthy Manuel I, in the early 16th century, echo the Moorish style. Gradual rebuilding of the palace has resulted in a fascinating amalgamation of various different styles.

★ Sala das Pegas
It is said that King João I had the ceiling panels painted as a rebuke to the court women for indulging in idle gossip like chattering magpies (pegas).

The Torre da Meca has dovecotes below the cornice decorated with armillary spheres and nautical rope.

The Sala das Galés (galleons) houses temporary exhibitions.

★ Sala dos Brasões
The domed ceiling of this majestic room is decorated with stags holding the coats of arms (brasões) of 72 noble Portuguese families. The lower walls are lined with 18th-century Delft-like tiled panels.

Jardim da Preta, a walled garden

Sala de Dom Sebastião, the audience chamber

TIMELINE

10th century Palace becomes residence of Moorish governor	**1281** King Dinis orders restoration of the Palácio de Oliva (as it was then known)	**1495–1521** Reign of Manuel I; major restoration and Manueline additions	**1683** Afonso VI dies after being imprisoned here for nine years by brother Pedro II		**1755** Parts of palace damaged in great earthquake (*see pp22–3*)

800	1000	1200	1400	1600	1800

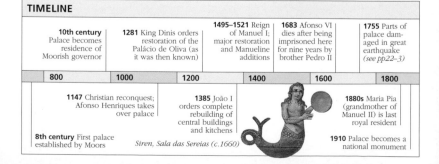

1147 Christian reconquest; Afonso Henriques takes over palace

1385 João I orders complete rebuilding of central buildings and kitchens

1880s Maria Pia (grandmother of Manuel II) is last royal resident

8th century First palace established by Moors

Siren, Sala das Sereias (c.1660)

1910 Palace becomes a national monument

★ Sala dos Cisnes
The magnificent ceiling of the former banqueting hall, painted in the 15th century, is divided into octagonal panels decorated with swans (cisnes).

Sala das Sereias
Intricate Arabesque designs on 16th-century tiles frame the door of the Room of the Sirens.

The Sala dos Árabes is decorated with fine *azulejos*.

The kitchens, beneath the huge conical chimneys, have spits and utensils once used for preparing royal banquets.

Entrance

Sala dos Archeiros, the entrance hall

Manuel I added the *ajimene* windows, a distinctive Moorish design with a slender column dividing two arches.

Chapel
Symmetrical Moorish patterns decorate the original 15th-century chestnut and oak ceiling and the mosaic floor of the private chapel.

STAR FEATURES

★ Sala dos Brasões

★ Sala dos Cisnes

★ Sala das Pegas

Sintra: Palácio da Pena

On the highest peaks of the Serra de Sintra stands the spectacular palace of Pena, an eclectic medley of architectural styles built in the 19th century for the husband of the young Queen Maria II, Ferdinand Saxe-Coburg-Gotha. It stands over the ruins of a Hieronymite monastery founded here in the 15th century on the site of the chapel of Nossa Senhora da Pena.

Triton Arch Ferdinand appointed a German architect, Baron Von Eschwege, to build his summer palace filled with oddities from all over the world and surrounded by a park. With the declaration of the Republic in 1910, the palace became a museum, preserved as it was when the royal family lived here. Allow at least an hour and a half to visit this enchanting place.

Entrance Arch
A studded archway with crenellated turrets greets the visitor at the entrance to the palace. The palace buildings are painted the original daffodil yellow and strawberry pink.

Manuel II's Bedroom
The oval-shaped room is decorated with green walls and stuccoed ceiling. A portrait of Manuel II, the last king of Portugal, hangs above the fireplace.

In the kitchen the copper pots and utensils still hang around the iron stove. The dinner service bears the coat of arms of Ferdinand II.

★ Ballroom
The spacious ballroom is sumptuously furnished with German stained-glass windows, precious Oriental porcelain and four life-size turbaned torchbearers holding giant candelabra.

★ Arab Room
Marvellous trompe-l'oeil frescoes cover the walls and ceiling of the Arab Room, one of the loveliest in the palace. The Orient was a great inspiration to Romanticism.

VISITORS' CHECKLIST

Estrada da Pena, 5 km (3 mile) S of Sintra. **Tel** *219 105 340.* *434 from Avenida Dr Miguel Bombarda, Sintra.* ◯ *Apr–Sep: 9:45am–7pm; Oct–Mar: 10am–5pm; last adm: 30 mins before closing.* ◯ *1 Jan, 25 Dec.* **www**.parquesdesintra.pt

★ Chapel Altarpiece
The impressive 16th-century alabaster and marble retable was sculpted by Nicolau Chanterène. Each niche portrays a scene of the life of Christ, from the manger to the Ascension.

The Triton Arch is encrusted with Neo-Manueline decoration and is guarded by a fierce sea monster.

The cloister, decorated with colourful patterned tiles, is part of the original monastery buildings.

Entrance

FERDINAND: KING CONSORT

Ferdinand was known in Portugal as Dom Fernando II, the "artist" king. Like his cousin Prince Albert, who married the English Queen Victoria, he loved art, nature and the new inventions of the time. He was himself a watercolour painter. Ferdinand enthusiastically adopted his new country and devoted his life to patronizing the arts. In 1869, 16 years after the death of Maria II, Ferdinand married his mistress, the opera singer Countess Edla. His life-long dream of building the extravagant palace at Pena was completed in 1885, the year he died.

STAR FEATURES

★ Arab Room

★ Ballroom

★ Chapel Altarpiece

Outdoor café in the popular holiday resort of Cascais

Cascais **7**

🏚 *27,800.* 🚉 🚌 **ℹ** *Rua Visconde da Luz 14 (214 820 085).* 🛒 *1st & 3rd Sun of the month.*

Having been a holiday resort for well over a century, Cascais possesses a certain illustriousness that younger resorts lack. Its history is most clearly visible in the villas along the coast, built as summer residences by wealthy *Lisboetas* during the late 19th century, after King Luís I had moved his summer activities to the 17th-century fortress here.

The sandy, sheltered bay around which the modern suburb has sprawled was a fishing harbour in prehistoric times. Fishing still goes on, and was recently given a municipal boost with the decision to build a quay for the landing and initial auctioning of the fishermen's catch. But Cascais today is

first of all a favoured suburb of Lisbon. It may sometimes seem more defined by its ceaseless construction boom than by any historic or even touristic qualities, but the beautiful, windswept coastline beyond the town has been left relatively undeveloped.

The **Museu Condes de Castro Guimaraes** is perhaps the best place to get a taste of Cascais as it was just over a century ago. A castle-like villa on a small creek by a headland, its grounds are today part of a park.

Across the road from the museum is the marina, one of the most emblematic developments in Cascais. With its small shopping centre, restaurants and cafés, it is a weekend magnet for today's car-borne Cascais residents and tourists.

The **Casa das Histórias**, designed by Eduardo Souto de Moura, was established by the artist Paula Rego to exhibit her works, which range from paintings and drawings to illustrations and lithographs.

🏛 **Museu Condes de Castro Guimarães**
Avenida Rei Humberto de Itália.
Tel *214 825 401.*
Museum ⬜ *10am–5pm Tue–Sun.*
Library Casa da Horta de Santa Clara. ⬜ *10am–7pm Mon–Sat.* ⬤ *1–2pm Mon, Sun & pub hols.*

🏛 **Casa das Histórias**
Avenida da República 300. **Tel** *214 826 970.* ⬜ *10am–6pm daily.*

Environs
At **Boca do Inferno** (Mouth of Hell), about 1.5 km (1 mile) west on the coast road, the sea rushes into clefts and caves in the rocks making an ominous booming sound and sending up spectacular spray in rough weather. The place is almost obscured by a roadside market and cafés but a small platform gives a good view of the rocky arch with the sea below.

The magnificent sandy beach of **Guincho**, 10 km (6 miles) further west, is backed by sand dunes with clumps of umbrella pines and a cycle path. A small fort (now a luxury hotel) stands perched on the rocks above the sea. Atlantic breakers rolling in make this a paradise for experienced windsurfers and surfers, but beware of the strong currents.

Spectacular view of the weatherbeaten coastline at Boca do Inferno, near Cascais

Estoril **8**

🏚 *24,000.* 🚉 🚌 **ℹ** *Arcadas do Parque (214 687 630).*

Despite once being the haunt of exiled royalty fleeing European republicanism, the lovely resort town of Estoril does not rest on its historical laurels. Today it is a tourist and business resort, and a place for comfortable retirement. As such, it relies equally on its historical reputation and on the natural attractiveness it has always possessed. There are also a number of good golf courses.

What separates Estoril from Cascais, besides a pleasant beach promenade of 3 km (2 miles) and a mansion covered ridge known as Monte Estoril, is its sense of place. The heart of Estoril is immediately accessible from the train station. On one side of the tracks is the riviera-like, but relaxed beach, on

Sandy beach and promenade along the bay of Estoril

the other a palm-lined park flanked by grand buildings, stretching up past fountains to what is said to be Europe's biggest casino. Dwarfing the casino is the Estoril Congress Centre, a vast multipurpose edifice that speaks confidently of Estoril's contemporary role.

Palácio de Queluz ❾

See pp108–9.

Alcochete ❿

🏛 8,000. 🚌 ℹ️ Largo da Misericórdia (212 348 655).

This delightful old town overlooks the wide Tagus estuary from the southern shore. Salt has long been one of the main industries here, and saltpans can still be seen to the north and south of the town, while in the town centre a large statue of a muscular salt worker has the inscription: "Do Sal a Revolta e a Esperança" (From Salt to Rebellion and Hope). On the outskirts of town, is a statue of Manuel I (see p18), who was born here on 1 June 1469 and granted the town a Royal Charter in 1515.

Statue of a salt worker in Alcochete (1985)

Environs
The **Reserva Natural do Estuário do Tejo** covers a vast area of estuary water, salt marshes and small islands around Alcochete and is a very important breeding ground for water birds. Particularly interesting are flocks of flamingos that gather here during the autumn and spring migration, en route from colonies such as the Camargue in France and Fuente de Piedra in Spain. Ask at the tourist office about boat trips to see the wildlife of the estuary, which includes wild bulls and horses.

🦌 **Reserva Natural do Estuário do Tejo**
Avenida dos Combatentes da Grande Guerra 1. **Tel** 212 348 021.

Pilgrims' lodgings, Cabo Espichel

Costa da Caparica ⓫

🏛 12,000. 🚢 to Cacilhas or Trafaria then bus. 🚌 to Pragal then bus. ℹ️ Avenida General Humberto Delgado (212 900 071).

Long beaches backed by sand dunes make this a popular holiday resort for Lisboetas, who come to sunbathe, swim, and enjoy the beach cafés and seafood restaurants. A railway with open carriages runs for 10 km (6 miles) along the coast in summer. The first beaches reached from the town are popular with families with children, while the furthest beaches suit those seeking quiet isolation. Further south, sheltered by pine forests, **Lagoa do Albufeira** is a peaceful windsurfing centre and camp site.

Cabo Espichel ⓬

🚌 from Sesimbra.

Sheer cliffs drop straight into the sea at this windswept promontory where the land ends dramatically. The Romans named it Promontorium Barbaricum, alluding to its dangerous location, and a lighthouse warns sailors of the treacherous rocks below. Stunning views of the ocean and the coast can be enjoyed from this bleak outcrop of land but beware of the strong gusts of wind on the cliff edge.

In this desolate setting is the impressive **Santuário de Nossa Senhora do Cabo**, a late 17th-century church with its back to the sea. On either side of the church a long line of pilgrims' lodgings facing inwards forms an open courtyard. Baroque paintings, ex votos and a frescoed ceiling decorate the church's interior. There are plans to fully restore the building and open it as a hotel. Nearby, a domed chapel has tiled blue and white azulejo panels depicting fishing scenes. The site became a popular place of pilgrimage in the 13th century when a local man had a vision of the Madonna rising from the sea on a mule. Legend has it that the mule tracks can be seen embedded in the rock. The large footprints, on Praia dos Lagosteiros below the church, are actually believed to be fossilized dinosaur tracks.

Spring flowers by the saltpans of the Tagus estuary near Alcochete

Palácio Nacional de Queluz ⑨

A sphinx in the gardens

In 1747, Pedro, younger son of João V, commissioned Mateus Vicente to transform his 17th-century hunting lodge into a Rococo summer palace. The central section, including a music room and chapel, was built, but after Pedro's marriage in 1760 to the future Maria I, the palace was again extended. The French architect, Jean-Baptiste Robillion, added the sumptuous Robillion Pavilion and gardens, cleared space for the Throne Room and redesigned the Music Room. During Maria's reign, the royal family kept a menagerie and went boating on the *azulejo*-lined canal.

Corridor of the Sleeves
Painted azulejo *panels (1784) representing the continents and the seasons, as well as hunting scenes, line the walls of the bright Corredor das Mangas (sleeves).*

The Lion Staircase is an impressive and graceful link from the lower gardens to the palace.

★ **Sala dos Embaixadores**
Built by Robillion, this stately room was used for diplomatic audiences as well as concerts. The trompe l'oeil ceiling shows the royal family attending a concert.

Neptune's Fountain

STAR FEATURES

- ★ Throne Room
- ★ Sala dos Embaixadores
- ★ Palace Gardens

To canal

Shell Waterfall

The Robillion Pavilion displays the flamboyance of the French architect's Rococo style.

Don Quixote Chamber
The royal bedroom, where Pedro IV (see p19) was born and died, has a domed ceiling and magnificent floor decoration in exotic woods, giving the square room a circular appearance. Painted scenes by Manuel de Costa (1784) tell the story of Don Quixote.

Music Room
Operas and concerts were performed here by Maria I's orchestra, "the best in Europe" according to English traveller, William Beckford. A portrait of the queen hangs above the grand piano.

VISITORS' CHECKLIST

Largo do Palácio, Queluz.
Tel 214 343 860. Queluz-Belas or Queluz-Massama. from Lisbon (Colégio Militar). **Palace & Gardens** 9am–5pm Wed–Mon (gardens to 6pm May–Oct). 1 Jan, Easter, 1 May, 25 Dec. (free 10am–2pm Sun).

Chapel

The royal family's living rooms and bedrooms opened out onto the Malta Gardens.

★ Throne Room
The elegant state room (1770) was the scene of splendid balls and banquets. The gilded statues of Atlas are by Silvestre Faria Lobo.

Entrance

Malta Gardens

The Hanging Gardens, designed by Robillion, were built over arches, raising the ground in front of the palace above the surrounding gardens.

MARIA I (1734–1816)
Maria, the eldest daughter of José I, lived at the palace in Queluz after her marriage to her uncle, Pedro, in 1760. Serious and devout, she conscientiously filled her role as queen, but suffered increasingly from bouts of melancholia. When her son José died from smallpox in 1788, she went hopelessly mad. Visitors to Queluz were dismayed by her agonizing shrieks as she suffered visions and hallucinations. After the French invasion of 1807, her younger son João (declared regent in 1792) took his mad mother to Brazil.

★ Palace Gardens
The formal gardens, adorned with statues, fountains and topiary, were often used for entertaining. Concerts performed in the Music Room would spill out into the Malta Gardens.

Sesimbra ®

🏠 42,000. 🚌 ℹ️ Largo da
Marinha 26–7 (212 288 540).
🗓️ 1st & 3rd Fri of month.

A steep narrow road leads
down to this busy fishing
village in a sheltered south-
facing bay. Protected from
north winds by the slopes
of the Serra da Arrábida, the
town has become a popular
holiday resort with Lisboetas.
It was occupied by the Romans
and later the Moors until King
Sancho II (see p18) conquered
its heavily defended forts in
1236. The old town is a maze
of steep narrow streets, with
the **Santiago Fort** (now a
customs post) in the centre
overlooking the sea. From the
terrace, which is open to the
public during the day, there
are views over the town, the
Atlantic and the wide sandy
beach that stretches out on
either side. Sesimbra is fast
developing as a resort, with
holiday flats mushrooming on
the surrounding hillsides and
plentiful pavement cafés and
bars that are always busy on
sunny days, even in winter.
    The fishing fleet of brightly
painted boats is moored in the
Porto do Abrigo to the west
of the main town. The harbour
is reached by taking Avenida
dos Náufragos, a sweeping

Colourful fishing boats in the harbour at Sesimbra

promenade that follows the
beach out of town. On the
large trawlers (traineiras), the
catch is mainly sardines, sea
bream, whiting and swordfish;
on the smaller boats, octopus
and squid. In the late afternoon, when the fishing boats
return from a day at sea, a
colourful, noisy fish auction
takes place on the quayside.
The day's catch can be tasted
in the town's excellent fish
restaurants along the shore.
    High above the town is
the **Moorish castle**, greatly
restored in the 18th century
when a church and small
flower-filled cemetery were
added inside the walls. There
are wonderful views from the
ramparts, especially at sunset.

Palmela ®

🏠 57,000. 🚌 🚉 ℹ️ Castelo de
Palmela (212 332 122). 🗓️ every
other Tue.

The formidable castle at
Palmela stands over the
small hilltown, high on a north-
eastern spur of the wooded
Serra da Arrábida. Its strategic
position dominates the plain
for miles around, especially
when floodlit at night. Heavily
defended by the Moors, it was
finally conquered in the 12th
century and given by Sancho I
(see p18) to the Knights of
the Order of Santiago. In
1423, João I transformed the
castle into a monastery for
the Order, which has been
restored and converted into a
splendid pousada (see p123),
with a restaurant in the monks'
refectory and a swimming
pool for residents, hidden
inside the castle walls. From
the castle terraces, and especially from the top of the
14th-century keep, there are
fantastic views all around,
over the Serra da Arrábida to
the south and on a clear day
across the Tagus to Lisbon. In
the town square below, the
church of **São Pedro** contains
18th-century tiles of scenes
from the life of St Peter.
    The annual wine festival, the
Festa das Vindimas, is held on
the first weekend of September
in front of the 17th-century
Paços do Concelho (town hall).
Traditionally dressed villagers
press the wine barefoot and on
the final day of celebrations
there is a spectacular firework
display from the castle walls.

The castle at Palmela with views over the wooded Serra da Arrábida

Serra da Arrábida ⑮

🚌 *Setúbal.* ℹ️ *Parque Natural da Arrábida, Praça da República, Setúbal (265 541 140).*

The Parque Natural da Arrábida covers the small range of limestone mountains that stretches east–west along the coast between Sesimbra and Setúbal. It was established to protect the wild, beautiful landscape and rich variety of birds and wildlife, including eagles, wildcats and badgers.

The name Arrábida is from Arabic meaning a place of prayer, and the wooded hillsides are indeed a peaceful, secluded retreat. The sheltered, south-facing slopes are thickly covered with aromatic and evergreen shrubs and trees, such as pine and cypress, more typical of the Mediterranean. Vineyards also thrive on the sheltered slopes and the town of **Vila Nogueira de Azeitão** is known for its wine, especially the Moscatel de Setúbal.

The **Estrada de Escarpa** (the N379-1) snakes across the top of the ridge and affords astounding views. A narrow road winds down to **Portinho da Arrábida**, a sheltered cove with a beach of fine white sand and crystal clear sea, popular with underwater fishermen. The sandy beaches of **Galapos** and **Figueirinha** are a little further east along the coast road towards Setúbal. Just east of Sesimbra, the Serra da Arrábida drops to the sea in the sheer 380-m (1,250-ft) cliffs of Risco, the highest in mainland Portugal.

Portinho da Arrábida on the dramatic coastline of the Serra da Arrábida

🛕 Convento da Arrábida

Serra da Arrábida. *Tel 212 197 620.* ⏰ *10am, 3pm Wed–Sun (by appt only).* 🚫 *Aug.* 🌐
Half-hidden among the trees of the Serra, this 16th-century building was once a Franciscan monastery. The five round towers were probably used for meditation. The building now houses a cultural centre.

🏛 Museu Oceanográfico

Fortaleza de Santa Maria, Portinho da Arrábida. *Tel 212 189 791.* ⏰ *10am–4pm Tue–Fri, 3–6pm Sat.* 🚫 *public hols, Sat in Aug.* 🌐
This small fort, just above Portinho da Arrábida, was built by Pedro, the Prince Regent, in 1676 to protect local communities from attacks by Moorish pirates. It now houses a Sea Museum and Marine Biology Centre where visitors can see aquaria containing many local sea creatures, including sea urchins, octopus and starfish.

🍷 José Maria da Fonseca

Rua José Augusto Coelho 11, Vila Nogueira de Azeitão. *Tel 212 198 940.* **Fax** *212 198 942.* ⏰ *10am–1pm, 2:30–6:30pm daily.* 🚫 *1 & 2 Jan, 31 May, 24 & 25 Dec.* 🌐 🅿️ 🛗
The Fonseca winery produces quality table wines and is famous for its fragrant dessert wine, Moscatel de Setúbal *(see p129).* Tours of the winery explain the process of making moscatel and a visit to a series of old cellars containing huge oak and chestnut vats. Tours last about 45 minutes and include a wine tasting.

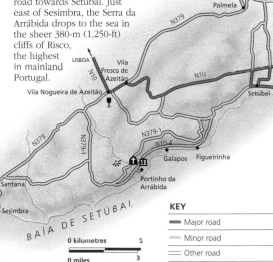

KEY

━━━ Major road

▬▬▬ Minor road

═══ Other road

0 kilometres — 5

0 miles — 3

Manueline interior of Igreja de Jesus, Setúbal

Setúbal 16

🏘 *92,000.* 🚉 🚌 🚢 🛈 *Travessa Frei Gaspar 10 (265 539 130).*

Although this is an important industrial town, and the third largest port in Portugal (after Lisbon and Oporto), Setúbal can be used to explore the area. To the south of the central gardens and fountains are the fishing harbour, marina and ferry port, and a lively covered market. North of the gardens is the old town, with attractive pedestrian streets and squares full of cafés.

The 16th-century **cathedral**, dedicated to Santa Maria da Graça, has glorious tiled panels dating from the 18th century, and gilded altar decoration. Street names commemorate two famous Setúbal residents: Manuel Barbosa du Bocage (1765–1805), whose satirical poetry landed him in prison, and Luísa Todi (1753–1833), a celebrated opera singer.

In Roman times, fish-salting was the most important industry here. Rectangular tanks, carved from stone, can be seen under the glass floor of the Regional Tourist Office on Travessa Frei Gaspar.

🏛 Igreja de Jesus

Largo de Jesus. *Tel 265 520 964.* ⭕ *9:30am–12:30pm, 2:30–5pm Tue–Fri, 9:30am–12:30pm, 2:30–3:30pm Sat & Sun.* ♿ **Museum** *Tel 265 537 890.* ⭕ *9am–12:30pm, 2–5:30pm Tue–Sat.* ⬤ *public hols.*
To the north of the old town, this striking Gothic church is one of Setúbal's architectural treasures. Designed by the architect Diogo Boitac in 1494, the lofty interior is adorned with twisted columns, carved in three strands from pinkish Arrábida limestone, and rope-like stone ribs decorating the roof, recognized as the earliest examples of the distinctive and ornate Manueline style.

On Rua do Balneário, in the old monastic quarters, a **museum** houses 14 remarkable paintings of the life of Christ. Painted in glowing colours, they are attributed to followers of Jorge Afonso (1520–30).

🏛 Museu de Arqueologia e Etnografia

Avenida Luísa Todi 162. *Tel 265 239 365.* ⭕ *9am–12:30pm, 2–5:30pm Tue–Sat.* ⬤ *public hols.*
The archaeological museum displays a wealth of finds from digs around Setúbal, including Bronze Age pots, Roman coins and amphorae. The ethnography display shows local arts, crafts and industries, including the processing of salt and cork over the centuries.

♟ Castelo de São Filipe

Estrada de São Filipe. *Tel 265 550 070.* ⭕ *daily.*
The star-shaped fort was built in 1595 by Philip II of Spain during Portugal's period under Spanish rule to keep a wary eye on pirates, English invaders and the local population. A massive gateway and stone tunnel lead to the sheltered interior, which now houses a *pousada (see p123)* and an exquisite small chapel, tiled with scenes from the life of São Filipe by Policarpo de Oliveira Bernardes (1695–1778). A broad terrace offers marvellous views over the city and the Sado estuary.

Environs
Setúbal is an excellent starting point for a tour by car of the unspoilt **Reserva Natural do Estuário do Sado**, a vast stretch of mud flats, shallow lagoons and salt marshes with patches of pine

Fisherman's boat on the shallow mud flats of the Reserva Natural do Estuário do Sado

forest, which has been explored and inhabited since 3500 BC. Otters, water birds (including storks and herons), oysters and a great variety of fish are found in the reserve. The old tidal water mill at Mouriscas, 5 km (3 miles) to the east of Setúbal, uses the different levels of the tide to turn the grinding stones. Rice-growing and fishing are the main occupations today, and pine trees around the lagoon are tapped for resin.

✕ Reserva Natural do Estuário do Sado
ℹ *Praça da República, Setúbal* (265 541 157).

Península de Tróia ⓱

🚌 ⛴ *Tróia.* **ℹ** *Tróia Tourist Information (265 499 000).*

Thatched fisherman's cottage in the village of Carrasqueira

High-rise holiday apartments dominate the tip of the Tróia Peninsula, easily accessible from Setúbal by ferry. The Atlantic coast, stretching south for 18 km (11 miles) of untouched sandy beaches, is now the haunt of sun-seekers in the summer.

Near Tróia, in the sheltered lagoon, the Roman town of **Cetóbriga** was the site of a thriving fish-salting business; the stone tanks and ruined buildings are open to visit. To the south, smart holiday villas and golf clubs are springing up along the lagoon.

Further on, **Carrasqueira** is an old fishing community where you can still see traditional reed houses, with walls and roofs made from thatch. The narrow fishing boats moored along the mud flats

View over Alcácer do Sal and the River Sado from the castle

are reached by walkways raised on stilts. From here to Alcácer do Sal, great stretches of pine forest line the road, and there are the first glimpses of the cork oak countryside typical of the Alentejo region.

∩ Cetóbriga
N253-1. **Tel** *265 499 400.*
◯ *Oct–May: 10am–1pm, 3–5:30pm Tue–Sat (to 6:30pm Jun–Aug).* 🏛

Alcácer do Sal ⓲

🏯 *14,000.* 🚉 🚌 **ℹ** *Largo Pedro Nunes 76 (265 610 071 or 265 610 076).* 🛍 *1st Sat of month.*

Bypassed by the main road, the ancient town of Alcácer do Sal (*al-kasr* from the Arabic for castle, and *do sal* from its trade in salt) sits peacefully on the north bank of the River Sado. The imposing castle was

a hillfort as early as the 6th century BC. The Phoenicians made an inland trading port here, and the castle later became a Roman stronghold. Rebuilt by the Moors, it was conquered by Afonso II in 1217. The buildings have now taken on a new life as a *pousada (see p122)*, with views over the rooftops.

There are pleasant cafés along the riverside promenade and several historic churches. The 18th-century **Santo António** holds a marble Chapel of the 11,000 Virgins, while the **Cripta Arqueológica** exhibits finds dating from the Iron Age to the modern era. The bullring is a focus for summer events and hosts the agricultural fair in October.

🏛 Cripta Arqueológico
Castelo de Alcácer do Sal. **ℹ** *265 612 058.* ◯ *10am–1pm, 3–7pm (summer); 9am–5:30pm (winter).*

BIRDS OF THE TAGUS AND SADO ESTUARIES

Many waterbirds, including black-winged stilts, avocets, Kentish plovers and pratincoles are found close to areas of open water and mud flats as well as the dried-out lagoons of the Tagus and Sado estuaries. Reed-beds also provide shelter for nesting and support good numbers of little bitterns, purple herons and marsh harriers. From September to March, the area around the Tagus estuary is extremely important for wildfowl and wintering waders.

Black-winged stilt, a wader that feeds in the estuaries

TRAVELLERS'
NEEDS

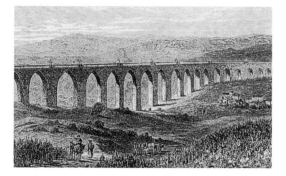

WHERE TO STAY

Porter services are available in Lisbon's top hotels

Lisbon and its environs offer a variety of accommodation, from restored palaces to family-run hostels. Hotels in Lisbon range from modern and luxurious or elegant and old-fashioned to comfortable chain hotels. There are many hotels around the main sightseeing areas of the city.

The hotels in Estoril and Cascais along the Lisbon coast are perhaps less varied with fewer characterful options. In the countryside around Lisbon, hotels are fairly scarce, though Sintra has a selection of places to stay and is a good base for exploring the area west of Lisbon. *Pousadas*, often historic buildings converted into hotels, are an alternative in the Lisbon Coast area. If you prefer self-catering, farmhouses, villas and apartments usually offer flexibility and good value. The hotels listed on pages 118–23 have been selected from every price category as offering the best value for money in each area.

Bedroom at the York House hotel in Lisbon, a converted 16th-century convent *(see p120)*

CHOOSING A HOTEL

The majority of the modern, luxury hotels in Lisbon are centrally situated around Parque Eduardo VII, at the north end of Avenida de Liberdade. As an alternative, the converted Expo 98 area, Parque das Nações, now has several top-range hotels with easy access to the airport and Oriente railway station.

The Baixa district has a number of more modest *pensões* with a wide choice of accommodation located around Rossio square.

Characterful smaller hotels are found in the Lapa district to the west. Most of the city's older districts, including Chiado, Barrio Alto, Graça and Alfama, have small hotels that offer atmosphere if not always top comforts and quiet.

TYPES OF HOTEL

Hotels in Lisbon vary greatly in terms of quality, price and facilities. At present there are two main types of lodging, as classified by the Portuguese tourist authority: hotels and *pensões*. *Pensões* are slowly being phased out, however, and will be upgraded to one-star hotels or more.

Hotels are distinguished mainly by the fact that they take up an entire building and are often purpose-built. *Pensões*, on the other hand, are always housed in shared premises, typically occupying several floors of a residential building. All hotels and *pensões* are meant to provide meals. If they only offer breakfast, they must also be called *residencial*.

The *estalagem* is an inn, usually with a garden, and located outside of city centres, but these are also being phased out. *Albergarias* are *pensões* that are the equivalent of 4- or 5-star hotels. *Pousadas* are either country inns or located in historic buildings such as castles or palaces. They are a state-owned chain run by **Pestana**.

HOTEL CHAINS

International luxury groups are represented in Lisbon by such hotels as the Lapa Palace and the Ritz Four Seasons *(see p120)*. Smaller luxury groups include **Tivoli Hotels**, which has three hotels in Lisbon and two in Sintra, and the **Pestana Group**, which owns the Pestana Palace Hotel *(see p118)* in Lisbon. **Heritage Hotels** runs five smaller luxury hotels in the city, including the Solar do Castelo *(see p119)*.

Lower down the scale, **Ibis Hotel**, a part of the French-owned Accor Group, has six

The impressive façade of the luxurious Olissippo Lapa Palace *(see p120)*

◁ Breakfasting beneath the wisteria at the Pousada da Palmela

View from the Tivoli Palácio de Seteais, Sintra, now a luxury hotel *(see p123)*

properties in the Lisbon area, while the local chain **VIP Hotels** has a number of units ranging from two to five stars.

GRADINGS

The Portuguese tourist authority grades hotels from one to five stars (five being the top rating). These ratings are based on a fixed set of criteria which covers most aspects of comfort. They do not take into account more subjective factors such as view or atmosphere. All graded establishments should have a sign showing their rating.

PRICES

In Portugal, establishments are free to set their own prices, but tariffs must be displayed at reception and in the rooms. The cost of the room usually includes all taxes and a continental breakfast. Other meals are charged as extras. It is sometimes possible to bargain for a better rate, especially in low season. As a rule, the cost of a single room is around 60 to 75 per cent of the cost of a double room. Cascais and Estoril can be expensive, but prices drop substantially out of season. *Pousadas* charge three rates: for low (Nov–Mar), mid (Apr–end Jul and mid-Sep–Oct) and high (end Jul–mid-Sep, carnival, Easter and New Year) seasons.

BOOKING

You will need to book in advance for Estoril and Cascais in high season, when much accommodation is taken by tour operators. Book ahead for central Lisbon, which can also get full. Most hoteliers speak English so it should not be a problem to book by phone. Deposits are not usually required but a written confirmation by fax or email, including a credit card number may be requested.

Pousadas can be booked through **Pestana** or at the *pousadas* website. The Portuguese tourist authority, **Turismo de Portugal**, publishes two official guides which are revised regularly, and are available in English, French and Spanish, as well as Portuguese: *Alojamento Turístico* (Tourist Accommodation and *Turismo no Espaço Rural* (Tourism in the Country). These list all of the establishments rated by the authority, but only the latter contains any description of individual settings.

TRAVELLING WITH CHILDREN

The Portuguese adore children and will welcome them warmly into hotels and restaurants. Travellers who have children with them will find an immediate point of contact with their hosts.

DISABLED TRAVELLERS

The Portuguese National Tourist Office lists hotels with facilities for the disabled, and produces a general information leaflet. Some youth hostels and camp sites provide special facilities and these are listed by the relevant organizations, and in a guide that is published by the **Instituto Nacional para o Reabilitação**.

DIRECTORY

HOTEL CHAINS

Heritage Hotels
Tel 213 218 200.
Fax 213 471 630.
www.heritage.pt

Ibis Hotel
www.ibishotel.com

Pestana Group
Tel 213 615 600; 808 252 252.
Fax 213 615 601.
www.pestana.com

Tivoli Hotels
Tel 213 198 900.
Fax 213 198 950.
www.tivolihotels.com

VIP Hotels
Tel 217 814 100.
Fax 217 814 101.
www.viphotels.com

POUSADAS

Pestana
Lisbon: *Tel* 218 442 000/01.
Fax 218 442 085/7.
www.pousadas.pt

INFORMATION

Portugal Hotel Guide
www.hotelguide.pt

Turismo de Portugal
Rua Ivone Silva 6,
1050-124 Lisbon.
Tel 211 140 200.
Fax 211 140 830.
www.turismodeportugal.pt

DISABLED TRAVELLERS

Instituto Nacional para o Reabilitação
Avenida Conde de Valbom 63,
1063 Lisbon.
Tel 217 929 500.
Fax 217 959 545.
www.inr.pt

Choosing a Hotel

The hotels in this guide have been selected across a wide price range for their good value, facilities and location. The hotels are listed alphabetically within each price category, both for central Lisbon and the Lisbon Coast. Map references refer to the Street Finder on pages 172–179.

PRICE CATEGORIES
For a standard double room per night, including breakfast, tax and service.

€ Under €55
€€ €55–€120
€€€ €120–€175
€€€€ €175–€230
€€€€€ Over €230

LISBON

ALCÂNTARA Pestana Palace Hotel
€€€€€
Rua Jau 54, 1300-314 **Tel** *213 615 600* **Fax** *213 615 601* **Rooms** *194*   **Map** *2 F3*

This magnificent hotel is partly housed in the 19th-century Palácio Valle-Flor and features luxuriously appointed rooms and suites. Most are located in a modern accommodation wing where there is also a conference centre, health club and indoor swimming pool. **www.pestana.com**

AVENIDA Alegria
€
Praça da Alegria 12, 1250-004 **Tel** *213 220 670* **Fax** *213 478 070* **Rooms** *35*   **Map** *4 F1*

A homely feel pervades this basic, good value *residencial* that offers clean and tidy rooms, some with their own balcony. The smart façade, dating from 1865, overlooks a palm-laden garden and borders the red-light district, although the vicinity is fairly quiet. **www.alegrianet.com**

AVENIDA VIP Inn Veneza
€€
Avenida da Liberdade 189, 1250-141 **Tel** *213 522 618* **Fax** *213 526 678* **Rooms** *37*   **Map** *5 C5*

A charming and elegantly designed property distinguished by an ornate staircase lined with colourful wall murals by Pedro Luiz-Gomes. The hotel was built in 1886 and the interior retains a wonderful 19th-century atmosphere. The rooms are spacious and well appointed and there is a wonderfully intimate bar. **www.viphotels.com**

AVENIDA Britânia
€€€
Rua Rodrigues Sampaio 17, 1150-278 **Tel** *213 155 016* **Fax** *213 155 021* **Rooms** *33*   **Map** *5 C5*

The only surviving original Art Deco hotel in Lisbon, this small boutique property is unique. The building was designed by the architect Cassiano Branco in 1944 and has been lovingly restored. Period detail has been faithfully maintained, with whimsical modern nuances. The polished marble lobby is beautiful. **www.heritage.pt**

AVENIDA Inspira Santa Marta Hotel
€€€
Rua de Santa Marta 48, 1150-297 **Tel** *210 440 900* **Fax** *210 435 993* **Rooms** *89*   **Map** *5 C5*

Style and ecological sustainability (such as use of environmentally friendly building materials, sustainable food and restricted use of paper) are the key elements at this hotel just off the Avenida da Liberdade. Billed as an urban retreat in downtown Lisbon, it has a Mediterranean restaurant and sumptuous spa. **www.inspirahotels.com**

AVENIDA Tivoli Jardim
€€€
Rua J. César Machado 7, 1250-135 **Tel** *213 591 000* **Fax** *213 591 245* **Rooms** *119*   **Map** *4 F1*

Popular with business executives, this is the sister hotel of the neighbouring Tivoli Lisboa. The hotel is named after the tropical gardens at the rear of the building where guests can relax and take a dip in the pool. Alternatively, take advantage of the extensive sports facilities at the Tivoli Lisboa. **www.tivolihotels.com**

AVENIDA Lisboa Plaza
€€€€
Travessa do Salitre 7, 1269-066 **Tel** *213 218 218* **Fax** *213 471 630* **Rooms** *112*   **Map** *4 F1*

Built in 1953, and situated off Praça da Alegria and Av. da Liberdade, this boutique hotel possesses an informal atmosphere and understated charm. The decor is by the Portuguese interior designer Graça Viterbo, and her characteristic colour-coordinated fabrics and furnishings feature throughout the property. **www.heritage.pt**

AVENIDA Sofitel Lisboa
€€€€
Avenida da Liberdade 127, 1269-038 **Tel** *213 228 300* **Fax** *213 228 310* **Rooms** *171*   **Map** *4 F1*

Comfort and modernity are the key features here. The bedrooms have opulent mattresses and soft, downy quilts that guarantee a good night's sleep. Slick, contemporary design and a first-class restaurant are some of the factors that make this 5-star deluxe hotel a city-centre favourite. **www.sofitel-lisboa.com**

AVENIDA Tivoli Lisboa
€€€€
Avenida da Liberdade 185, 1269-050 **Tel** *213 198 900* **Fax** *213 198 950* **Rooms** *308*   **Map** *4 F1*

One of Lisbon's most emblematic hotels, the Tivoli holds court over Avenida da Liberdade and is renowned for its high degree of service and personal attention. The rooftop Terrace Grill is a gourmet hotspot. The hotel regularly hosts VIP conferences. **www.tivolihotels.com**

Key to Symbols *see back cover flap*

BAIRRO ALTO Pensão Londres
€

Rua Dom Pedro V 53, 1250-092 **Tel** *213 462 203* **Fax** *213 465 682* **Rooms** *36* **Map** *4 F2*

Housed in a lofty, angular building, the rooms here are sparsely decorated but are clean, tidy and all have satellite TV. Those on the fourth floor command glorious panoramic views of the city. The owners provide a laundry service and helpful advice on where to go and what to see. **www.pensaolondres.com.pt**

BAIXA Beira Minho
€

Praça da Figueira 6, 1100-240 **Tel** *213 461 846* **Fax** *218 867 811* **Rooms** *19* **Map** *7 B3*

With a strikingly colourful entrance, the corridor leading to this comfortable and centrally located *pensão* passes straight through a flower shop, and the scent is wonderful. Facilties are basic but *en suite* rooms are equipped with TVs and direct-dial telephones.

BAIXA Norte
€

Rua dos Douradores 161, 1100-205 **Tel** *218 878 941* **Fax** *218 868 462* **Rooms** *34* **Map** *7 B3*

Wedged in between a row of shops on a semi-pedestrianized street near Praça de Figueira, this centrally positioned functional *pensão* offers spotless rooms with private bathroom facilities and TV but no breakfast. Guests will have no problem finding a café or restaurant, however, as the area is full of them.

BAIXA Portugal
€

Rua João das Regras 4, 1100-294 **Tel** *218 877 581* **Fax** *218 867 343* **Rooms** *59* **Map** *7 C3*

The rather drab façade of this hotel situated off Praça Martim Moniz belies a stylish old-fashioned decor. The large rooms are light and airy and carpeted throughout. An attractive, well-stocked bar provides a handy meeting point and the hotel is within easy reach of Rossio metro station. **www.hotelportugal.com**

BAIXA Duas Nações
€€

Rua da Vitória 41, 1100-618 **Tel** *213 460 710* **Fax** *213 470 206* **Rooms** *54* **Map** *7 B4*

The "Two Nations" is a rather grand building straddling the corner of Rua Augusta and Rua da Vitória, both pedestrianized, and the property is fashioned as a traditional Lisbon boarding house. Rooms are well appointed and have private bathroom facilities. Those overlooking Rua Augusta can be noisy at times. **www.duasnacoes.com**

BAIXA Lisboa Tejo
€€

Rua dos Condes de Monsanto 2, 1100-159 **Tel** *218 866 182* **Fax** *218 865 163* **Rooms** *58* **Map** *7 B3*

This stylish hotel, housed within an 18th-century building, has a modern interior. Situated in the heart of the capital's downtown district, it is close to several reasonably priced eateries. The rooms are bright and comfortable. There is a Moorish well in the lobby. Special rates for parking are available nearby.

BAIXA Internacional Design Hotel
€€€

Rua da Betesga 3, 1100-090 **Tel** *213 240 990* **Fax** *213 240 999* **Rooms** *55* **Map** *7 B3*

Thanks to a skilled team of architects, decorators, designers and artists, the four floors of this property each have a special theme: Minimalism; Zen philosophy; pop culture; and Afro-style. The hotel is run on holistic principles and only uses biological and organic products. **www.internacionaldesignhotel.com**

BAIXA Mundial
€€€

Praça Martim Móniz 2, 1100-341 **Tel** *218 842 000* **Fax** *218 842 110* **Rooms** *350* **Map** *7 B3*

This typical four-star property has comfortable rooms, modern facilities and the added bonus of a private car park. The hotel looms large over Praça Martim Moniz but provides some fine cityscapes. The best views are from the top-floor restaurant, particularly at night. **www.hotel-mundial.pt**

CASTELO Ninho das Águias
€

Costa do Castelo 74, 1100-179 **Tel** *218 854 070* **Rooms** *16* **Map** *7 C3*

Easily identified by its rooftop turret, the unusual "Eagle's Nest" *pensão* perches under the castle walls. A huge stuffed eagle greets visitors on arrival. The rooms are bright and breezy and the hotel is very popular so it is wise to book ahead. The terraced flower garden offers peace and solitude. Breakfast is not served.

CASTELO Olissippo Castelo
 €€€

Rua Costa do Castelo 126, 1100-179 **Tel** *218 820 190* **Fax** *218 820 194* **Rooms** *24* **Map** *7 C3*

Located at the foot of the Castelo de São Jorge, between the ancient districts of Alfama and Mouraria, the Olissippo is ranked as one of the best four-star hotels in town. With their understated luxury, rooms are both modern and welcoming. Free Wi-Fi is available, and half of the rooms have balconies with a view. **www.olissippohotels.com**

CASTELO Solar do Castelo
€€€€€

Rua das Cozinhas 2, 1100-181 **Tel** *218 806 050* **Fax** *218 870 907* **Rooms** *14* **Map** *7 C3*

Hidden within the walls of the castle is this sparkling gem of a hotel, incorporated into the architecture of a renovated 18th-century mansion, itself constructed on the site of the former Alcáçova Palace. Some rooms face a central courtyard and guests can enjoy a complimentary decanter of port upon arrival. **www.heritage.pt**

CHIADO Hotel do Chiado
 €€€

Rua Nova do Almada 114, 1200-290 **Tel** *213 256 100* **Fax** *213 256 161* **Rooms** *40* **Map** *7 B4*

Occupying the top two floors of the historic Armazens do Chiado building, which was rebuilt after the 1988 fire, this hotel boasts head-spinning views of the Castelo de São Jorge, which can be enjoyed from many of the rooms and the bar's terrace. Free Wi-Fi is available throughout the hotel. **www.hoteldochiado.com**

GRAÇA Senhora do Monte
€€

Calçada do Monte 39, 1170-250 **Tel** *218 866 002* **Fax** *218 877 783* **Rooms** *28*   **Map** *7 D1*

This unique little hilltop *albergaria* is somewhat off the beaten track but rewards those who make the effort with some memorable views. The interior features cosy sofas and large tables and lamps. All the guest rooms have balconies and the small decorative touches make all the difference. **www.albergariasenhoradomonte.com**

LAPA York House
€€€

Rua das Janelas Verdes 32, 1200-691 **Tel** *213 962 435* **Fax** *213 972 793* **Rooms** *32*   **Map** *4 D3*

Behind the rose-pink walls of this enchanting hotel are luxurious rooms with wooden or terracotta floors and elegant antique furniture. Housed in the 17th-century Covento dos Marianos and set around a charming, plant-filled patio, York House is peaceful, serene and wholly inviting. **www.yorkhouselisboa.com**

LAPA As Janelas Verdes
€€€€

Rua das Janelas Verdes 47, 1200-690 **Tel** *213 968 143* **Fax** *213 968 144* **Rooms** *29*   **Map** *4 D3*

This romantic and luxurious hotel is housed in an 18th-century mansion, once owned by the Portuguese novelist Eça de Queirós *(see p55)*. It has Neo-Classical decor and a peaceful, charming patio. The property has its own library and is a short walk from the Museu Nacional de Arte Antiga *(see pp56–9)*. **www.heritage.pt**

LAPA Olissippo Lapa Palace
€€€€€

Rua do Pau da Bandeira 4, 1249-021 **Tel** *213 949 494* **Fax** *213 950 665* **Rooms** *109*   **Map** *3 C3*

The *grande dame* of Lisbon hotels, this gracious, historical property dates from 1870. The palace was once the home of the Count of Valanças and each room in the Palace Wing is uniquely decorated in its own Portuguese style – from 18th-century Neo-Classical to Art Deco. Leisure options include a spa. **www.olissippohotels.com**

MARQUES DE POMBAL Castilho
€

Rua Castilho 57, 1250-068 **Tel** *213 860 822* **Fax** *213 862 910* **Rooms** *25*   **Map** *4 F1*

A stone's throw from Marquês de Pombal metro station, this is an ideal option for those seeking a city-centre location at an out-of-town price. The hotel is on the fourth floor of the building and the comfortable rooms, some with three or four beds, are well equipped. **www.turisplan.pt/residencialcastilho**

MARQUES DE POMBAL Jorge V
€€

Rua Mouzinho da Silveira 3, 1250-165 **Tel** *213 562 525* **Fax** *213 150 319* **Rooms** *49*   **Map** *5 C5*

Considering the central location, this pleasant, comfortable hotel offers good value for money. Roughly half the rooms have balconies, so request one when checking in. There are also six suites. The downstairs bar is a good place to mingle with fellow guests and there are Internet facilities in the lobby. **www.hoteljorgev.com**

MARQUES DE POMBAL Nacional
€€

Rua Castilho 34, 1250-070 **Tel** *213 554 433* **Fax** *213 561 122* **Rooms** *61*   **Map** *5 B5*

This interesting glass-fronted hotel has comfortable rooms and all the services you would expect from a three-star property, including a private car parking facility. Its location near Praça Marquês de Pombal makes it a handy base from which to explore the city. **www.hotel-nacional.com**

MARQUES DE POMBAL Tiara Park Atlantic Lisboa
€€€€

Rua Castilho 149, 1099-034 **Tel** *213 818 700* **Fax** *213 890 500* **Rooms** *331*   **Map** *5 B4*

This elegant 18-floor structure overlooks Eduardo VII Park. Part of the exclusive Tiara chain, with plush furnishings and an ultra-modern interior, this is one of Lisbon's top hotels. The L'Appart restaurant is a favoured spot among fine-dining Lisboetas. Guests can enjoy very special rates at nearby Club VII health club. **www.tiara-hotels.com**

MARQUES DE POMBAL Four Seasons Hotel Ritz Lisbon
€€€€€

Rua Rodrigo da Fonseca 88, 1099-039 **Tel** *213 811 400* **Fax** *213 831 783* **Rooms** *282*   **Map** *5 B5*

Hospitality at the legendary Ritz combines luxury and elegance in a grand style. The hotel is a prominent landmark and a stunning base from which to experience the city. A major draw is the spa with its Zen-inspired decor in marble and rich oak and a wealth of treatments and therapies. **www.fourseasons.com**

PARQUE DAS NAÇOES Tivoli Oriente
€€€

Avenida Dom João II, 1990-083 **Tel** *218 915 100* **Fax** *218 915 345* **Rooms** *279*

Parque das Nações, on the riverfront east of the city centre, boasts major attractions such as the Oceanarium and the Pavilhão Atlántico concert hall, all within easy reach of this handsome hotel. The impressive Vasco da Gama shopping mall is opposite, and there is a delicious choice of nearby bars and restaurants. **www.tivolihotels.com**

RATO Amazónia
€€

Travessa Fábrica dos Pentes 12–20, 1250-106 **Tel** *213 877 006* **Fax** *213 879 090* **Rooms** *192*   **Map** *5 B5*

Conveniently close to the city centre but with an informal side-street ambience, this mid-range hotel has an attractive interior decorated with ethnic artwork and sculpture. The guest rooms are comfortable and the grounds boast a modest swimming pool that is closed during winter. **www.amazoniahoteis.com**

RATO Altis
€€€€€

Rua Castilho 11, 1269-072 **Tel** *213 106 000* **Fax** *213 106 262* **Rooms** *300*   **Map** *4 F1*

This huge hotel has every expected facility, including a well-equipped health club that offers massage and physiotherapy among its many treatments, and an indoor swimming pool. There is a rooftop grill and the Herald Bar where guests can unwind over a drink while listening to live piano music. **www.altishotels.com**

Key to Price Guide *see p118* **Key to Symbols** *see back cover flap*

RESTAURADORES Nova Goa

Rua do Arco do Marquês do Alegrete 13, 1100-034 **Tel** *218 881 137* **Fax** *218 867 811* **Rooms** *41*   **Map** *7 C3*

Just around the corner from Praça da Figueira *(see p45)*, this *pensão* is clean, comfortable and fairly basic. The rooms do, however, have *en suite* bathrooms and cable TV. Some knowledge of Portuguese will help foreign guests as little English is spoken. **www.pensaonovagoa.com**

RESTAURADORES Restauradores

Praça dos Restauradores 13, 1250-187 **Tel** *213 475 660* **Fax** *213 424 104* **Rooms** *28*   **Map** *7 A2*

If the lift is out of order it will be a bit of a hike to the fourth floor where this small *pensão* is situated. The *en suite* rooms are surprisingly well furnished, with those at the front of the building commanding a giddy view of the busy street below. Breakfast is not served.

RESTAURADORES Roma

Travessa da Glória 22a, 1250-118 **Tel** *213 460 557* **Fax** *213 460 557* **Rooms** *39*   **Map** *7 A2*

A first-class *pensão* that differs from many others in that some of the rooms are in fact small apartments, complete with kitchenettes. A 24-hour reception means guests can arrive any time of day or night, and there is a secure luggage room. Good restaurants and bars are close at hand. **www.residenciaroma.com**

RESTAURADORES Turim Suisso Atlântico

Rua da Glória 3, 1250-114 **Tel** *213 400 270* **Fax** *213 469 018* **Rooms** *100*   **Map** *7 A2*

In a small side street by the Elevador da Glória, this slightly outdated hotel has large old-fashioned rooms and public areas with stone arches and wooden beams. Note that room 117 does not have a window. Its great advantage is the location, just a short step away from bustling Praça dos Restauradores. **www.turimhoteis.com**

RESTAURADORES Florescente

Rua das Portas de Santo Antão 99, 1150-266 **Tel** *213 426 609* **Fax** *213 427 733* **Rooms** *68*   **Map** *7 A2*

For a modest *pensão*, the rooms here put a three-star hotel to shame. They are spotless and well appointed and all have *en suite* bathrooms. The Florescente stands on a pedestrianized street and is near the Coliseu dos Recreios concert venue, so the *pensão's* exclusive car parking option is a real plus. **www.residencialflorescente.com**

RESTAURADORES VIP Executive Suites Eden

Praça dos Restauradores 24, 1250-187 **Tel** *213 216 600* **Fax** *213 216 666* **Rooms** *134*   **Map** *7 A2*

This building used to be a theatre-cinema and part of the interior is decorated with old film posters. The refurbishment project won its architects a "Best Tourism Project in Portugal" award for the 75 studios and 59 apartments they incorporated into the original structure. **www.vlphotels.com**

RESTAURADORES Avenida Palace

Rua 1de Dezembro 123, 1200-359 **Tel** *213 218 100* **Fax** *213 422 884* **Rooms** *82*   **Map** *7 B3*

Built in 1892, this sumptuous building with its Neo-Classical façade is the oldest hotel in Lisbon. The stunning interior retains many charming period details and evokes romantic images of Paris during the Belle Epoque. The rooms are decorated in a classical style. **www.hotelavenidapalace.pt**

ROSSIO Metrópole

Praça Dom Pedro IV 30, 1100-200 **Tel** *213 219 030* **Fax** *213 469 166* **Rooms** *36*   **Map** *7 B3*

Inaugurated in 1917, this hotel was a favourite haunt of spies and double agents during World War II. The individually styled and elegant rooms are partly furnished with original pieces from the 1920s and the whole building has a distinctly retro atmosphere. The balcony views across Rossio are idyllic. **www.almeidahotels.com**

SALDANHA Horizonte

Avenida António Augusto de Aguiar 42, 1050-017 **Tel** *213 539 526* **Fax** *213 538 474* **Rooms** *53*   **Map** *5 B4*

This large *pensão* offers good value for money for this area, situated as it is near Parque Eduardo VII. Accommodation is roomy and amenities include satellite TV and a safe. There is also a daily laundry service. The *pensão* faces Parque metro station and rooms at the front can be noisy. **www.hotelhorizonte.com**

SALDANHA Hotel Marquês de Sá

Avenida Miguel Bombarda 130, 1050-167 **Tel** *217 911 014* **Fax** *217 936 983* **Rooms** *164*   **Map** *6 B2*

A four-star hotel in a modern building standing over the older townhouses that characterize this area of Lisbon. The interior design is fairly conventional save for some fetching abstract carpet designs. The hotel is a short walk from the Museu Calouste Gulbenkian *(see pp76–9)*. **www.olissippohotels.com**

SALDANHA Real Parque

Avenida Luís Bivar 67, 1069-146 **Tel** *213 199 000* **Fax** *213 570 750* **Rooms** *153*   **Map** *5 C3*

Smart and impressive, this hotel loves children and can even supply kid's toys and furniture, and a special children's menu. The adults meanwhile can make use of the health and fitness centre which is decorated with lovely turquoise and aquamarine mosaic tiles. **www.realhotelsgroup.com**

SALDANHA Sheraton Lisboa Hotel & Spa

Rua Latino Coelho 1, 1069-025 **Tel** *213 120 000* **Fax** *213 547 164* **Rooms** *369*   **Map** *5 C3*

Housed in Lisbon's tallest building, this Sheraton has a choice of gourmet and bistro restaurants, including the Panorama restaurant and bar on the top floor with stunning views. Chic guest rooms and suites are complemented in mood and design by a state-of-the-art spa with 10 specialist treatment rooms. **www.sheraton.com/lisboa**

THE LISBON COAST

ALCÁCER DO SAL Pousada Dom Afonso II
Castelo de Alcácer do Sol, 7580-197 **Tel** *265 613 070* **Fax** *265 613 074* **Rooms** *35*

This historic and atmospheric *pousada* occupies a converted castle on a strategic hilltop whose foundations overlay vestiges of Roman, Moorish, Phoenician and even Neolithic remains. Chunky, whitewashed walls embrace tidy rooms with floor-to-ceiling shuttered windows plus views of the town and the River Sado. **www.pousadas.pt**

CARCAVELOS Praia Mar
Rua do Gurué 16, 2775-581 **Tel** *214 585 100* **Fax** *214 573 130* **Rooms** *154*

You can almost keep one foot in the swimming pool while dipping the other in the sea, such is this wonderful hotel's proximity to the beach. The ultra-modern rooms and suites are extremely stylish, with flat-screen TVs and incredible ocean views or garden vistas. **www.almeidahotels.com**

CASCAIS Cidadela
Avenida 25 de Abril, 2754-517 **Tel** *214 827 600* **Fax** *214 867 226* **Rooms** *115*

An easy walk from the town centre, most of the rooms and suites at this typical holiday hotel offer spectacular views over the bay. One- and three-bed apartments are also available, complete with kitchenette. The swimming pool is surrounded by pretty gardens where barbecues take place during the evening. **www.hotelcidadela.com**

CASCAIS Solar Dom Carlos
Rua Latino Coelho 104, 2750-408 **Tel** *214 828 115* **Fax** *214 865 155* **Rooms** *18*

This wonderful building is a former Royal Cottage and was once the summer residence of King Carlos I. As befitting a monarch, some of the bedrooms are rather grand. So, too, is the breakfast room, which is decorated with wall-to-ceiling frescos. The rear gardens contain an historic chapel. **www.solardomcarlos.com**

CASCAIS Casa da Pérgola
Avenida Valbom 13, 2750-508 **Tel** *214 840 040* **Fax** *214 834 791* **Rooms** *10*

A beautiful 19th-century Mediterranean-style mansion with white marble floors and staircases, a stucco ceiling and ornate furniture set in its own landscaped gardens. The façade is adorned with decorative handpainted tiles. It has been owned by the same family for over a century. Closed from 1 Dec–28 Feb. **www.pergolahouse.com**

CASCAIS Albatroz
Rua Frederico Arouca 100, 2750-353 **Tel** *214 847 380* **Fax** *214 844 827* **Rooms** *52*

Built in the 19th century as a retreat for the Portuguese royal family, the Albatroz sits perched on the rocks directly overlooking the ocean. Notable for its traditional style of luxury and exceptional design, the service is first class. The hotel has its own outdoor saltwater swimming pool. **www.albatrozhotels.com**

COSTA DA CAPARICA Praia do Sol
Rua dos Pescadores 12, 2825-386 **Tel** *212 900 012* **Fax** *212 902 541* **Rooms** *54*

A small hotel, Praia do Sol has comfortable rooms specially designed for leisure stays. The interior design, with leather armchairs and tiled flooring, is not the most stylish but the advantage is that the hotel is located in a popular resort town near one of the largest beaches in Portugal. **www.hotelpraiadosol-caparica.com**

COSTA DA CAPARICA Hotel Costa da Caparica
Avenida General Humberto Delgado 47, 2829-506 **Tel** *212 918 900* **Fax** *212 910 687* **Rooms** *353*

This attractive hotel, with an unusual semi-circular entrance, has a spa that offers guests hot stone massage, among other treatments and therapies. Many of the rooms, some non-smoking and seven of which are adapted for the disabled, overlook the beach. There is a piano bar and à la carte restaurant. **www.hotelcostacaparica.pt**

ERICEIRA Vilazul
Calçada da Baleia 10, 2655-238 **Tel** *261 860 000* **Fax** *261 862 927* **Rooms** *21*

Only 500 m (0.5 km) from the sea, this bright and airy hotel is family-owned and the staff are friendly and helpful. Although basic, the rooms are spotless and some have great panoramic views of the beach. The hotel has its own restaurant. Book ahead if planning a stay during the summer. **www.hotelvilazul.com**

ESTORIL São Cristóvão
Avenida Marginal 7079, 2765-607 **Tel** *214 680 913* **Fax** *214 649 286* **Rooms** *14*

This charming *pensão* is housed in an interesting old villa that commands an outstanding spot on the ocean side of the Avenida Marginal. The sturdy, beige-coloured building stands alone on the esplanade and has its own garden. The owners are generous with their hospitality. **www.residencial-saocristovao.com**

ESTORIL Hotel da Inglaterra
Rua do Porto 1, 2765-271 **Tel** *214 684 461* **Fax** *214 682 108* **Rooms** *55*

This impressive and charismatic hotel started life in the early 20th century as a palace mansion and is endowed with some fine examples of period furniture. Carefully modernized over the years, the hotel features an excellent gymnasium and massage facility, and an outdoor swimming pool. **www.hotelinglaterra.com.pt**

Key to Price Guide *see p118* **Key to Symbols** *see back cover flap*

ESTORIL Palácio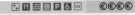

€€€€

Rua Particular, 2769-504 **Tel** *214 648 000* **Fax** *214 648 159* **Rooms** *161*

The impressive façade, classically styled interiors and gourmet restaurant make Estoril's landmark hotel a favourite with visiting heads of state, film stars and royalty. Most of the elegantly appointed rooms benefit from garden and sea views, and guests have access to an 18-hole golf course and tennis courts. **www.palacioestorilhotel.com**

GUINCHO Fortaleza do Guincho

€€€€

Estrada do Guincho, 2750-642 **Tel** *214 870 491* **Fax** *214 870 431* **Rooms** *27*

The most westerly hotel on the European mainland, this magical property is perched on a windy bluff near Cabo da Rocha and overlooks the ocean. Renovated from the shell of an old fortress, it has arched ceilings and a medieval decor. The restaurant is Michelin-starred. Reservations are essential. **www.guinchotel.pt**

GUINCHO Senhora da Guia

€€€€€

Estrada do Guincho, 2750-642 **Tel** *214 869 239* **Fax** *214 869 227* **Rooms** *41*

This fashionable *estalagem* is set in its own beautiful, carefully maintained grounds alongside the Quinta da Marinha golf course. Guests who are passionate about the sport can buy a "Golf Passport", which allows play on three or five different courses. There is also a luxury health club. Most rooms have sea views. **www.senhoradaguia.com**

PALMELA Pousada do Castelo de Palmela

€€€

Castelo de Palmela, 2950-317 **Tel** *212 351 226* **Fax** *212 330 440* **Rooms** *28*

The fortified walls of this 12th-century castle enclose a tranquil *pousada* of great historical interest. Housed within a former convent, its whitewashed rooms are large and comfortable and have incredible views. The 15th-century Igreja de Santiago, lined with wonderful 17th-century *azulejo* tiles, stands next door. **www.pousadas.pt**

QUELUZ Pousada Dona Maria I

€€€

Largo do Palácio Nacional, 2745-191 **Tel** *214 356 158* **Fax** *214 356 189* **Rooms** *26*

This impressive *pousada* is located in a building traditionally referred to as the "Clock Tower", which was once used by staff serving the Royal Court at the nearby 18th-century Palácio de Queluz. Careful renovation has preserved the character of the annexe while making sure guests are afforded every modern amenity. **www.pousadas.pt**

SESIMBRA Hotel do Mar

€€€

Rua General Humberto Delgado 10, 2970-628 **Tel** *212 288 300* **Fax** *212 233 888* **Rooms** *168*

It is easy to lose your way in this sprawling complex. The hotel is built on different levels on the cliffside and is linked by a catacomb of corridors and several lifts. Rooms are clean and simply furnished. However, guests staying in the presidential suite have a private swimming pool. **www.hoteldomar.pt**

SETÚBAL Ibis Setúbal

€

Rua do Alto da Guerra, 2914-518 **Tel** *265 700 900* **Fax** *265 700 909* **Rooms** *102*

Featuring the usual combination of Ibis comforts and economy, this hotel is an ideal base from which to explore the Arrábida Natural Park and the Sado Estuary Nature Reserve. The friendly staff can also arrange dolphin-watching excursions. Guests have the use of a swimming pool and a free car park. **www.ibishotel.com**

SETÚBAL Pousada de São Filipe

€€€

Castelo de São Filipe, 2900-300 **Tel** *265 550 070* **Fax** *265 539 240* **Rooms** *16*

This historic *pousada* is integrated within the Castelo de São Filipe, built on the orders of Philip of Spain (*see p112*) in 1590. Guests can tread the ramparts and admire fine views over the estuary and the Tróia peninsula. Five of the rooms are located in the castle's former cells. **www.pousadas.pt**

SINTRA Hotel Sintra Jardim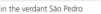

€€

Travessa dos Avelares 12, 2710-506 **Tel** *219 230 738* **Fax** *219 230 738* **Rooms** *15*

This rambling, family-run *pensão* is in a serene location just east of the town centre, in the verdant São Pedro residential area. Comfortable rooms look out over lush grounds and a splendid view of Sintra's Moorish castle. Private car parking is available. **www.residencialsintra.blogspot.com**

SINTRA Lawrence's

€€€

Rua Consigliéri Pedroso 38, 2710-550 **Tel** *219 105 500* **Fax** *219 105 505* **Rooms** *17*

Dating from 1764, Lawrence's is believed to be the oldest hotel on the Iberian Peninsula. Guest rooms are not numbered but instead are named after personalities from the world of art, theatre and literature, including Lord Byron, who is said to have stayed here in 1809 while writing "Childe Harold". **www.lawrenceshotel.com**

SINTRA Tivoli Palácio de Seteais

€€€€

Rua Barbosa do Bocage 8, 2710-517 **Tel** *219 233 200* **Fax** *219 234 277* **Rooms** *30*

One of the most cherished and romantic hotels in the country, this splendid property is a magnificent example of 18th-century architecture, with rooms that dazzle in the classical style of the era. Rare period furniture graces the public areas and guests are free to wander the beautifully landscaped topiary gardens. **www.tivolihotels.com**

SINTRA Penha Longa

€€€€€

Estrada da Lagoa Azul-Linhó, 2714-511 **Tel** *219 249 011* **Fax** *219 249 007* **Rooms** *194*

A luxury hotel and golf resort, Penha Longa is famed for its outstanding blend of culture and leisure. Rooms and suites are fabulously appointed, with many facing the Robert Trent Jones Jr designed Atlantic golf course. The Midori restaurant serves Japanese gourmet cuisine, and there is also a lavish spa. **www.penhalonga.com**

RESTAURANTS, CAFES AND BARS

Particularly in Lisbon and along the coast, there are many restaurants dedicated to cooking all manner of freshly caught fish and seafood. It may be grilled, pan-fried or turned into soup or a stew. However, meat dishes are also plentiful, some of the most popular being made of pork and lamb. Lisbon has an abundance of cheap restaurants and cafés, as well as more expensive ones. There are not

Drinks waiter at the Palácio de Seteais *(see p135)*

only typically Portuguese restaurants in Lisbon, but also Chinese, Indian, Brazilian and African, all of which reflect Portugal's colonial past. This section gives tips on the different types of restaurants and cafés, as well as advice on menus, drinks and ordering your meal. The listings found on pages 130–35 are a selection of the best restaurants in all price ranges that are to be found throughout the capital and in the Lisbon Coast area.

TYPES OF RESTAURANT

Eating venues in Lisbon come in all shapes and sizes and at all price levels. Among the most reasonable is the local *tasca* or tavern, often just a room with half-a-dozen tables presided over by a husband-and-wife team. *Tascas* are often frequented by locals and professionals at lunchtime, which is a good indication of quality food. The *casa de pasto* offers a budget three-course meal in a large dining room, while a *restaurante* is more formal and offers a wider choice of dishes. At a typical *marisqueira*, the emphasis is on seafood and fresh fish. A *churrasqueira*, originally Brazilian, specializes in spit-

roasted foods. A *cervejaria* is the ideal place to go for a beer and snack, maybe of delicious seafood. The restaurants in better hotels are generally of good quality. *Pousadas (see p116)*, found mainly in country areas, offer a network of traditional restaurants, with the focus on local gastronomic specialities.

The pleasant courtyard of Lautasco *(p130)* along Beco do Azinhal in the Alfama

EATING HOURS

Lunch is usually served between 1 and 3pm, when many restaurants get very crowded. Dinner is served from 7pm until at least 10pm in most places, and can

often be later. An alternative for a late dinner would be a *fado* house *(see pp144–5)*, usually open from about 9:30pm to 3 or 4am. However, a meal here will be somewhat more expensive as the price includes a show.

RESERVATIONS

It is a good idea to book ahead for expensive restaurants, and for those in popular locations in high season. Disabled people should certainly check in advance on facilities and access. Special facilities are generally lacking but most places will try to be helpful.

THE MENU

Some restaurants, in tourist areas particularly, offer an *ementa turística*, a cheap, daily-changing menu. This is served with coffee and a drink (a glass of wine or beer, a soft drink or water) and provides a full meal at a good price with no hidden costs. Lunch

The impressive interior of Cozinha Velha *(see p135)* at Queluz

Eating outside in Cascais along the Lisbon coast

(almoço) generally consists of a soup or starter and a fish or meat dish with potatoes or rice. To sample a local speciality, you should ask for the *prato do dia* – dish of the day. The choice of sweets can be limited, but there is usually a good selection of fresh fruits in season or you can try a pastry such as a *pastel de nata*.

Dinner *(jantar)* may be two or more courses, perhaps rounded off with ice cream, fruit, a simple dessert or cheese. Casserole-style dishes, such as *cataplana* (a kind of tightly sealed wok in which the food is steamed, often used for fish and seafood) or *porco à alentejana* (pork with clams), are brought to the table in a pot for diners to share. This is similarly done with large fish, such as sea bass, which are sold by weight. One serving is large and can easily be shared by two people, and it is perfectly acceptable to ask for a *meia dose* or half-portion. If requested, Portuguese restaurants will be more than happy to supply these half-portions for adults as well as for any children present.

Peculiar to Portugal is the plate of assorted appetizers – perhaps olives, cheese and sardine pâté – which are served with bread at the start of a meal. However, these are not usually included in the price of the meal and an extra charge will be made for each item consumed.

Pasteis de nata (custard pastries)

VEGETARIANS

Vegetarians will not eat as well as fish lovers, although local cheeses and breads can be excellent. Chefs are usually happy to provide something meatless, although this will probably mean just a salad or omelette. A greater variety of vegetarian dishes can be found in ethnic restaurants.

WHAT TO DRINK

It would be a pity to visit Portugal without sampling port *(see pp128–9)* and Madeira, the country's two most famous drinks. Some restaurants may suggest a glass of white port as an aperitif while you wait for your meal. As far as house wine is concerned, it is usually of an acceptable quality to wash down your meal whatever the standard of the restaurant. Otherwise, ask for the wine list *(carta de vinhos)* and choose one of the Portuguese wines *(see pp128–9)*. As a complement to the wine, mineral water is recommended. This is either *com gás* (sparkling) or *sem gás* (still). If you prefer to drink beer, Sagres and Super Bock are both good lagers. *Cervejarias*, such as the lively Cervejaria Trindade in the Bairro Alto *(see pp48–59)*, are ideal places to get a snack late at night and enjoy an excellent range of beers, from lagers to dark beers, many of which are draught.

PAYING

It is common practice to add a five or ten per cent tip to bills. Although service is included, it provides a low wage which the tip is meant to supplement. Note that not all restaurants accept credit cards.

CHILDREN

The Portuguese view children as a blessing rather than a nuisance, so Lisbon is an ideal city for families to eat out together. Half portions *(meia dose)* at reduced prices are advertised in restaurants or are provided on request.

SMOKING

Smoking is not permitted in restaurants and other public places in Portugal, unless the establishment has an efficient smoke-extractor system.

DRINKING COFFEE IN LISBON

Coffee is widely drunk in Lisbon and served in many forms. The most popular, *uma bica*, is a small cup of strong black coffee like an espresso. For a weaker version, ask for *uma carioca de café*. A strong *bica* is called *uma italiana*. *Uma meia de leite* is half coffee, half milk. Strong coffee with a dash of milk is known as *um garoto escuro (um garoto claro* is quite milky). If you like coffee with plenty of milk, ask for *um galão* (a gallon). It is served in a glass, and again you can order *um galão claro* (very milky) or *escuro* (strong).

Uma bica   **Um galão**

The Flavours of Lisbon

Gastronomically, the Lisbon region is immensely varied, bringing together many different foods from all over Portugal. There is roast suckling pig from the north, an excellent choice of fish and seafood from the Atlantic coastline plus unique cheeses and hearty stews from the mountains. One popular dish, originating in the south of the country and reflecting this diversity, is *porco à alentejana*, a mixture of pork and clams spiced with paprika. Cuisines old and new, exotic and familiar, blend with one another in cosmopolitan Lisbon's many quality restaurants.

Sardines

Fresh cheeses on sale at Lisbon's celebrated Mercado de Ribera

MEAT AND DAIRY

Pork is the most commonly eaten meat in Portugal. Spit-roasted suckling pig *(leitão)* is a traditional favourite, but pork meat is also popular roasted *(porco preto)* and in rich, hearty stews. Pigs' trotters with coriander *(pézinhos de coentrada)* are considered a delicacy. Cured pork products *(embutidos)* –

spiced, salted or smoked – are an essential part of the national cuisine, from paprika-hued *chouriço* sausage to dark and intensely flavoured *Ibérico* ham (made from pigs fed on acorns) and *morcela* blood sausage seasoned with cloves and cumin. Kid *(cabrito)* is also popular as a roast or in stews. Beef is served less often but is of high quality (look for the names Barrosã, Mirandesa or

Maronesa), while sheep tend to be kept more for cheese production than meat. Ewe's and goat's milk cheeses are of exceptional quality, and are as delicious when they are fresh and soft as when they are long matured, firm and piquant. Portugal's most famous cheese, the distinctive and buttery Serra, is made from ewe's milk, and the rounds are wrapped in muslin to maintain their shape.

Serra da Estrela
Saloio
Palhais
Qurijo fresco
Alavão

Fine ewe's and goat's milk cheeses from Portugal

LOCAL DISHES AND SPECIALITIES

Much traditional Portuguese cuisine is that of a hardworking, frugal people who preserved and used everything they could produce. Hence the predominance of cured meats and dried bean stews (often incorporating ham or sausage for flavour). *Favas à Portuguesa* is a Lisbon favourite. The capital is not just the place where all the flavours of Portugal come together, but also where the influences of Portugal's 16th-century overseas expansion get their strongest expression. This applies equally to older influences, long since assimilated into local cuisine, as well as to newer ones, from Cape Verdean restaurants to sushi bars. *Frango à piri-piri*, barbecued chicken with chilli, is a favourite dish, originating from Portugal's former colonies in Africa.

Paprika

Feijoada *is a paprika-spiced stew of beans, vegetables and cured meat (usually pork), with many local variations.*

Lisbon's famed lettuces take pride of place on a vegetable stall

FISH AND SEAFOOD

With its long Atlantic coast-line, it is no surprise that Portugal's fish dishes are unmissable. The range on sale at any fish market is vast. Squid *(lula)*, cuttlefish *(choco)*, sea bass *(robalo)*, gilthead bream *(dourada)*, sardines *(sardinhas)* and shellfish such as oysters *(ostras)* and cockles *(ameijoas)* are found in abundance and often come together in the rich, steamed fish stew *cataplana de peixe e mariscos*. Traditional salt cod *(bacalhau)* is still much in evidence but today, river fish are less commonly served – trout *(trutas)* is often farmed and the once-common lamprey *(lampreia)* may be imported. Snails *(caracóis)* sometimes appear in dishes, including *feijoada*.

VEGETABLES AND FRUIT

A visit to Lisbon's superb food market, Mercado de Ribera (Avenida 24 de Julio, Cais do Sodré) will reveal just how fertile the inland regions are, with heaps of

Waiter with a tray of traditional pastéis de nata pastries

every kind of vegetable (peppers and tomatoes are especially flavourful) and ripe, perfumed fruits including figs, melons, grapes, greengages, apricots and citrus fruits. Portuguese olives and their oil are omni-present – the essential trio of ingredients, key to many a dish, is olive oil, garlic and coriander. Both wheat and maize are grown for bread, which is often hard and long-lasting and used to give extra volume to soups. The nickname *alfacinhas* for natives of Lisbon may have a connection with *alface* (lettuce) – the city has long been famous for an especially delicious variety.

ON THE MENU

Açorda de marisco Shellfish soup thickened with bread and favoured with garlic.

Bacalhau à gomes de sá Salt cod layered with potato and onion, and garnished with egg and olives.

Caldo verde A popular, bright green soup made from a type of kale.

Pastéis de bacalhau Little salt-cod cakes eaten cold as a snack or hot as a main dish. A national addiction.

Queijadas de Sintra Cheese tarts spiced with cinnamon.

Sardinhas assadas Chargrilled fresh sardines.

Caldeirada de peixe, *a fish stew, uses a selection of sea-food along with potatoes, tomatoes and peppers.*

Favas à Portuguesa *combines broad (fava) beans with* morcela *(blood sausage) and chopped pork ribs.*

Arroz doce *is a delicious dessert of lemon zest-scented rice pudding topped with a decoration of cinnamon.*

The Wines of Portugal

Although still overshadowed by the excellence and fame of port, Portuguese table wine deserves to be taken seriously. After years of investment in the industry, many of the reds, such as the full-bodied wines from the Douro (made with some of the same grapes as port), have established an attractive style all their own. Great whites are fewer, but most regions have some. And of course there is *vinho verde*, the usually white, light, slightly carbonated wine from the north.

Sparkling rosés, *such as Mateus and Lancers, have been Portugal's great export success. But the country now has many excellent wines that reach beyond the easy-drinking charms of these.*

WINE REGIONS

Many of Portugal's wine regions maintain their individual style by specializing in particular Portuguese grape varieties. The introduction of modern wine-making techniques has improved overall quality, and as yet the increasing use of imported grape varieties seems no threat to Portuguese individuality.

KEY

☐ Vinhos Verdes
☐ Douro
☐ Dão
☐ Bairrada
☐ Estremadura
☐ Ribatejo
☐ Setúbal
☐ Alentejo

0 kilometres   50

0 miles   25

***Vinho verde* vineyards in the village of Lapela, near Monção in the Minho**

Cellar of the Bussaco Palace Hotel, near Mealhada, famous for its red wine

HOW TO READ A WINE LABEL

Tinto is red, *branco* is white, *seco* is dry and *doce* is sweet. Beyond that, the essential information concerns the producer, the region and the year. Wines made to at least 80 per cent from a single grape variety may give the name of that grape on the front label. *Denominação de Origem Controlada* (DOC) indicates that the wine has been made according to the strictest regulations of a given region, but, as elsewhere, this need not mean higher quality than the nominally simpler *Vinho Regional* appellation. The back label often describes grape varieties and wine-making techniques.

This wine is from the Douro and is made according to DOC regulations for the region.

The name of this wine means "banks of the River Tua", further specifying its geographical origin.

***Reserva* means that** the wine has been aged, probably in oak casks. It also implies that the wine is of higher quality than non-reserva wine from the same producer.

The Sociedade Agricola e Comercial dos Vinhos Vale da Corça, Lda, produced and bottled this wine.

Vinho verde, *"green wine"*, *from the Minho region, can be either red or white, but the fizzy, dry reds are generally consumed locally. Typical white* vinho verde *is bone dry, slightly fizzy, low in alcohol and high in acidity. A weightier style of white* vinho verde *is made from the Alvarinho grape, near the Spanish border. Among the best brands are Soalheiro and Palácio da Brejoeira.*

Bairrada *is a region where the small and thick-skinned Baga grape dominates. It makes big, tannic wines, sometimes with smoky or pine-needle overtones and, like the older Dão wines, they need time to soften. Modern winemaking and occasional disregard for regional regulations have meant more approachable reds (often classified as* Vinho Regional das Beiras*) and crisper whites. Quality producers include Luís Pato and Caves Aliança.*

Ribatejo *is the fertile valley of the Tagus to the north and east of Lisbon. After Estremadura, it is Portugal's biggest wine region measured by volume, but its potential for quality wines has only just begun to be realized. As in Estremadura,* Vinho Regional *bottlings are frequently better than DOC ones. Producers to look for include Quinta da Alorna, Casa Branco and Fiuza & Bright.*

The Douro *region is best known as the source of port wine, but in most years about half of the wine produced is fermented dry to make table wine, and these wines are now at the forefront of Portuguese wine-making. The pioneer, Barca Velha, was launched half a century ago and is both highly regarded and among the most expensive. Other quality producers include Calheiros Cruz, Domingos Alves de Sousa, Quinta do Crasto, Niepoort and Ramos-Pinto.*

Picking grapes for *vinho verde*

Setúbal, *to the south of Lisbon, is best known for its sweet, fortified Muscat wine, Moscatel de Setúbal. In addition, the region also produces excellent, mostly red, table wine. Two big quality producers dominate the region: José Maria da Fonseca (see p111) and J.P. Vinhos. The co-operative at Santo Isidro de Pegões makes good-value wines, while interesting smaller producers include Venâncio Costa Lima, Hero do Castan-heiro and Ermelinda Freitas.*

The Dão region *now offers some of Portugal's best wines. Small producers, such as Quinta dos Roques, Quinta da Pellada and Quinta de Cabriz, and the large Sogrape company make fruity reds for younger drinking; fresh, dry whites; and deeper, richer reds which retain their fruit with age – a far cry from the heavy, hard-edged, often oxidized wines of the past.*

Estremadura *is Portugal's westernmost wine area and has now emerged as a region in its own right. Several producers make modern* Vinho Regional *wines with character; look for wines by DFJ, Casa Santos Lima, Quinta de Pancas and Quinta do Monte d'Oiro. The most interesting DOC is Alenquer, a full-bodied wine. Bucelas, to the south of the region, produces characterful white wines.*

Alentejo *wine has possibly made the biggest leap in quality in recent years. Long dismissed by experts as a region of easy-drinking house reds for restau-rants, this area now produces some of Portugal's most serious red wines and a surprising number of excellent whites. Among the best producers are Herdade de Esporão, Herdade dos Coelheiros, Cortes de Cima and João Portugal Ramos.*

Choosing a Restaurant

The restaurants in this guide have been selected for their good value, exceptional food, or interesting location. These listings highlight some of the factors that may influence your choice, such as whether you can opt to eat outdoors or if the venue offers live music. Entries are alphabetical within each price category.

PRICE CATEGORIES
Price categories include a three-course meal for one with half a bottle of wine, including cover charge, service and VAT.

€ Under €20
€€ €20–€25
€€€ €25–€30
€€€€ €30–€40
€€€€€ Over €40

LISBON

ALCÂNTARA Espaço Lisboa
€€€

Rua da Cozinha Económica 16, 1300-149 **Tel** *213 610 210*

Map *3 A4*

Near Lisbon's main cruise terminal, with a stylish interior, Espaço Lisboa specializes in traditional Portuguese cuisine. It has a good range of fish and seafood, as well as some classic meat dishes such as veal in Port wine and grilled lamb chops. Open for dinner only.

ALCÂNTARA Alcântara Café
€€€€€

Rua Maria Luisa Holstein 15, 1300-388 **Tel** *213 637 176*

Map *3 A4*

Established in the 1980s, this is a classic Lisbon dining venue. The vast interior is styled on the Nautilus, the submarine from Jules Verne's *Twenty Thousand Leagues Under the Sea*. The menu leans towards contemporary Portuguese, with dishes like *escalopes de salmão* (salmon escalopes). Open Tue–Sun for dinner only. Closed Mon; 2 wks Aug.

ALFAMA Hua-Ta-Li
€

Rua dos Bacalhoeiros 109–115, 1100-068 **Tel** *218 879 170*

Map *7 C4*

This large and popular Chinese restaurant is located in a semi-pedestrianized street close to the docks. A long list of great soups and all the regular rice and noodle dishes are available, plus one or two surprises, such as prawn casserole and frogs' legs with chillis. Service is swift and somewhat perfunctory.

ALFAMA Lautasco
€€

Beco do Azinhal 7a (off Rua de São Pedro), 1100-067 **Tel** *218 860 173*

Map *8 E4*

Rustically decorated with wooden panelling and wagon-wheel chandeliers, Lautasco specializes in typical Portuguese cuisine that can be enjoyed on the outside terrace. Decorative streamers and colourful spotlights enhance an already atmospheric setting. It is especially popular during the Santo António festivities *(see p23)*. Closed Sun.

ALFAMA Santo António de Alfama
€€€

Beco de São Miguel 7, 1100-538 **Tel** *218 881 328*

Map *8 E4*

Good-quality Portuguese and international fare is served here in a little corner of the Alfama. The choice on the menu is impressive, with two dozen starters alone as well as the popular *petiscos* (Portuguese tapas). The restaurant prides itself on its cod *(bacalhau)* and steak *(bife)* dishes. Photos of film stars line the walls.

AMOREIRAS Mezzaluna
€€€

Rua Artilharia Um 16, 1250-039 **Tel** *213 879 944*

Map *5 A4*

This attractive restaurant located in a quiet neighbourhood is arguably one of the best Italian restaurants in the city. On the menu are classics such as *spaghetti alla carbonara* and tagliatelle with shrimp and vodka sauce. They have a marvellous wine list. Closed Sat lunch & Sun.

AVENIDA Os Tibetanos
€€

Rua do Salitre 117, 1250-198 **Tel** *213 142 038*

Map *4 F1*

Perfumed with incense and decorated with colourful Tibetan prayer flags and images of the Dalai Lama, this lovely informal restaurant is an oasis for vegetarians. The imaginative, healthy menu is full of suggestions like *tofu com pesto e queijo de cabra* (tofu with pesto and goat's cheese). There is an open-air terrace at the rear. Closed Sun.

AVENIDA Ribadouro
€€€€

Rua do Salitre 2-12, 1250-200 **Tel** *213 549 411*

Map *4 F1*

Set on the corner of Avenida da Liberdade, Ribadouro is a great place to meet after a late film or show. Roomy, functional but with prompt service, the menu reads like a fisherman's wish list: oysters, *buzios* (whelks), crab, lobster and other seafood (all priced by the kilo) stand alongside more conventional meat dishes. Closed 24 & 25 Dec.

BAIRRO ALTO Bota Alta
€€

Travessa da Queimada 35, 1200-364 **Tel** *213 427 959*

Map *7 A3*

In the heart of the bohemian quarter, the "High Boot" has been around since the '70s. The attractive interior is decorated with original paintings and ceramics, including an enormous clay boot on the bar. The traditional menu includes *costeletas fumados à algarvia* (smoked ribs Algarve style) and *bacalhau real* (codfish). Closed Sat lunch, Sun; Sep.

Key to Symbols *see back cover flap*

BAIRRO ALTO Casanostra

Travessa do Poço da Cidade 60, 1200-334 **Tel** *213 425 931* **Map** *7 A3*

Ask for Italian food and Casanostra will certainly be one of the places mentioned. A favourite haunt of Lisbon's artistic and intellectual set, the restaurant is renowned for its creative six-page menu. Popular choices include *penne all'arrabbiata* (pasta with bacon in hot tomato and garlic sauce). Closed Sat lunch.

BAIRRO ALTO Imperio dos Sentidos

Rua da Atalaia 35–37, 1200-037 **Tel** *213 431 822* **Map** *4 F2*

Snuggling inside an early 20th-century building, this understated eatery, though not billed as a seafood restaurant nonetheless entices clients with dishes such as pasta with creamed spinach sauce and shrimp, and salmon loin in red wine sauce. It is also well known for its desserts. Open for dinner only. Closed Mon.

BAIRRO ALTO Pap'Açorda

Rua da Atalaia 57, 1200-037 **Tel** *213 464 811* **Map** *4 F2*

One of Lisbon's gastronomic landmarks, Pap'Açorda was one of the first to modernize Portuguese food and remains one of the city's most successful restaurants. Both Lisboetas and tourists come for the *açorda de mariscos* (bread stew and seafood). The wine list is comprehensive and reflects the diversity of the menu. Closed Sun & Mon.

BAIRRO ALTO Tavares Rico

Rua da Misericórdia 35–37, 1200-270 **Tel** *213 421 112* **Map** *7 A4*

Few restaurants anywhere can boast a more than 200-year-old history and it is this rich heritage that makes Tavares a very special place to dine. The gilt and mirrors of the restored dining room exude 18th-century charm and elegance. The menu, however, is modern, international gourmet cuisine. Closed Sun & Mon.

BAIXA Muni

Rua dos Correeiros 128, 1100-163 **Tel** *218 884 203* **Map** *7 B4*

Discreet and unassuming, this delightful restaurant does wonderful justice to traditional Portuguese fare. Taster dishes include an excellent octopus salad and *peixinhos da horta* (runner beans deep-fried in crispy batter). The *cabrito assado no forno* (oven-baked kid) is mouthwateringly succulent.

BELÉM Nosolo Italia

Avenida de Brasília 202, 1400-038 Lisbon **Tel** *213 015 969* **Map** *1 B5*

Located by the river facing the Monument to the Discoveries, Nosolo Italia serves traditional Italian cuisine. With 25 different pasta dishes and up to 30 pizzas on the menu, not to mention a dozen freshly prepared salads, there's plenty of choice, even for vegetarians. A large outdoor terrace provides fine river views.

BELÉM Rosa dos Mares

Rua de Belém 2–6, 1300-085 **Tel** *213 639 055* **Map** *1 C4*

This restaurant is named after a seafaring legend that dates back to the Age of Discoveries. After months at sea, a crew member spied roses floating in the water. The flowers heralded land. He collected the roses and upon return to Portugal presented them to the queen. Naturally, specialities here are fresh seafood. Closed Mon.

BELÉM Vela Latina

Doca do Bom Sucesso, 1400-038 **Tel** *213 017 118* **Map** *1 B5*

The relatively high prices here reflect Vela Latina's enviable waterfront location and its menu of classic Portuguese cuisine. The high-ceiling interior and large bay windows lend the place a peaceful air and, of course, the view of the Tagus and nearby Torre de Belém is priceless. Closed Sun.

CAMPO DE OURIQUE Tasquinha d'Adelaide

Rua do Patrocínio 70–74, 1350-231 **Tel** *213 962 239* **Map** *3 C2*

The menu choice at this cosy restaurant has its origins in the Tras-os-Montes and as such diners can feast on regional dishes like *rojões à transmontana* (fried pork Tras-os-Montes) and *paletilha e sela de borrego no forno* (saddle of oven-baked lamb). A wide variety of wines are available. Arrive early to beat the crowds. Closed Sun.

CAMPO PEQUENO Rodízio Grill

Campo Pequeno 79, 1000-082 **Tel** *217 939 760* **Map** *5 C1*

A large restaurant built to serve a high turnaround of custom. The menu lists 40 starters alone! The theme is South American, and dishes include the Brazilian BBQ – ribs of buffalo flavoured with spicy garlic and served with black beans and banana fritters. The buffet "pay as you weigh" price depends on how much you stack on your plate.

CAMPO PEQUENO Laurentina

Avenida Conte de Valbom 71a, 1050-067 **Tel** *217 960 260* **Map** *5 B2*

Located close to the Museu Calouste Gulbenkian, Laurentina has been serving fine Portuguese fare for more than 30 years. It offers an exhaustive range of *bacalhau* dishes, including *couvada de bacalhau* (cod with cabbage and potatoes) as well as some meat-based favourites, such as *cabrito assado no forno* (roast kid). Closed Sun.

CASTELO Restô do Chapitô

Costa do Castelo 7, 1149-079 **Tel** *218 867 334* **Map** *7 C3*

Chapitô is actually a school for performing arts and the cheerful ambience is carried through to the informal restaurant where you can enjoy dishes like trout with bacon and flame-grilled sausages. Some tables offer incredible views of downtown Lisbon. Live jazz enlivens the weekends. The first floor is closed for lunch at the weekend.

CASTELO Casa do Leão

Castelo de São Jorge, 1100-129 **Tel** *218 875 962*

Map 8 D3

Chef's suggestions here include the excellent goat's cheese terrine with cherry tomato confit followed by leg of duck with ratatouille. The restaurant is in the grounds of Castelo de São Jorge *(see pp38–9)* and customers must book in advance in order to ensure the entrance fee is discounted from their final bill. On warm days, tables are set outside.

CHIADO La Brasserie de l'Entrecôte

Rua do Alecrim 117, 1200-016 **Tel** *213 473 616*

Map 7 A4

There is only one fixed menu here, a crunchy green salad garnished with pine nuts and French dressing followed by prime cutlets of entrecôte steak, prepared as you wish, swamped in a cream and herb sauce and served with French fries. There is a choice of three desserts. You cannot book ahead here so arrive early to make sure of a table.

GRAÇA Via Graça

Rua Damasceno Monteiro 9b, 1170-108 **Tel** *218 870 830*

Map 8 D1

Via Graça is singular in its position, perched as it is on the edge of a hill and with a panorama that includes the Castelo de São Jorge *(see pp38–9)*. The well-presented Portuguese cuisine includes dishes such as *empada de caça* (game pie). There is an excellent wine list. Closed Sat & Sun lunch.

LAPA Picanha

Rua das Janelas Verdes 96, 1200-692 **Tel** *213 975 401*

Map 4 D4

For a set price you can eat all you want, but the meal is based around one ingredient: *picanha* (rump steak grilled on an open fire). Tread carefully and you will have room for dessert, the choice of which includes cheesecake, chocolate cake and tropical fruit. The interior is decorated with some beautiful *azulejo* tiles.

LAPA A Confraria

Pensão York House, Rua das Janelas Verdes 32, 1200-691 **Tel** *213 962 435*

Map 4 D3

This charming hotel-restaurant offers an eclectic menu and boasts a delightful setting. Customers can sit inside and admire the tiled walls, or outside below a palm in the flower-laden garden. The cuisine is typically Portuguese and includes monkfish in a mustard sauce and partridge in a vinegar-flavoured marinade. Closed Mon & Tue.

LAPA Terreiro do Paço

Praça do Comércio, 1100-148 **Tel** *210 995 679*

Map 7 B5

With a great location on the western side of the city's main square, this is a first-choice restaurant for both tourists and locals alike. Specialities include *tentáculos de polvo com batata doce* (octopus tentacles with sweet potato) and an oxtail stew with mashed potato and spinach. A lunchtime buffet and sushi menus are also available.

MARQUÊS DE POMBAL Marisqueira Santa Marta

Travessa do Enviado de Inglaterra 1d, 1150-139 **Tel** *213 525 638*

Map 5 C5

At lunchtime, this place heaves with hungry mouths and it is often difficult to get a table. The restaurant is known for its wide range of fish and shellfish dishes, as well as for a good choice of traditional Portuguese fare. Value for money and a loyal clientele are two reasons why you may have to wait before taking your seat.

MARQUÊS DE POMBAL Restaurante 33A

Rua Alexandre Herculano 33a, 1250-008 **Tel** *213 546 079*

Map 5 C5

This restaurant has a small lounge space that resembles the interior of a hunting lodge, with stuffed deer and boar heads staring down impassively from the wall. In fact, the whole place has a rural ambience and a decor to match. The menu is traditional Portuguese and features many impressive seafood dishes. Closed Sat lunch & Sun.

MARQUÊS DE POMBAL Pabe

Rua Duque de Palmela 27a, 1250-097 **Tel** *213 537 484*

Map 5 C5

A city-centre restaurant with a difference: the building is designed as a mock-Tudor house, complete with stained-glass windows. Pabe's medieval atmosphere is further accentuated by wooden beams and copper tables. The charcoal-grilled baby goat and the breaded squid in mayonnaise sauce are recommended.

MARQUÊS DE POMBAL Eleven

Rua Marquês de Fronteira, Jardim Amália Rodrigues, 1070-310 **Tel** *213 862 211*

Map 5 B4

Named after 11 entrepreneurs who wanted to establish Lisbon's first world-class design-driven restaurant, this is a Michelin-starred gastronomic tour de force. The contemporary-styled interior and sophisticated ambience is complemented by a provocative, international menu. Closed Sun.

MOURARIA Tentações de Goa

Rua S. Pedro Mártir 23, 1100-555 **Tel** *218 875 824*

Map 7 C3

A little gem hidden in a cobblestone backstreet, this modest restaurant is the recipient of a best ethnic food award for its exotic Goan menu. Dishes include lentils with lamb, fish massala and baby shark. The service is prompt and friendly and great value for money considering this is in the heart of the city centre. Closed Sun, Mon lunch & hols.

PRAÇA ESPANHA A Gôndola

Avenida de Berna 64, 1050-043 **Tel** *217 970 426*

Map 5 B2

The menu at A Gôndola is bursting with Portuguese and Italian dishes. It features a vegetarian selection and some wicked desserts, including vodka sorbet. It is a charming place to unwind, especially during the summer when you can enjoy your meal in the gardens.

Key to Price Guide *see p130* **Key to Symbols** *see back cover flap*

PRAÇA ESPANHA O Polícia

Rua Marquês Sá da Bandeira 112a, 1050-158 **Tel** *217 963 505* **Map** *5 B2*

So named because the owner's father was a policeman, the menu here changes daily but is based around seafood and shellfish. The *espetada de tamboril* (monkfish kebab) is particularly good. The restaurant has won numerous awards and attracts loyal patrons. Closed Sat dinner & Sun.

PRAÇA DO CHILE Cervejaria Portugalia

Avenida Almirante Reis 117, 1115-014 **Tel** *213 140 002* **Map** *6 E5*

This cavernous, atmospheric beer hall is the original of a national chain and serves excellent seafood dishes such as *açorda de camarão* (bread stew with prawns). The *presuntos* (cured hams) are also very good. A huge aquarium lines one side of the bar, where, if you prefer, you can just order a beer and enjoy the atmosphere.

RATO Real Fábrica

Rua da Escola Politécnica 275, 1250-101 **Tel** *213 852 090* **Map** *4 E1*

Between 1735 and 1835 this was a factory used for manufacturing silk under royal patronage. Later abandoned, the building has been refurbished and now has a roomy interior with a wood and stone decor. Starters here include spicy Mozambique prawns. The signature dish is *entrecote à Real Fábrica* – steak fit for a king. Closed Sun.

RATO Casa da Comida

Travessa das Amoreiras 1, 1250-025 **Tel** *213 885 376* **Map** *5 B5*

A refined and discreet restaurant with a charming patio overflowing with purple bougainvillea, this is the place for a romantic evening when good food is more important than the price. The menu is haute cuisine in style and international in outlook, with caviar, frogs' legs, duck and pheasant all on the menu. Closed Mon, Sat lunch & Sun.

RESTAURADORES Casa do Alentejo

Rua das Portas de Santo Antão 58, 1150-268 **Tel** *213 405 140* **Map** *7 A2*

Visitors to this extraordinary 19th-century house are in for a surprise. Behind the unremarkable façade is a beautiful Moorish-style courtyard decorated with tiles inlaid with intricate Arabic calligraphy. Art exhibitions regularly take place here, as do choral recitals. The food is fairly standard regional fare.

RESTAURADORES Solar dos Presuntos

Rua das Portas de Santo Antão 150, 1150-269 **Tel** *213 424 253* **Map** *7 A2*

This restaurant is proud of its reputation as one of Lisbon's best places to sample *presunto* – leg of cured ham. The window display is devoted to hams and also allows passers-by to see cuts being prepared. Solar dos Presuntos is also well known for its fish and seafood dishes. Reservations are advisable. Closed Sun & public hols.

RESTAURADORES Gambrinus

Rua das Portas de Santo Antão 23, 1150-264 **Tel** *213 421 466* **Map** *7 B2*

One of the best seafood restaurants in the country, Gambrinus is exclusive and expensive. But people do not come here just for the shellfish. The menu lists Iranian Beluga caviar and truffle foie gras among the starter options. Fresh fish is the mainstay, however. The extensive wine list includes an array of vintage ports.

SALDANHA António

Rua Tomás Ribeiro 63, 1050-226 **Tel** *213 538 780* **Map** *5 C3*

António's is a good stop for lunch. The cooking is straightforward and served up with a polite but no-nonsense attitude. The portions are generous, with the steak and fries or roast chicken a popular order. The dessert menu leans heavily towards ice cream. A handy and cheaper takeaway service is available. Closed Sun.

SANTA APOLÓNIA Casanova

Avenida Infante Dom Henrique, at Cais da Pedra, 1900-264 **Tel** *218 877 532* **Map** *8 F3*

This rather trendy Italian eatery enjoys a prime position overlooking the river. A scribbled version of the menu is stencilled on the wall near the entrance and pizzas are the speciality. There is even an unusual but delicious chocolate-spread pizza for dessert. Bookings are not accepted.

SANTA APOLÓNIA Bica do Sapato

Avenida Infante Dom Henrique, at Cais da Pedra, 1900-000 **Tel** *218 810 320* **Map** *8 F3*

Part owned by American actor John Malkovich, this minimalist, stylish restaurant in a converted riverfront warehouse has three dining options: contemporary interpretations of Portuguese dishes in the gourmet area; tasty bistro food in the café; and a mix of Asian fusion and sushi specials upstairs. Book well in advance. Closed Sun lunch & Mon lunch.

SANTA APOLÓNIA Faz Figura

Rua do Paraíso 15b, 1100-396 **Tel** *218 868 981* **Map** *8 F2*

The tables on the covered terrace at this fashionable restaurant are hard to come by given the incredible views of the Tagus, but you can always linger over a drink at the bar while you wait. The menu is eclectic, with traditional Portuguese and international cuisine.

SANTOS Kais

Cais da Viscondessa, Rua da Cintura do Porto de Lisboa, 1200-109 **Tel** *213 932 930* **Map** *4 D4*

A superb example of how an old warehouse can be transformed into a fashionable venue, Kais is two restaurants in one. Downstairs is the "Adega" where typical Portuguese food is served. Upstairs, a refined international menu is on offer. The decor is best described as "industrial chic". Open for dinner only. Closed Sun & Mon.

SÃO BENTO Clube de Journalistas

Rua das Trinas 129, 1200-857 **Tel** *213 977 138*   **Map** *4 D3*

Housed in an exquisite 18th-century building where Lisbon's São Bento district merges with Lapa, this restaurant is a rare find and well off the tourist trail. The menu is extensive and offers fine Portuguese fare with a Mediterranean twist. Highlights include the roast leg of lamb. There's an inner courtyard garden, too. Closed Sun.

THE LISBON COAST

CASCAIS Mayura

Rua Freitas Reis 15b, 2750-357 **Tel** *214 846 540*

Flavours from the subcontinent abound at this excellent restaurant located in a quiet neighbourhood away from the beach. The menu is what you would expect from any quality curry house but the presentation is first class. Besides the tandoori specialities, the kitchen also serves a variety of spicy Goan dishes.

CASCAIS Eduardo's

Largo das Grutas 3, 2750-367 **Tel** *214 831 901*

With its wooden panels and squat appearance, this Belgian-run restaurant could be mistaken for a forester's lodge. Inside, an aquarium forms part of a dividing wall. The food slants towards French European, with options such as *ragoût de borrego à flamenga* (Flemish-style lamb ragoût). Try the delicious crêpes for dessert. Closed Sun.

CASCAIS Casa Velha

Avenida Valbom 1, 2750-508 **Tel** *214 832 586*

Located in the heart of Cascais, this property resembles a traditional farmhouse but with a maritime-themed interior, complete with mock red oil lanterns hanging over the tables. The menu is predominantly seafood, with *caldeirada de peixe* (fish stew) and *cherne grelhado* (grilled halibut) among the favourites. Closed Wed.

CASCAIS O Pescador

Rua das Flores 10b, 2750-348 **Tel** *214 832 054*

Mick Jagger and Julio Iglesias are just two of the famous personalities that have been lured to this well-established seafood restaurant, decorated with quirky maritime artifacts. An ocean of choice leaps from the menu, such as lobster soup, rose shrimp cocktail and swordfish steak. Closed Mon lunch in summer and Sun dinner.

ERICEIRA Dom Carlos

Estrada Nacional 247, 2655-319 **Tel** *261 866 371*

One of the best fish and seafood restaurants in the region, Dom Carlos boasts a grand interior with seating for almost 300 people, so getting turned away is unlikely even in the high season. House specialities include paella, fish casserole and *mariscada á Dom Carlos* (seafood platter), a particular favourite with locals. Closed Mon & Tue.

ESTORIL Pinto's

Arcadas do Parque 18b, 2765-087 **Tel** *214 687 247*

Close to the Palácio hotel *(see p123)* and with pleasant views of the esplanade gardens, Pinto's is a mix between bar, cafeteria and restaurant and is a great standby if you want a quick meal without breaking the bank. Pizzas, pastas, omelettes and burgers share the menu with a large selection of shellfish and some generous salads.

ESTORIL Estoril Mandarin

Casino Estoril, 2765-237 **Tel** *214 667 270*

This is the best place in Portugal to sample authentic Chinese cuisine. The Peking duck is sautéed, sliced and served wrapped in crisp lettuce leaves. Lunchtimes are popular, with delicious dim sum "snacks" a favourite choice. The menu also includes mini deep-fried spring rolls and shredded pork congee soup with egg. Closed Mon & Tue.

ESTORIL Four Seasons Grill

Hotel Palácio Estoril, Rua do Parque, 2765-000 **Tel** *214 680 400*

Located in the Palácio hotel *(see p123)*, this is one of Estoril's most sophisticated fine-dining venues. Set within a stylishly designed mezzanine and lower floor, the restaurant's decor changes according to each season of the year. The *à la carte* menu offers superb Portuguese and international cuisine.

GUINCHO Estalagem Muchaxo

Praia do Guincho, 2750-642 **Tel** *214 870 221*

Housed in the *estalagem* of the same name, Muchaxo affords splendid views over Cabo da Roca, the most westerly point of the European mainland. The restaurant offers a good seafood menu, with the lobster in a tomato, cream and port sauce typical of the dishes on offer. The kitchen has its own shellfish beds.

GUINCHO Porto de Santa Maria

Estrada do Guincho, 2750-642 **Tel** *214 879 450*

With its stunning location overlooking Guincho beach and the Sintra Hills beyond, this restaurant is enormously popular. The well-crafted menu pays tribute to the ocean with stuffed crab, rock lobster, oyster and shrimp just for starters. One of the house specialities is fish baked in crusty bread smothered with olive oil and garlic. Closed Mon.

MONTE ESTORIL O Sinaleiro
 €€

Avenida de Sabóia 595, 2765-278 **Tel** *214 685 439*

Unassuming but welcoming with friendly, efficient service, O Sinaleiro is both a bar and restaurant. At first glance the menu appears to list fairly standard Portuguese fare, though the cooking is excellent. Look more closely though and you will spy incongruities such as *espetada mista de caça* (barbecued wild boar and deer kebab). Closed Wed.

MONTE ESTORIL Com Sentido's
 €€€€

Avenida de Sabóia 515d, 2765-502 **Tel** *214 682 838*

Large, abstract canvasses adorn the walls of this fashionable and contemporary-looking restaurant. The menu is equally well presented. Customers can opt for dishes such as the duck *magret* in orange sauce or milk-fed veal cutlet confit with sautéed Swiss chard. The dessert list is equally appealing. Closed Sun & Mon lunch.

PAÇO D'ARCOS Aquarela do Brasil
 €

Praça 5 de Outubro 12a, 2770-029 **Tel** *214 415 412*

This charming establishment resembles an art gallery more than a restaurant at times. Aquarela means "water-colour" but the owners encourage artists to submit work for the walls in all mediums. The Brazilian food is wonderful, with generous portions offered in a polite, easy-going manner. It can get very busy. Closed Sun dinner in winter.

PALMELA Pousada do Castelo de Palmela
 €€€€

Pousada do Castelo de Palmela, 2950-317 **Tel** *212 351 226*

The converted refectory of this 15th-century monastery provides an elegant and suitably romantic setting for a restaurant that offers discreet service. The dining hall is partly illuminated by a chandelier that throws light across such delicacies as oyster soup or Dover sole in a beer marinade.

PORTINHO DA ARRÁBIDA Beira-Mar
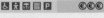 €€

Portinho da Arrábida, 2925-378 **Tel** *966 337 352*

On warm days, the most sought-after tables at this appealing restaurant are on the balcony overlooking the harbour. The stunning seaside setting helps whet the appetite for a robust selection of food and guests can enjoy specials like *arroz de tamboril* (monkfish rice) and *arroz de marisco* (seafood rice). Closed Wed (except Jun–Aug).

QUELUZ Cozinha Velha
 €€€€

Largo Palácio Nacional de Queluz, 2745-191 **Tel** *214 356 158*

Set in the old kitchens of the Palácio de Queluz (*see pp108–9*), this venerable restaurant draws its inspiration from traditional Portuguese recipes. The building retains much of its impressive 18th-century architecture, with the original stone chimney acting as a design centrepiece.

SESIMBRA Ribamar
 €€€

Avenida dos Náufragos 29, 2970-637 **Tel** *212 234 853*

Comfortable, cheerful and flooded with light, Ribamar sits right on the waterfront and is considered one of the best restaurants in the region. Along with the sea views, it serves up some wonderfully original concoctions, and there is always something new on the menu. Be daring and opt for the fish with seaweed, or cream of sea urchin soup.

SETÚBAL Poço das Fontainhas
 €€

Rua das Fontainhas 96, 2910-082 **Tel** *265 534 807*

Tucked away in the backstreets near the Tróia ferry terminal, this popular restaurant is a bit tricky to find but worth the effort. Fresh Atlantic fish and seafood dominate the menu, with *caldeirada à Setubalense* (Setúbal-style fish and potato casserole) a favourite among locals. Other highlights include *espetada de lulas* (squid kebab). Closed Mon.

SETÚBAL Pousada de São Filipe
 €€€€

Pousada de São Filipe, Castelo de São Filipe, 2900-300 **Tel** *265 550 070*

There is a jaw-dropping view of Setúbal and the Sado estuary and if it is warm tables are set outside on the esplanade. The ambience is late 16th-century Portugal and the food reflects the country's centuries-old culinary tradition. Regional dishes include pumpkin cream soup, fried red mullet and grilled lamb with orange sauce.

SINTRA Tulhas
 €

Rua Gil Vicente 4-6, 2710-568 **Tel** *219 232 378*

The mysterious hole near the entrance to this restaurant is the last vestige of a series of medieval granaries that once stood on the site (the Portuguese word for granary is *tulhas*). Small and unpretentious, the home-made food is wholesome and great value for money. The veal steak in Madeira wine is particularly flavoursome. Closed Wed.

SINTRA Lawrence's
€€€€€

Rua Consigliéri Pedroso 38-40, 2710-550 **Tel** *219 105 500*

The owners describe Lawrence's as a restaurant with rooms rather than a hotel, such is the esteem in which they hold this gourmet venue. Indeed, Lord Byron and William Beckford are just two of the historical figures said to have eaten here. The à la carte cuisine is served with finesse and there are over 200 wines to choose from.

SINTRA Restaurante Palácio de Seteais
€€€€€

Rua Barbosa du Bocage 8, Seteais, 2710-517 **Tel** *219 233 200*

The palace, now a hotel, is a breathtaking example of 18th-century splendour, and is home to a splendid gourmet restaurant. The building features a grand dining room decorated with mythological motifs and frescoes, and has outstanding views of the landscaped gardens and the coast. The menu is essentially Portuguese haute cuisine.

Cafés and Bars

Coffee is a vital element of the Portuguese way of life and a vibrant culture has developed around the simple pleasure of relaxing over a cup of coffee and a pastry in one of Lisbon's many cafés. The Portuguese have a complex classification system for coffee options (see p125), which modern coffee fashions will not change. Although shortcomings of service and gastronomy may be allowed to pass in a restaurant, a bad coffee at the end of the meal is a cardinal sin.

Bar culture is a younger phenomenon. While traditional drinking places such as ginjinha bars live on, the bars that make Lisbon's nightlife one of Europe's liveliest and most varied are rarely more than a decade or two old. Bairro Alto is the city's best-known bar territory and has the widest choice, but Santos, Bica/Santa Catarina and Cais do Sodré are good areas for bar-hopping too.

CLASSIC CAFÉS

Foremost among the grand cafés from the turn of the last century is **A Brasileira**, perfectly sited at the top of one of Lisbon's best shopping streets. The intellectuals who made it famous are long gone (there is a café-table bronze of poet Fernando Pessoa on the popular esplanade), but the atmosphere is cosmopolitan. **Nicola**, down in Rossio, has an elegant Art Deco interior and a busy outdoor seating area with plenty to watch. Across the square is **Pastelaria Suiça**, another boulevard-style café where the long promenade is its main attraction. **Martinho da Arcada**, under the arcades in Praça do Comércio, has an illustrious history and a beautifully tiled interior. Traffic makes the tables outside less of a treat, unless you opt for the restaurant, which has tables further in.

PARK/GARDEN CAFÉS

Those who appreciate a bit of greenery and no traffic with their coffee should seek out **Linha d'Água** at the top of Parque Eduardo VII. As with many Lisbon cafés it also serves meals at lunchtime. The pond-side café in **Jardim da Estrela** is another attractive option. **Pão de Canela** is a small café with a terrace on Praça das Flores, a quiet square with a garden in one of Lisbon's cosiest neighbourhoods. **Cafetaria Quadrante** in the modern complex of the Centro Cultural de Belém is set in an attractive, minimalist garden overlooking the river. Inside it can feel a bit like a canteen, but there is also a quieter upstairs bar, Terraço. Vegetarians will appreciate **Psi**, with its small garden and spiritual vibe.

CONTEMPORARY CAFÉS

A contemporary approach means more froth in your milky coffee (do not call it latte though), a wider range of sandwiches and a lighter touch with meals. It may also mean a lounge-like atmosphere, plenty of magazines and a serious take on music. Exponents of this approach include **Café no Chiado** with a very relaxed atmosphere; **Vertigo**, also in Chiado; and the inimitable **Pois, Café** with its cosy vaulted living room near the Sé. There is no Starbucks in Lisbon, but homegrown chains **LA Caffé** and **Magnolia Caffé** offer style and quality.

PASTRY SHOPS

Pastelarias are a crucial institution in Lisbon. Less raucous and smoky than normal cafés and snack bars, they are the preferred haunt of ladies of a certain age. However, as with any other customer, they would not bother coming in if the glass counter was not laden with freshly made pastéis de nata or amêndoas (custard or almond tarts), bolos de arroz (rice-flour cakes) or queijadas (cottage cheese tarts). **Bénard** is next to A Brasileira and gets some of the surplus custom from there, but its pastries are fresher. **Confeitaria Nacional** has been around for nearly two centuries and still does a booming over-the-counter business. The café section gets crowded quickly. Uptown is **Pastelaria Versailles** which is airier and has an atmosphere of faded grandeur. By far the most famous pastry shop is **Antiga Confeitaria de Belém**, where the pastel de nata (known as pastel de Belém in Lisbon) is said to have been invented.

DJ BARS

Bairro Alto has more bars than most people can ever manage to remember, but among those where music is taken particularly seriously are **Clube da Esquina** and **Mexe Café**. In nearby Bica/Santa Catarina, **Bicaense** has a coolly informal groove. Closer to the river, **Lounge** is less low key than it was, but remains dedicated to non-mainstream sounds. With a prime location overlooking the river, **Clube Ferroviário** features top DJs, live concerts and outdoor film screenings.

OUTDOOR BARS

Good bars for sunset viewing, warm nights and occasional sunrises include **Meninos do Rio**, whose irresistible chaises longues on the quayside need to be grabbed early. **Op Art** is a beacon of good taste and music in the otherwise slightly tacky Docas area under the bridge. **Noobai** combines great music with great views from the Santa Catarina viewpoint, and is one of Lisbon's most popular spots on warm summer evenings. Below the Castle, **Bar das Imagens** is a long-standing, or leaning, terrace over the city.

CLASSICS AND GINJINHAS

Pavilhão Chinês is on every tourist's itinerary, but it is worth a visit for its curio-shop interior. It is also one of the few places that give cocktails proper respect. The **British Bar** is a remnant from a bygone era and its wall clock goes backwards, but it attracts a very present-day crowd. **Portas Largas** could be said to be the engine that runs Bairro Alto – its street party is electric (and gay, but far from exclusively so). *Ginjinha* bars are a uniquely Portuguese institution: small, hole-in-the-wall bars that serve morello-cherry liqueur, *ginjinha* and almost nothing else. Pop into **A Ginjinha** or **Ginjinha Sem Rival** for a taste.

WINE BARS

There are surprisingly few bars that offer a good range of wines by the glass in Lisbon. Among the few that exist, **Enoteca** is perhaps the best, where tasty small dishes are served alongside an excellent selection of Portuguese and some foreign wines. In a similar vein, the **Néctar Wine Bar** in the heart of the Baixa serves a selection of wines by the glass. And **Lux**, Lisbon's premier nightclub, now has a bar dedicated to Bacchus. Port by the glass can also be had at the **Solar do Vinho do Porto**, run by the Port Wine Institute of Oporto.

DIRECTORY

CLASSIC CAFÉS

A Brasileira
Rua Garrett 120.
Map 7 A4.
Tel 213 469 541.

Martinho da Arcada
Praça do Comércio 3.
Map 7 C5.
Tel 218 879 259.

Nicola
Praça D. Pedro IV 24–25.
Map 7 B3.
Tel 213 460 579.

Pastelaria Suiça
Praça D. Pedro IV 96–101.
Map 7 B3.
Tel 213 214 090

PARK/GARDEN CAFÉS

Cafetaria Quadrante
Centro Cultural de Belém,
Praça do Império. **Map** 1
B5. **Tel** 213 612 400
(ext. 3130).

Jardim da Estrela
Jardim da Estrela, Praça
da Estrela. **Map** 4 D2.

Linha d'Água
Jardim Amália Rodrigues
(top of Parque Eduardo VII).
Map 5 B3.
Tel 213 814 327.

Pão de Canela
Praça das Flores 27.
Map 4 E2.
Tel 213 972 220.

Psi
Alameda Santo António
dos Capuchos.
Map 6 D5.
Tel 213 590 573.

CONTEMPORARY CAFÉS

Café no Chiado
Largo do Picadeiro 10–12.
Map 7 A4.
Tel 213 460 501.

LA Caffé
Avenida da Liberdade
129B (branch in Campo
Grande 3A). **Map** 4 F1.
Tel 213 256 736.

Magnolia Caffé
Campo Pequeno 2A.
Map 5 C1.
Tel 217 959 852.

Pois, Café
Rua S. João da Praça,
93–95. **Map** 8 D4.
Tel 218 862 497.

Vertigo
Travessa do Carmo 4.
Map 7 A4.
Tel 213 433 112.

PASTRY SHOPS

Antiga Confeitaria de Belém
Rua de Belém 84/92. **Map** 1
C4. **Tel** 213 638 077.

Bénard
Rua Garrett 104. **Map** 7
A4. **Tel** 213 473 133.

Confeitaria Nacional
Praça da Figueira 18B.
Map 7 B3.
Tel 213 424 470.

Pastelaria Versailles
Avenida da República 15A.
Map 5 C3.
Tel 213 546 340.

DJ BARS

Bicaense
Rua da Bica de Duarte
Belo 42 A. **Map** 4 F3.
Tel 213 257 940.

Clube da Esquina
Rua da Barroca 30. **Map** 4
F2. **Tel** 213 427 149.

Clube Ferroviário
Rua da Santa Apolónia 59.
Map 8 F2.
Tel 218 153 196.

Lounge
Rua da Moeda 1.
Map 4 F3.

Mexe Café
Rua da Trombeta. **Map** 4
F2. **Tel** 213 474 910.

OUTDOOR BARS

Bar das Imagens
Calçada Marquês de
Tancos 1. **Map** 7 C3.
Tel 218 884 636.

Meninos do Rio
Rua da Cintura do Porto
de Lisboa, Armazém 255.
Map 4 E4.
Tel 213 220 070.

Noobai
Miradouro de Santa
Catarina. **Map** 4 F3.
Tel 213 465 014.

Op Art
Doca de Santo Amaro.
Map 3 A5.
Tel 213 956 787.

CLASSICS AND GINJINHAS

A Ginjinha
Largo de São Domingos 8.
Map 7 B3.

British Bar
Rua Bernardino Costa 52.
Map 7 A5.
Tel 213 422 367.

Ginjinha Sem Rival
Rua das Portas de Santo
Antão 7. **Map** 7 B2.

Pavilhão Chinês
Rua Dom Pedro V 89.
Map 4 F2.
Tel 213 424 729.

Portas Largas
Rua da Atalaia 105.
Map 4 F2.
Tel 213 466 379.

WINE BARS

Enoteca
Rua da Mãe d'Água.
Map 4 F1.
Tel 213 422 079.

Lux
Cais da Pedra,
Av. Infante D. Henrique.
Map 8 F3.
Tel 218 820 890.

Néctar Wine Bar
Rua dos Douradores 33.
Map 7 C4.
Tel 912 633 368.

Solar do Vinho do Porto
Rua de São Pedro
de Alcântara 45.
Map 7 A3.
Tel 213 475 707.

SHOPPING IN LISBON

Lisbon offers a wide variety of shops to the visitor, with its combination of elegant high street shops, flea markets and modern shopping centres. The cobbled streets of the Baixa and the chic Chiado district have traditionally been Lisbon's main shopping areas, but the numerous indoor shopping centres are becoming increasingly popular.

Portuguese ceramic cockerel

Markets in Lisbon, Sintra and Cascais provide more adventurous shopping. If you are after something typically Portuguese, the hand-woven tapestries and lacework are worth buying. Most of all, choose from a range of ceramics, such as *azulejos* or Vista Alegre porcelain. For lovers of wine, Lisbon's wine merchants offer the best from all over the country.

A delicatessen in the Bairro Alto

OPENING HOURS

Traditional shopping hours are Monday to Friday 9am to 1pm and 3pm to 7pm, and Saturday 9am to 1pm.

However, in order to satisfy consumer demand, many shops, especially those in the Baixa, are now staying open during the lunch hour and on Saturday afternoons. Specialist shops such as hardware stores generally close for lunch at 12:30pm and reopen at 2:30pm. Shopping centres are open daily from 10am to midnight with most shops closing at 11pm. Generally, convenience stores are open daily from 7am to 2am.

HOW TO PAY

Most shops in Lisbon accept Visa and, to a lesser extent, American Express and MasterCard. Many smaller shops outside the main shopping areas will not.

An alternative is to obtain a cash advance with a credit card from one of the many Multi-banco teller machines (ATMs). Note that these charge interest on the withdrawal from day one, in addition to a currency conversion fee.

VAT AND TAXES

Non-European Union residents are exempt from IVA (Value Added Tax) in Portugal provided they remain in the country for no longer than 180 days. However, obtaining a rebate may be complicated in small shops or in areas less frequented by tourists. It is much simpler to buy in shops with a Global Blue Tax Free sign outside.

To get your rebate, ask the shop assistant for an *Isençâo na Exportaçâo* form. This must then be presented to a customs officer on your departure from Portugal. The original of the document will be returned to the vendor who is responsible for the reimbursement.

SHOPPING CENTRES

Large shopping centres are now very much part of the shopping landscape in Lisbon. They combine vast supermarkets, international chain stores and small specialist shops. All have restaurants and underground car parks; most also have cinemas. The oldest is **Amoreiras**, which has 230 shops, seven cinemas and 40 restaurants. **Dolce Vita Monumental** is one of three smaller centres clustered near Praça Duque de Saldanha. **Armazéns do Chiado** in the Chiado area has an historic façade but a modern interior. The huge **Colombo Shopping Centre** (*see p74*) in Benfica boasts a large children's leisure centre. The **Vasco da Gama** centre connects Oriente Station with Parque das Naçoes. The Spanish department store **El Corte Inglés** is at the top of Parque Eduardo VII. **Cascaishopping**, located between Estoril and Sintra, is one of many suburban centres.

The vast Amoreiras Shopping Centre, home to international chain stores

Shoppers browsing among the bric-à-brac in the popular Feira da Ladra

MARKETS

There are markets of every variety in Lisbon, from municipal markets selling fresh produce to the famous **Feira da Ladra** (Thieves' Market), a flea market on the slopes of the Alfama district. Although some stalls just sell junk, some bargains can be found among the array of bric-à-brac, second-hand clothes and general arts and crafts.

For more specialized markets, head to Oriente station, where you will find the **Feira de Antiguidades E Velharias**, an antiques market, or to the Chiado district for the **Feira dos Alfarrabistas**, for old books. The **Feira de Colec-cionismo** (collectors' market) takes place in Cais do Sodré every Sunday (9am–1pm).

Set in picturesque surroundings outside Lisbon, the **Feira de São Pedro**, in Sintra, is a wonderful market selling everything from new clothes and old bric-à-brac, to maturing cheeses and cackling fowl.

Along the Lisbon Coast, the **Feira de Cascais** has some good clothes bargains, as does the **Feira de Carcavelos**. Arrive early to beat the crowds.

FOOD SHOPS

It is almost impossible to window shop in Lisbon's delicatessens (*charcutarias*) without buying. Lined with a vast array of mouth-watering foods, from superb cheeses to tasty smoked meats and exquisite sweets, establishments

such as **Charcutaria Brasil** are a must for all seasoned gourmets. Here you can buy almost all regional specialities, from cheeses such as *serra* and *ilhas* to wild game such as partridge. Smoked hams and spicy sausages are also popular. If you have a sweet tooth, try some delicious *ovos moles* (egg sweets) or an assortment of dried or crystallized fruits, including delicious Elvas plums.

Other good food shops include **Charcutaria Carvalho & Morais** and **Manuel Tavares**, which has a large selection of port and madeira. **Celeiro Dieta** is a good health food shop, and is well known for stocking organic foods.

WINES AND SPIRITS

Portugal has a large variety of wines, fortified wines and spirits, ranging from light *vinhos verdes* to powerful *tintos* (reds), from fruity young ruby ports to ancient tawny ports or madeira, from sweet *amêndoa amarga* (bitter almond liqueur) to fiery *bagaceira* (grapeskin distillate). **Napoleão**, the best-known wine merchants in Lisbon, has outlets in many parts of the city, with its oldest shop in the Baixa. For port specifically, visit the **Solar do Vinho do Porto** (*see p54*) in Bairro Alto: this slightly fusty institution is actually a bar where you can sample a vast range of ports before deciding what to buy. **Garrafeira de Campo de Ourique** is one of Lisbon's best smaller wine merchants, and **Coisas do Arco do Vinho** has a good selection. Alternatively, large supermarkets are good for bargains, with frequent special offers on wines and spirits. You could visit the cellars of **J.M. da Fonseca** in Azeitão, where you can taste and buy many of the wines.

Fresh fish for sale at one of Lisbon's municipal markets

MUSIC AND MULTIMEDIA

The music scene in Portugal is a lively mix of traditions and the very latest trends. *Fado* music remains hugely popular, while techno and trance dance music have a dedicated following. Lisbon is also an important centre for contemporary music from former African colonies such as Cape Verde.

FNAC operates two mega-stores in Lisbon, and these are widely regarded as the city's best music shops in terms of variety. FNAC also sells most kinds of electronic hardware and software as well as books. **Discoteca Amália** in the Baixa specializes in *fado*.

Frontage of Livraria Bertrand, one of Lisbon's oldest bookshops

BOOKSHOPS

Portugal enjoys a great literary tradition with a range of authors, past and present, including Luís de Camões, Eça de Queiróz, Fernando Pessoa and José Saramago. Translations of their works, and those of other well-known Portuguese writers, are available in most large bookshops.

Livraria Bertrand and **Livraria Portugal**, both in the Chiado, are among Lisbon's oldest bookshops. **Livraria Buchholz** near the top of Avenida da Liberdade, was founded by a German and has a particularly large section of books in languages other than Portuguese, including travel guides, paperback fiction and history.

For an interesting selection of second-hand books, try visiting the **Feira dos Alfarrabistas** market, held in the Chiado district on the first Sunday of every month.

Terracotta ware for sale in Setúbal

CLOTHES

Many of the large chain stores, have outlets in Lisbon, particularly in the shopping centres *(see p138)*. Perhaps most noticeable is the Spanish **Zara** chain, whose shops sell affordable clothes for everyone.

More exclusive shops, including designer outlets, can be found on and around Avenida da Liberdade. **Rosa & Teixeira**, sells classic menswear, **Loja das Meias** is a mid- range chain with several shops. **Ana Salazar** is one of an increasing number of known Portuguese designers.

CERAMICS

Portugal's ceramics are famous for their quality and variety. In Lisbon you can find everything, from delicate porcelain to rustic terracotta, and from tiles to tableware.

The very fine **Vista Alegre** porcelain tableware is internationally known. Also famous are the hand-painted ceramics, including tiles from **Viúva Lamego**, **Santana** and **Cerâmica Artística de Carcavelos**. Known as *azulejos*, glazed tiles have long been used in Portugal to brighten up buildings. They may be plain, patterned or make up large figurative paintings. In Cascais, **Ceramicarte** is one of the largest ceramic centres. Perhaps the most ubiquitous pottery originates from Barcelos, famous for its decoratively painted cockerel which has become the unofficial national symbol.

REGIONAL CRAFTS

Portugal has a long and rich history of fine regional craftwork *(artesanato)*, in particular embroidery and fine lace, hand-knitted woolens, and delicate jewellery made from silver and gold thread. There are plenty of handicraft and gift shops in the Restauradores and Rossio areas of Lisbon, though these can be a little touristy. **Arte Rustica**, in the Baixa, is excellent for genuine crafts and a fascinating place to spend time browsing.

Regionália, in Estoril, and **Sintra Bazar**, in central Sintra, are also both good for arts.

Between July and August a wide variety of crafts can be seen at the Estoril Craft Fair, at which artisans from all over Portugal gather to exhibit their work. Cork

Lisbon offers regional crafts from all over Portugal

carvings and pottery can be found at **Santos Ofícios**.

ANTIQUES

Antiques often tend to be overpriced in Portugal, especially in Lisbon where the shops are mostly geared to a fairly upmarket clientele. You will generally find better value in towns outside the city. It is a good idea to look for shops that are members of APA *(Associação Portuguesa de Antiquários)*. These are usually identified by a sign in the shop window.

The majority of Lisbon's antique shops are located either in Rua Dom Pedro V, at the top of the Bairro Alto, or in Rua de São Bento, by the Parliament building, and around the cathedral, in the Alfama. There are numerous religious artifacts to be found in the area and **Solar** specializes in 16th–20th-century tiles *(azulejos)*. Beautiful prints (known as *gravuras*), sold at various second-hand bookshops in the Bairro Alto, are usually good value for money. **Livraria Olisipo** stocks books and also old prints of landscapes, fauna and maps. For a good range of quality antiques it is worth visiting the auctions held at **Cabral Moncada Leilões** (which are held every Monday evening) and also the Antiques Fair, which is held in Lisbon annually during April.

SIZE CHART

Lisbon uses both British and American systems.

Women's dresses, coats and skirts

Portuguese	34	36	38	40	42	44	46
British	8	10	12	14	16	18	20
American	6	8	10	12	14	16	18

Women's shoes

Portuguese	36	37	38	39	40	41
British	3	4	5	6	7	8
American	5	6	7	8	9	10

Men's suits

Portuguese	44	46	48	50	52	54	56	58
British	34	36	38	40	42	44	46	48
American	34	36	38	40	42	44	46	48

Men's shirts

Portuguese	36	38	39	41	42	43	44	45
British	14	15	15½	16	16½	17	17½	18
American	14	15	15½	16	16½	17	17½	18

Men's shoes

Portuguese	39	40	41	42	43	44	45	46
British	6	7	7½	8	9	10	11	12
American	7	7½	8	8½	9½	10½	11	11½

DIRECTORY

SHOPPING CENTRES

Amoreiras
Avenida Eng. Duarte Pacheco, Amoreiras.
Map 5 A5.
Tel 213 810 200.
www.amoreiras.com

Armazéns do Chiado
Rua do Carmo 2,
Chiado. **Map** 7 B4.
Tel 213 210 600.

Cascaishopping
Estrada Nacional 9,
Alcabideche, Estoril.
Tel 210 121 620.

Colombo Shopping Centre
Avenida Lusíada, Benfica.
Tel 217 113 600/36.
www.colombo.pt

Dolce Vita Monumental
Avenida Fontes Pereira de Melo 51, Saldanha.
Map 5 C4.
Tel 213 510 500.

El Corte Inglés
Avenida António Augusto Aguiar 31. **Map** 5 B5.
Tel 213 711 700.
www.elcorteingles.pt

Vasco da Gama
Avenida Dom João II,
Parque das Nações.
Tel 218 930 600.
www.centrovasco dagama.pt

MARKETS

Feira dos Alfarrabistas
Rua da Anchieta, Chiado (10am–5pm Sat).

Feira de Antiguidades Velharas
Estação Oriente.

Feira de Carcavelos
Carcavelos (Thu).

Feira de Cascais
Cascais.

Feira de Coleccionismo
Mercado da Ribeira,
Avenida 24 de Julho.
Map 4 F4.

Feira da Ladra
Alfama (Tue & Sat).
Map 8 E3.

Feira de São Pedro
Sintra.

FOOD SHOPS

Celeiro Dieta
Avenida António Augusto de Aguiar 130, Saldanha.
Map 5 B3.
Tel 213 558 164.

Charcutaria Brasil
Rua Alexandre Herculano 90–92, Rato. **Map** 5 C5
Tel 213 885 644.

Charcutaria Carvalho & Morais
Avenida João XXI 54,
Areeiro. **Map** 6 E1.
Tel 217 973 412.

Manuel Tavares
Rua da Betesga 1,
Baixa. **Map** 7 B3.
Tel 213 424 209.

WINES AND SPIRITS

Coisas do Arco do Vinho
Centro Cultural de Belém.
Map 1 B5.
Tel 213 642 031.

Garrafeira de Campo de Ourique
Rua Tomás de Anunciação 29a, Campo de Ourique.
Tel 213 973 494.

J.M. da Fonseca
Vila Nogueira de Azeitão,
Azeitão.
Tel 212 197 500.

Napoleão
Rua dos Fanqueiros 70,
Baixa. **Map** 7 C4.
Tel 218 872 042.

Solar do Vinho do Porto
Rua São Pedro de Alcântara 45, Bairro Alto.
Map 7 A3.
Tel 213 475 707.
www.ivdp.pt

MUSIC AND MULTIMEDIA

Discoteca Amália
Rua do Ouro, 272.
Baixa. **Map** 7 B4.
Tel 213 420 939.

FNAC
Rua Nova do Almada 102,
Chiado. **Map** 7 B4.
Tel 707 313 435.

BOOKSHOPS

Livraria Bertrand
Rua Garrett 73, Chiado.
Map 7 A4.
Tel 213 476 122.

Livraria Buchholz
Rua Duque de Palmela 4,
Marquês Pombal. **Map** 5 C5. *Tel 213 535 095.*

Livraria Portugal
Rua do Carmo 70–74,
Chiado. **Map** 7 B4.
Tel 213 474 982.

CLOTHES

Ana Salazar
Rua do Carmo 87,
Chiado. **Map** 7 B3.
Tel 213 472 289.

Loja das Meias
Rua Castilho 39.
Map 4 F1.
Tel 213 710 303.

Rosa & Teixeira
Avenida da Liberdade 204,
Avenida. **Map** 5 C5.
Tel 213 110 350.

Zara
Rua Garrett 1, Chiado.
Map 7 B4.
Tel 213 243 710.

CERAMICS

Cerâmica Artística de Carcavelos
Avenida Loureiro 47b,
Carcavelos.
Tel 214 563 267.

Ceramicarte
Largo da Assunção 3–4,
Cascais. *Tel 214 840 170.*

Santana
Rua do Alecrim 95,
Chiado.
Map 7 A5.
Tel 213 422 537.

Vista Alegre
Largo do Chiado 20–21,
Chiado.
Map 7 A4.
Tel 213 461 401.

Viúva Lamego
Largo do Intendente 25.
Map 7 C1.
Tel 218 852 408.

REGIONAL CRAFTS

Arte Rústica
Rua do Ouro 246–8,
Baixa.
Map 7 B4.
Tel 213 421 127.

Regionália
Arcadas do Parque 87,
Estoril.
Tel 214 681 619.

Santos Ofícios
Rua da Madalena 87,
Baixa.
Map 7 C4.
Tel 218 872 031.

Sintra Bazar
Praça da República 37,
Sintra.
Tel 219 248 245.

ANTIQUES

Cabral Moncada Leilões
Rua Miguel Lupi 12,
Estrela.
Map 4 E2.
Tel 213 954 781.

Livraria Olisipo
Largo Trindade Coelho 7–8,
Bairro Alto.
Map 7 A3.
Tel 213 462 771.

Solar
Rua Dom Pedro V 68–70,
Bairro Alto. **Map** 4 F2.
Tel 213 465 522.

ENTERTAINMENT IN LISBON

For a smallish European capital, Lisbon has a good and varied cultural calendar. Musical events range from classical and opera performances to intimate *fado* evenings, and large rock concerts. Dance, both classical and modern, is well represented in Lisbon. The Gulbenkian Foundation, long the only major arts patron, has been joined by other private funds as well as state institutions.

Football is a consuming passion of the Portuguese, and Lisbon's Sporting and Benfica teams play regularly at home. Lisbon outparties many larger capitals, with a nightlife known for its liveliness.

BOOKING TICKETS

Tickets can be reserved by phoning the Agência de Bilhetes para Espectáculos Públicos (**ABEP**). Pay in cash when you collect them from the kiosk. Some cinemas and theatres accept phone or credit card bookings – it is best to check first.

ABEP kiosk selling tickets on Praça dos Restauradores

LISTINGS MAGAZINES

Previews of forthcoming events and listings of bars and clubs appear weekly in major newspapers. English-language events publications include the monthly *Follow Me Lisboa*, which is free and widely available throughout the city, including most hotel reception areas. The monthly *Agenda Cultural* is in Portuguese.

CINEMA AND THEATRE

Movie-goers are very well served in Lisbon. Films are shown in their original language with Portuguese subtitles, and tickets are inexpensive. On Mondays most cinemas offer reductions. The city's traditional cinemas have now largely given way to modern multiplexes, usually in shopping centres such as Amoreiras or El Corte Inglés *(see p141)*. While these screen mainstream Hollywood fare,

cinemas such as **King Triplex** show more European films. Classics and retrospectives can be seen at the **Cinemateca Portuguesa**, whose monthly programme is available at tourist offices.

Theatre performances are most often in Portuguese, but large institutions such as the **Teatro Nacional Dona Maria II** and the **Teatro da Trindade** occasionally stage guest performances by visiting companies. Less formally, **Chapitô** sometimes has open-air shows.

CLASSICAL MUSIC, OPERA AND DANCE

The **Centro Cultural de Belém** *(see p68)* and the **Fundação Calouste Gulbenkian** *(see pp76–9)* host national and international events including concerts and ballet. The **Teatro Nacional de São Carlos** is Portugal's national opera, with a season that mixes its own productions with guest performances. The **Teatro Camões** hosts the Lisbon symphony orchestra and the Portuguese national ballet. The **Coliseu dos Recrejos** offers a variety of events.

Performance at the Chapitô circus school, Alfama

WORLD MUSIC, JAZZ, POP AND ROCK

Lisbon's musical soul may be *fado* (see pp144–5), but the city is no stranger to other forms of musical expression. African music, particularly that of former Portuguese colony Cape Verde, plays an big part in Lisbon's music scene. Venues include **B.Léza**, which has frequent live performances.

The **Hot Clube** has been Lisbon's foremost jazz venue for as long as anyone can

The house orchestra playing at the Fundação Calouste Gulbenkian

Musician at a live music venue

remember, and has the right intimate atmosphere. **Speakeasy** is younger, slightly bigger, and varies live jazz with up-tempo blues, particularly at weekends.

Large rock and pop concerts are held at outdoor venues, such as football stadiums, or indoors at **Pavilhão Atlântico** or Coliseu dos Recreios.

NIGHTCLUBS

Bairro Alto remains a lively area for Lisbon nightlife, although its mostly small bars don't usually have dance floors or keep very late hours. However, there are a few exceptions, including the doyen of Bairro Alto clubs, **Frágil**, still at the cutting edge after 20 years.

Among the larger and more mainstream dance venues are **Urban Beach** and **Kapital**; the former is a nearly historic house club, while the latter is an up-market club right by the river.

Further along the riverfront are **Belém Bar Café** and **Alcântara-Mar**, while eastwards along the river near Santa Apolónia station, is **Lux**, the cream of Lisbon's current club scene.

Details of recommended bars in Lisbon, Estoril, Cascais and Sintra can be found on pages 134–5.

SPECTATOR SPORTS

Lisbon's main football stadiums, built for the 2004 European Football Championship, are **Estádio José Alvalade** and **Estádio da Luz**.

The Portuguese football cup finals as well as other events, such as the Estoril Open tennis tournament, are held at the **Estádio Nacional-Jamor**. The Pavilhão Atlântico is also used for indoor sporting events such as tennis, volleyball and basketball. Estoril's **Autódromo** Fernanda Pires da Silva is a motor-racing venue.

DIRECTORY

BOOKING TICKETS

ABEP
Praça dos Restauradores.
Map 7 A2.
Tel 213 425 360.

FNAC
Centro Colombo
Avenida Luisada Benfica.
Tel 707 313 435.

CINEMA AND THEATRE

Chapitô
Costa do Castelo 7.
Map 7 C3.
Tel 218 867 334.

Cinemateca Portuguesa
Rua Barata Salgueiro 39.
Map 5 C5.
Tel 213 596 262.

King Triplex
Avenida Frei Miguel Contreiras 52a.
Map 6 E1.
Tel 218 480 808.

Teatro Nacional Dona Maria II
Praça Dom Pedro IV.
Map 7 B3.
Tel 213 250 800.

Teatro da Trindade
Largo da Trindade 9.
Map 7 A3.
Tel 213 423 200.

CLASSICAL MUSIC, OPERA AND DANCE

Centro Cultural de Belém
Praça do Império.
Map 1 C5.
Tel 213 612 400.

Coliseu dos Recreios
Rua das Portas de Santo Antão 92.
Map 7 A2.
Tel 213 240 580.

Fundação Calouste Gulbenkian
Avenida de Berna 45.
Map 5 B2.
Tel 217 823 000.

Teatro Camões
Parque das Nações.
Tel 218 923 477.

Teatro Nacional de São Carlos
Rua Serpa Pinto 9.
Map 7 A4.
Tel 213 253 000.

WORLD MUSIC, JAZZ, POP AND ROCK

B.Léza
Cais da Riberia Nova, Armazem. **Map** 4 F4.
Tel 213 888 738.

Hot Clube
Praça da Alegria 48. **Map** 4 F1. *Tel 213 619 740.*

Pavilhão Atlântico
Parque das Nações.
Tel 218 918 409.

Speakeasy
Cais das Oficinas, Armazém 115, Rocha Conde d'Óbidos.
Map 4 D4.
Tel 213 964 257.

NIGHTCLUBS

Alcântara-Mar
Rua da Cozinha Económica 11.
Tel 213 636 830.

Belém Bar Café
Av. Brasilia, Belém.
Map 3 A4.
Tel 213 624 232.

Frágil
Rua da Atalaia 128. **Map** 4 F2. *Tel 213 469 578.*

Kapital
Avenida 24 de Julho 68.
Map 4 E3.
Tel 213 957 101.

Lux
Avenida Infante Dom Henrique. **Map** 8 D5.
Tel 218 820 890.

Urban Beach
Cais da Viscondessa, Rua da Cíntura, Santos.
Map 3 C4.
Tel 961 312 712.

SPORTS

Autódromo Estoril
Alcabideche.
Tel 214 609 500.

Estádio José Alvalade
(Sporting) Rua Francisco Stromp 2.
Tel 707 204 444.

Estádio da Luz
(Benfica) Avenida General Norton Matos 1500.
Tel 707 200 100.

Estádio Nacional-Jamor
Cruz Quebrada.
Tel 214 156 402.

Fado: the Music of Lisbon

Like the blues, *fado* is an expression of longing and sorrow. Literally meaning "fate", the term may be applied to an individual song as well as the genre itself. The music owes much to the concept known as *saudade*, meaning a longing both for what has been lost and for what has never been attained, which perhaps accounts for its emotional power. The people of Lisbon have nurtured this poignant music in back-street cafés and restaurants for over 150 years, and it has altered little in that time. It is sung as often by women as men, always accompanied by the *guitarra* and *viola* (acoustic Spanish guitar). *Fado* from Coimbra has developed its own lighter hearted style.

A *guitarra* accompanist

A graphic depiction of the music's low-life associations from the 1920s

All female *fadistas* wear a black shawl in memory of Maria Severa.

The *guitarrista* plays the melody and will occasionally perform a solo instrumental piece.

Maria Severa (1810–36) *was the first great* fadista *and the subject of the first Portuguese sound film in 1931. Her scandalous life and early death are pivotal to* fado *history, and her spiritual influence has been enormous, inspiring* fados, *poems, novels and plays.*

Most instruments have 12 paired strings, like this one. The double strings produce a resonant, silvery-sweet tone.

Delicate mother-of-pearl inlaid flower motifs

Mother-of-pearl finger plate

THE GUITARRA

Peculiar to Portuguese culture, the *guitarra* is a flat-backed instrument shaped like a mandolin, with eight, ten or twelve strings, arranged in pairs. It has evolved from a simple 19th-century design into a finely decorated piece, sometimes inlaid with mother-of-pearl. The sound of the *guitarra* is an essential ingredient of a good *fado*, echoing and enhancing the singer's melody line.

Alfredo Duarte *(1891–1982)*
was a renowned writer of
fado lyrics dealing with love,
death, longing, tragedy and
triumph. Affectionately
known as O Marceneiro
(the master carpenter)
because of his skill as a
joiner, he is still revered and
his work widely performed.

All kinds of themes *may occur in fado.*
This song of 1910, for example, celebrates
the dawning of the liberal republic. Such
songsheets remained a favoured means of
dissemination, even after the first records
were made in 1904.

A cultural icon *for the*
Portuguese, Amália
Rodrigues (1921–99)
was the leading
exponent of fado
for over 50 years. She
crystallized the music's
style in the post-war
years and made it
known around
the world.

The viola provides rhythm accompaniment,
but the player will never take a solo.

The music has long inspired *great writers and*
painters. O Fado (1910) by José Malhôa (1855–1933)
shows it in an intimate setting with the fadista
captivating his listener. The air of abandonment
underlines the earthiness of many of the songs.

THE FADO HOUSE

Lisbon's best *fado* houses are
those run by *fadistas* themselves.
Based on a love of the music and
on relationships with other performers, such houses usually offer
a truer *fado* experience than the
larger, tourist-oriented houses. A
good example is the Parreirinha
de Alfama, owned by Argentina
Santos *(shown above)*. Less slick,
but more emotionally charged,
are performances of *fado vadio*,
"itinerant" *fado*, in humbler
restaurants and bars such as
Tasca do Chico in Bairro Alto.

WHERE TO ENJOY FADO IN LISBON

Any of these places offer good food, wine and music. Or visit the
Museu do Fado for a fascinating exhibition on the history of *fado*.

Bacalhau de Molho
Beco dos Armazéns do Linho 2.
Map 8 E4. *Tel* 218 865 088.

Clube de Fado
Rua São João da Praça 92.
Map 8 D4. *Tel* 218 852 704.

O Faia
Rua da Barroca 54–6.
Map 4 F2. *Tel* 213 426 742.

Parreirinha de Alfama
Beco do Espírito Santo 1.
Map 7 E4. *Tel* 218 868 209.

**Restaurant Museu
do Fado**
Largo do Chafariz de Dentro 1.
Map 8 E4. *Tel* 218 823 470.

Senhor Vinho
Rua do Meio à Lapa 18.
Map 4 D3. *Tel* 213 977 456.

SURVIVAL GUIDE

PRACTICAL INFORMATION

Lisbon has become increasingly modern and cosmopolitan, with the advantages and disadvantages that this brings. The city is well equipped to receive visitors, and has professional tourist services, particularly at the Lisboa Welcome Center in the Baixa area and the Ask Me Lisboa

Tourist information sign

tourist office in Restauradores. However, it has also become rather expensive and traffic-ridden. Visitors seeking the old Lisbon can still find it in the Alfama, or any of the city's smaller areas. One of the best ways to appreciate Lisbon is on foot, using trams for the steeper hills and pausing to enjoy the varied views.

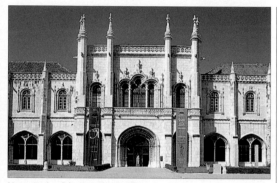

Museu Nacional de Arqueologia, which is free to visit on Sunday mornings

VISAS AND PASSPORTS

Nationals of the EU need only a valid passport to enter Portugal, which is a signatory to the Schengen Convention; for stays longer than six months, a residence permit is required. Americans, Canadians, Australians and New Zealanders may stay for up to 90 days without a visa. All travellers from outside the EU should check with their nearest Portuguese embassy or consulate, as regulations may change.

UK passport holders should note that lost or stolen passports can no longer be replaced by the **British Embassy** in Lisbon; instead, you will need to apply to the British Embassy in Madrid for a replacement.

TOURIST INFORMATION

The opening hours of tourist offices in Lisbon are generally the same as those of local shops *(see p138)*. Those that are more centrally located, such as **Ask Me Lisboa** and the **Lisboa Welcome Center**

remain open throughout weekends. Offices in the centre of Lisbon are indicated on the Street Finder maps *(see pp172–9)*. Other offices may be found at Portela airport *(see p156)* and at Santa Apolónia station (Map 8 F3). Addresses of offices in the Lisbon Coast area are given in the information at the top of each sight entry. Portuguese tourist offices outside Portugal, such as those listed on *page 149*, can provide you with useful information before you travel.

LANGUAGE

Written Portuguese is fairly similar to Spanish, so if you know Spanish you should have little difficulty reading Portuguese text. Spoken Portuguese, however, sounds very different from Spanish. Although English is more widely spoken in Portugal than in neighbouring Spain, the Portuguese are proud of their language and appreciate

visitors' efforts to communicate in Portuguese. A phrasebook with some useful words and phrases is on *pages 191–2*.

ADMISSION PRICES

Most museums and monuments charge an entrance fee, which often increases in the summer. Entry is usually free on Sunday mornings and public holidays. Pensioners and children under 14 are entitled to a 40 per cent discount. Visitors under 26 with a *Cartão Jóvem* (youth card; www.geracao-c.com) or an ISIC card (International Student Identity Card; www.isic.org) are entitled to half-price entrance.

Museum tickets

Visitors can also buy a Lisboa Card *(see p158)*, which includes free or discounted entry to many of Lisbon's state museums, historic monuments and places of special interest as well as discounted travel on the city's public transport.

OPENING HOURS

Most museums are open from 10am to 5pm Tue–Sun, with many closing for lunch from noon to 2pm or from 12:30 to 2:30pm. Smaller or privately owned museums may have different opening times. Note that state-run museums and some sights close on Mondays and public holidays. Major churches are open all day, although some may close from noon to 4pm. Smaller churches may only open for services.

◁ **View across Lisbon's skyline, with the Elevador de Santa Justa in the foreground**

TRAVELLERS WITH SPECIAL NEEDS

Facilities in Lisbon have improved greatly. Some buses (marked with a blue-and-white wheelchair logo at the front) can carry wheelchair-bound passengers, and ramps and lifts are common in many public places, including shopping centres, theatres, museums and across the rail and Metro network, though access to platforms is not always easy. Adapted toilets are available at airports and main train stations, and reserved car parking is clearly marked. The use of Braille to indicate directions and telephone numbers is on the increase. A number of tour companies, such as **Accessible Portugal**, **Access at Last** and **Choose Portugal**, offer specialist holiday packages to Lisbon or give advice on accessible accommodation for travellers with limited mobility.

TIME

Portugal follows Britain in adopting Greenwich Mean Time (GMT) in winter and moving the clocks forward 1 hour in summer. The 24-hour clock is commonly used.

ELECTRICITY

Voltage in Portugal is 220 volts. Plugs have two round pins and most hotel bathrooms offer built-in adaptors for shavers only.

CONVERSION CHART

Imperial to Metric
1 inch = 2.54 centimetres
1 foot = 30 centimetres
1 mile = 1.6 kilometres
1 ounce = 28 grams
1 pound = 454 grams
1 pint = 0.6 litres
1 gallon = 4.6 litres

Metric to Imperial
1 millimetre = 0.04 inches
1 centimetre = 0.4 inches
1 metre = 3 feet 3 inches
1 kilometre = 0.6 miles
1 gram = 0.04 ounces
1 kilogram = 2.2 pounds
1 litre = 1.8 pints

RESPONSIBLE TOURISM

Lisbon is taking environmental issues seriously, as demonstrated by special "eco-points" for the correct disposal of rubbish. Colour-coded bins (blue for card/paper, yellow for plastic and tin, and green for glass) in strategic locations around the city encourage the public to

Organic cakes at Quinoa

recycle their litter. The Inspira Santa Marta *(see p118)* is Lisbon's first eco-hotel. Awarded a Green Globe Certificate, it is constructed from ecologically sustainable building materials such as wood and stone, is designed to make maximum use of natural light and serves organic food in its restaurant.

Some shops have garnered green credentials too – for instance, the bread sold at **Quinoa**, a city-centre bakery, is 100 per cent organic. The Saturday market at Praça do Príncipe Real sells organic produce.

Slowly, Lisbon is reducing its carbon footprint, exemplified by its use of nearly 3 million energy-efficient light bulbs to illuminate its municipal Christmas decorations.

DIRECTORY

EMBASSIES AND CONSULATES

Australia
Avda da Liberdade 200, 2°,
E Edifício Victoria,
1269-121, Lisbon.
Map 5 C5. *Tel 213 101
500.* www.portugal.
embassy.gov.au

British Embassy
Lisbon
Rua de São Bernardo 33,
1249-082, Lisbon.
Map 4 D2.
Tel 213 924 000.
www.ukinportugal.fco.
gov.uk

Madrid
Torre Espacio
Paseo de la Castellana,
28046 Madrid, Spain.
Tel +34 917 146 400.

Canada
Avda da Liberdade
198–200, 3°, Edifício
Victoria, 1269-121, Lisbon.
Map 5 C5. *Tel 213 164
600.* www.canada
international.gc.ca/
portugal

United States
Avenida das Forças
Armadas, 1600-081,
Lisbon. *Tel 217 273 300.*
http://portugal.us
embassy.gov

TOURIST INFORMATION

Ask Me Lisboa
Palácio Foz, Praça dos
Restauradores. **Map** 7 A2.
*Tel 213 463 314,
808 781 212.*
www.askmelisboa.com

Lisboa Welcome Center
Praça Comércio (next to
post office), 1100-038.
Map 7 B5. *Tel 210 312
810.* www.visitlisboa.com

TOURIST OFFICES ABROAD

www.visitportugal.com

Canada
(see United States office).

United Kingdom
11 Belgrave Square,
London SW1X 8PP.
Tel +44 207 201 6666.

United States
590 Fifth Avenue,
Fourth Floor, New York
10036-4704.
Tel +1 646 723 0200.

TRAVELLERS WITH SPECIAL NEEDS

Access at Last
www.accessatlast.com

Accessible Portugal
Estrada do Paço do Lumiar,
Lispólis, Lote 1, 207B,
1600-546, Lisbon.
Tel 217 203 130.
www.accessible
portugal.com

Choose Portugal
www.chooseportugal.
com

RESPONSIBLE TOURISM

Quinoa
Rua do Alecrim 54,
Chiado, 1200-018 Lisbon.
Map 7 A4.
Tel 213 479 326.

Personal Security and Health

Pharmacy sign

Lisbon does not have a serious crime problem, but simple precautions can and should be taken. Watch out for pickpockets in busy areas and on public transport, avoid carrying large amounts of cash and don't leave valuables in parked cars. The police are generally helpful, but bureaucratic; reporting a crime can take time. In case of a medical emergency, dial 112 and ask for an ambulance. For minor medical complaints, consult a pharmacist first.

POLICE

In Lisbon and other main towns in Portugal, the police force is the *Polícia de Segurança Pública* (PSP). A division of the PSP, a special Metro unit, patrols Lisbon's rail and Metro network, most notably at night. In rural areas, law and order is kept by the *Guarda Nacional Republicana* (GNR). The *Brigada de Trânsito* (traffic police) is a division of the GNR, and its members are recognizable by their red armbands. They are responsible for patrolling roads.

If you have any property stolen, you should contact the nearest police station at the earliest opportunity. Theft of a passport should also be reported to your embassy. Many insurance companies insist that policy holders report any theft to the police within 24 hours.

The police will file a report; note that you will need this in order to claim from your insurance company on your return home.

There is a Tourist Police Station at Palácio Foz, in Praça dos Restauradores *(see p151)*, manned by English-speaking officers, that deals exclusively with complaints from tourists. Rail and Metro carriages display dedicated telephone numbers for use in the event of emergencies.

In all situations, try to keep calm and be polite to the authorities to avoid delays. The same applies should you be involved in a car accident. In rural areas you may be asked to accompany the other driver to the nearest police station to complete the necessary paperwork. Ask for an interpreter if no one there speaks English.

Traffic policeman **PSP officer** **GNR officer**

WHAT TO BE AWARE OF

Violent crime is fairly rare in Lisbon and in Portugal generally, and the majority of visitors will experience no problems whatsoever. Nonetheless, a few sensible precautions are worth taking: avoid quiet areas such as the Baixa after dark, and don't stroll alone through Bairro Alto, Alfama or around Cais do Sodré after bars have closed. In the daytime, be alert to the possibility of pickpockets or, more rarely, bag-snatchers. Be vigilant when withdrawing cash from an ATM (*Multibanco* or MB). Whenever possible, carry out the transaction in daylight and be aware of anyone standing too close behind you who could see your PIN number. Ideally, use an ATM together with someone you know and trust, or one that is housed within the bank's premises. Some poorer neighbourhoods and outlying slums see more serious daytime crime, but they are not on the typical visitor's itinerary.

Other general precautions include not carrying or showing large amounts of cash (carry only the amount needed for daily purchases), not leaving possessions visible in parked cars, not leaving bags unattended (especially at outdoor cafés and restaurants) and by holding on to valuable equipment such as mobile phones and cameras. Beware of pickpockets on crowded Metro trains. If you are robbed, you are advised not to put up any resistance.

Vaccinations are not needed for visitors to Portugal although doctors recommend being up-to-date with tetanus, diptheria and measles jabs. Tap water is safe to drink throughout the country. If you are visiting during the summer, it is advisable to bring insect repellent, as mosquitoes, while they do not present any serious health problems, can be a nuisance. The use of a good sun block is also recommended, and try to drink plenty of water.

Ambulance

Fire engine

Police car

IN AN EMERGENCY

The number to contact in the event of an emergency is **112**. Dial the number and then indicate which service you require – the police (*polícia*), an ambulance (*ambulância*) or the fire brigade (*bombeiros*). If you need medical treatment, the casualty department (*serviço de urgência*) of the closest main hospital will treat you. On motorways and main roads, use the orange SOS telephone to call for help should you have a car accident. The service is in Portuguese; press the button and wait for an answer. The operator will put you through.

HOSPITALS AND PHARMACIES

Social security coverage is available for all EU nationals in Portugal. To claim, you must obtain the European Health Insurance Card (EHIC) from the UK Department of Health or from a post office before you travel. The card comes with a booklet, *Health Advice for Travellers*, which explains exactly what health care you are entitled to and where and how to claim. You may find you have to pay and reclaim the money later. Not all treatments are covered by the card, and some are costly, so all travellers are advised to arrange for comprehensive medical insurance before travelling.

The **British Hospital** in Lisbon has English-speaking doctors, as do international health centres on the Lisbon Coast. Pharmacies (*farmácias*) can diagnose simple health problems and suggest appropriate treatment. Pharmacists can dispense a range of drugs that would normally be available only on prescription in many other countries. The sign for a *farmácia* is a green cross. They are open 9am–1pm and 3–7pm Mon–Fri (9am–1pm Sat). Each pharmacy displays a card in the window showing the address of the nearest all-night pharmacy and a list of those that are open until late (10pm). Two centrally located pharmacies are **Farmácia Barral** and **Farmácia Estácio**.

LEGAL ASSISTANCE

An insurance policy that covers the costs of legal advice, issued by companies such as Europ Assistance or Mondial Assistance, will help with the legal aspects of your insurance claim should you have an accident. If you have not arranged this cover phone your nearest consulate or the **Ordem dos Advogados** (Lawyers' Association), who can give you names of English-speaking lawyers and help you with obtaining representation. Lists of interpreters are given in the local Yellow Pages (*Páginas Amarelas*) under *Tradutores e Intérpretes*, or contact **AP Portugal**, based in Lisbon.

PUBLIC CONVENIENCES

The Portuguese for toilets is *casa de banho*. If the usual figures of a man or woman are not shown, look for the words *homens* (men) and *senhoras* (ladies). Toilet facilities are provided at motorway service areas every 40 km (25 miles) and at some drive-in rest areas. They can also be found in most modern shopping malls and at major transport hubs, such as coach and railway stations. In addition, a number of specially designed coin-operated toilets can be found in the streets. As a last resort, all cafés and restaurants provide toilet facilities; these, however, are often open only to customers – some are accessed by a key kept behind the counter.

DIRECTORY

EMERGENCY NUMBERS

General Emergency (Fire, Police, Ambulance)
Tel 112.

Central Police Station
Largo do Regedor 2, Rossio, Lisbon. **Map** 7 B3.
Tel 213 427 380.

Tourist Police Station
Palácio Foz, Restauradores, Lisbon. **Map** 7 A3.
Tel 213 421 623/634.

HOSPITALS AND PHARMACIES

British Hospital
Rua Tomás da Fonseca, Edifício B, Lisbon. *Tel 217 213 400.*

Farmácia Barral
Rua Augusta 225, Baixa, Lisbon. **Map** 7 B3.

Farmácia Estácio
Praça D. Pedro IV 61, Rossio, Lisbon. **Map** 7 B3.

LEGAL ASSISTANCE

AP Portugal
Avda João Crisóstomo 30–5°, Lisbon. **Map** 5 B3.
Tel 213 303 759.

Ordem dos Advogados
Largo de São Domingos 14, 1°, Lisbon. **Map** 7 B3.
Tel 218 823 550.

Banking and Local Currency

BPI bank logo

Portugal is one of the founding members of the European Monetary Union and one of the countries that launched the euro in 2002. Credit and debit cards are widely accepted, and funds can be readily obtained from ATMs; those offering the best exchange rates are found mainly in the Baixa district. It is always a good idea to arrive with enough euro in cash to cover one or two days' expenditure. Bank exchange rates can vary, while bureaux de change may provide a faster service than banks.

Bank façade on Rua do Ouro

BANKS AND BUREAUX DE CHANGE

Banks are open between 8:30am and 3pm, Monday to Friday. Some branches stay open for longer, usually until 6pm – check at individual branches. Some banks are open on Saturday mornings, but most banks are closed throughout weekends, and all are closed on public holidays. ATM services, however, are available 24 hours daily. Money can be changed at banks, bureaux de change (*agências de câmbios*) and at many hotels. Be aware that in Portugal, larger denomination banknotes such as the €200 and €500 note have a limited circulation, and some establishments may not accept them.

There are several major banks, which have branches everywhere, but their rates of exchange and commission vary. Waiting times and bureaucratic practices at banks may also make them a slow option. There are many bureaux de change,

such as **Nova Câmbios**, throughout the city. They often charge higher commissions than banks, but this is not always the case. It's worth shopping around, especially in and around Rossio, for the best rates. Bureaux de change also offer a speedier service, as well as longer opening hours (including weekends). As a rule, hotels have the worst rates of exchange.

Traveller's cheques are a safe but not very convenient way of carrying money; it is rare for shops or hotels to accept them as payment, and cashing them may be quite expensive. In general, bureaux de change are better for this than banks, where commissions may be high.

Funds may also be obtained using money-transfer companies like **Western Union**, which has several offices based in Lisbon. Recipients can pick up money at a participating Western Union agent in the city selected by the sender.

At banks, bureaux de change and money-transfer companies you may be asked to show your passport or some other form of photographic identification for exchange transactions.

CREDIT AND DEBIT CARDS

The most practical and convenient way to obtain cash is from an ATM (*Multibanco* or MB) using your credit or debit card. Note that many banks impose a small charge for international ATM transactions. Check the

charges with your bank in advance. *Multibanco* machines for withdrawing cash are widely available, typically outside banks or in shopping centres.

Smaller, wireless chip-and-PIN *Multibanco* machines are found at shop counters and can be used to pay for a range of purchases including rail tickets, clothes, and meals and drinks in restaurants. Some are even used in taxis. Most *Multibanco* machines accept Visa, MasterCard, American Express, Maestro and Cirrus cards and operate in several different languages.

Be sure to notify your bank and credit card providers before leaving for Portugal. Some banks forbid foreign transactions for security reasons unless they have been notified ahead of time.

THE EURO

The euro (€) is the common currency of the European Union. It went into general circulation on 1 January 2002, initially for 12 participating countries, including Portugal. EU members using the euro as their sole official currency are known as the eurozone. Several EU members have opted out of joining this common currency.

Euro notes are identical throughout the eurozone countries, each one including designs of fictional architectural structures and monuments. The coins, however, have one side identical (the value side), and one side with an image unique to each country. Both notes and coins are exchangeable in each country in the eurozone.

Banknotes

Euro banknotes, each a different colour and size, have seven denominations. The €5 note (grey in colour) is the smallest, followed by the €10 note (pink), €20 note (blue), €50 note (orange), €100 note (green), €200 note (yellow) and €500 note (purple).

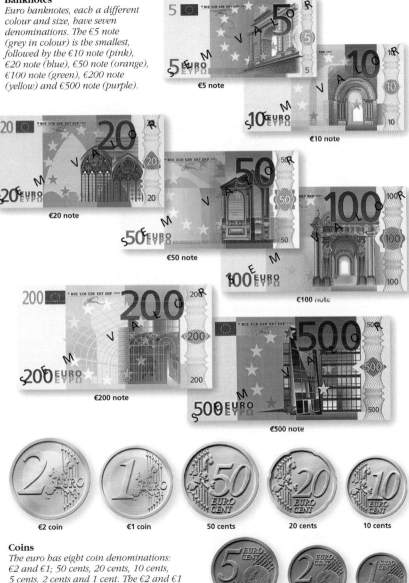

€5 note

€10 note

€20 note

€50 note

€100 note

€200 note

€500 note

€2 coin

€1 coin

50 cents

20 cents

10 cents

Coins

The euro has eight coin denominations: €2 and €1; 50 cents, 20 cents, 10 cents, 5 cents, 2 cents and 1 cent. The €2 and €1 coins are both silver and gold in colour. The 50-, 20- and 10-cent coins are gold. The 5-, 2- and 1-cent coins are bronze.

5 cents

2 cents

1 cent

Communications and Media

ctt correios

Correios (postal service) logo

Information and telecommunications technology in Portugal has advanced at a swift pace. Public telephones are widely available, and the country's mobile phone operators have roaming agreements with most international phone companies; there is good coverage across the city. Lisbon has numerous Internet cafés, and Wi-Fi access is available at the airport, most of the bigger hotels and in many public spaces. Foreign-language newspapers and magazines are on sale the same day of home publication. Portuguese terrestrial television is complemented by an array of foreign cable and satellite channels. Domestic radio broadcasts exclusively in Portuguese.

MOBILE PHONES

If you want to guarantee that your mobile phone will work in Portugal, make sure you have a quad-band phone. Tri-band phones are also usually compatible, but they may have limited global coverage. Contact your service provider to check your phone's compatibility.

To use your mobile phone abroad, you may need to request permission from your network provider before travelling so that they can set your phone to allow "roaming". Check roaming charges with your provider as making and receiving calls can be very expensive.

A popular and cheaper option is to purchase a local SIM card (the electronic chip that links your phone to a particular network); this will use the local mobile phone networks and can be topped up with credit. There are three main mobile phone operators in Portugal: TMN, Vodafone and Optimus. However, you can use a local SIM card only if your handset is "unlocked" – some operators lock their phones to specific networks. Visitors who intend to remain in the city for an extended period would benefit from hiring or even purchasing a mobile phone from one of the main phone operators' shops, such as **TMN** or **Vodafone**, listed opposite. The cost of both local and international calls will be significantly cheaper.

It is worth keeping your network operator's helpline number to hand in case of difficulties.

PUBLIC TELEPHONES

Public telephones are plentiful in Lisbon, with options to pay by coin, phonecard or credit card. They are found in booths in the streets as well as in bars, cafés and shopping centres. Card-operated phones are more common and more convenient, accepting a variety of phonecards that can be purchased from post offices, newsagents, tobacconists *(tabacaria)* and Portugal Telecom company outlets. They also tend to be cheaper, charging about 3 cents for a local call. Some phones also accept credit cards, although that incurs a small extra charge.

International calls and calls to mobile phones are more expensive. An alternative is to phone from a post office, without having either change or a card. You simply step

A public phone booth outside a café in Lisbon

into a free booth, make your call, and pay the cashier afterwards. The cost per unit is relatively low. Some cafés, restaurants and bars have a units meter connected to their phone that calculates the cost of your call, for which you pay afterwards. They charge more than the post office but less than hotels.

For international calls and calls to mobile phones in particular, bear in mind that rates are lower between 9pm and 9am, at weekends and on public holidays. All Lisbon landlines start with 21 and mobile numbers start with a 9.

Accessing the Internet at an Internet café

INTERNET ACCESS

Internet access is widely available in Lisbon, where an abundance of Internet cafés can be found in every major district, especially in tourist enclaves such as Bairro Alto and Chiado. Charges vary, but expect to pay between €1 and €3 per hour. Public Internet facilities can also be found at the city's coach and rail terminals, most of the large hotels, some guesthouses and the city's main youth hostel, Lisboa Central Hostel on Rua Rodrigues Sampaio (just off Marquês de Pombal square, Map 5 C5), as well as some other newer youth hostels.

Wi-Fi hotspots, such as those found at Lisbon airport and some modern shopping malls, enable users to log in on the go, but this facility is not always free.

People using mobile phones, laptop computers or palmtops and wishing to access the Web while abroad need to check that their Internet service provider offers a global roaming option.

POSTAL SERVICES

The postal service in Portugal is known as the *Correios* (the sign depicts a horse and rider in red). A letter sent to a country within the EU should take five to seven days to arrive, and a letter sent to the USA or further afield should take about seven to ten days.

First-class mail, known as *correio azul*, is posted in blue postboxes; second-class mail, or *normal*, in red ones. Post offices may have separate slots for national and international mail. There is also an express mail service *(EMS)* and a recorded delivery service *(correio registado)* for valuable letters.

Prepaid Easy Mail envelopes for domestic and international destinations are available. They do not need to be stamped or weighed, thus allowing for immediate dispatch. Stamps *(selos)* can be bought from post offices, from any shop displaying the *Correios* sign and from vending machines found at the airport, in railway stations and the larger shopping malls.

Post offices are usually open 9am–6pm Monday to Friday; larger post offices open 8:30am–10pm Monday to Friday and 9am–6pm on Saturday and Sunday.

If mailing larger items, use an international courier company. **FedEx** and **DHL** both have offices in Lisbon but are not centrally located.

LISBON'S ADDRESSES

Lisbon's addresses often include both the storey of a building and the location within that floor. The ground floor is the *rés-do-chão* (r/c), the first floor *primeiro andar* (1°), the second floor is expressed as 2°, and so on. Each floor is divided into left, *esquerdo* (E or Esqdo), and right, *direito* (D or Dto).

NEWSPAPERS AND MAGAZINES

English-language newspapers printed in Europe, including the *International Herald Tribune*, are available at larger newsagents on the day of publication except following a bank holiday. The same is true of various other European newspapers and periodicals. Foreign newspapers and magazines are more expensive, and some sections, notably weekend supplements, are not included.

Portuguese daily newspapers include *Diário de Notícias* and *Público*. The weekly *Portugal News*, published on Friday, is the country's main English-language publication. Catering to the expats living along the Estoril coast, it provides news and information on local events. Listings magazines available include the weekly *Time Out Lisbon*, published in Portuguese. A special edition, *Lisbon for Visitors*, is printed monthly in English.

Lisbon's Postboxes
First-class letters should be posted in blue (Correio Azul) boxes, and second-class letters in red boxes.

Portuguese newspapers

RADIO AND TELEVISION

Portugal has two state-owned TV channels, RTP1 and RTP2, and two privately owned ones, SIC and TVI. Most foreign programmes are broadcast in their original language, with Portuguese subtitles. Other English-language channels such as the BBC and CNN are available via satellite and cable. RDP radio (10 723 MHz) broadcasts in English in the summer only.

DIRECTORY

MOBILE PHONES

TMN
Loja 4.09, Armazéns Chiado, Rua do Carmo 2. **Map** 7 B4.

Vodafone
Praça D. Pedro IV 4–5, Rossio. **Map** 6 D3.

INTERNET ACCESS

Fábulas
Calçada Nova de São Francisco 14 (off Rua Garrett), Chiado. **Map** 7 B4.

NetCenter Café
Rua Diário de Notícias 157–159, Bairro Alto. **Map** 4 F2.

Unicâmbio
Praça da Figueira 2, Rossio. **Map** 7 B3.

POSTAL SERVICES

DHL
Av. Marechal Gomes da Costa 27, Olivais. **Tel** 707 505 606.

FedEx
Av. Severiano Falcão 12, Prior Velho, Lisbon. **Tel** 707 244 144

Main Post Office
Praça dos Restauradores. **Map** 7 A2. **www**.ctt.pt

Information on collection times   First-class postbox

Correio Azul
última hora .30

Second-class postbox

CORREIO

TRAVEL INFORMATION

Lisbon has an international airport, good rail links and a port that is popular with cruise liners. Its road network has improved greatly, with ring roads, motorways and a second bridge across the Tagus, however, traffic can be slow at rush hour. Trams provide fascinating trips through some of the city's oldest neighbourhoods; no other

Logo of TAP Portugal

form of public transport can negotiate their steep hills and narrow streets. For the rest of the city, the Metro is the best way to get around. The bus network is huge, but buses do get held up in traffic. The Lisbon Coast and Sintra are easily accessible by train, and ferries are a pleasant way of crossing the Tagus to reach Caparica's beaches.

ARRIVING BY AIR

Lisbon has regularly scheduled flights from European capitals and major cities, including London, Paris, Madrid, Rome, Frankfurt, Munich, Zurich and Milan. Airlines with regular flights include **British Airways**, **Air France**, **Iberia** and **Lufthansa**. Most of these are daily, and in many cases there are several connections. **TAP Portugal**, Portugal's national carrier, currently operates five daily flights from London (three from Heathrow and two from Gatwick) to Lisbon.

Travellers from North America will usually have to change at a European hub. **Delta** flies to Lisbon via Paris (using a partner airline) once or twice daily. **United Airlines** flies to Lisbon direct from Newark, New Jersey, daily. **Aer Lingus** operates a daily summer schedule to Lisbon from Boston and New York via Dublin. TAP's only direct flights from the US are also out of Newark.

South America is better served thanks to Portugal's ties with Brazil: TAP has direct flights to and from several Brazilian destinations.

There are no direct flights to Lisbon from Canada, Australia or New Zealand; London is a popular hub for flights from these countries.

TAP Portugal (code-sharing with PGA Portugália Airlines) also flies to domestic destinations, including Oporto, Faro and Funchal.

Signs at Lisbon's Portela Airport

SATA, in partnership with TAP, serves the Azores. A number of budget airlines, including **easyJet** and **Monarch**, serve Lisbon. Charter airlines' tickets have fixed outward and return dates, but as they are often cheaper than a regular one-way ticket, many one-way passengers buy a return ticket but only use the outward flight. Some charter companies re-sell empty return seats at lower prices. Students can get reduced rates through specialist travel agencies such as STA, and it is also worth checking Internet travel companies such as Expedia.com for deals. Tickets tend to be pricier during high season in summer.

LISBON AIRPORT

Portela Airport is located 7 km (4 miles) north of Lisbon's city centre. It has two terminals linked by a bus service: Terminal 1 handles international flights (and TAP Portugal flights to Porto, Faro, Madeira and the Azores), and Terminal 2 is used for domestic flights. Airport facilities include a bank and a post office.

CONNECTIONS WITH THE AIRPORT

The airport's proximity to the city centre means that it is reasonably fast and cheap to get to the heart of Lisbon. Taxis are available from the taxi rank just outside

the arrivals hall. Fares to the city centre are metered and cost between €10 and €15, with a small extra charge for luggage.

The Carristur-operated AeroBus and AeroShuttle bus services depart every 20–30 minutes between 7am and 11pm from the airport bus stop immediately beyond the taxi rank. They stop at major points in the city centre near to many hotels, such as Oriente, Entrecampos, Sete Rios, Saldanha, Marquês de Pombal, Restauradores, Rossio, Praça do Comércio and Cais do Sodré station. Tickets cost €3.50 and are then valid for the rest of the day for travel on buses, trams and funiculars.

Cheaper regular city buses can be caught at stops a little further to the right as you exit the arrivals hall. Tickets can be bought on boarding. Bus numbers 22, 44, 83, 705 and 745 stop at numerous locations around central Lisbon.

The exterior of Lisbon's large Portela airport

Entrance to the Ponte 25 de Abril, one of the main routes into Lisbon, from the south

ARRIVING BY RAIL

To the east of the Alfama district, on Avenida Infante Dom Henrique, is **Santa Apolónia**, the main station for long distance trains from Coimbra, Oporto and the north as well as from Madrid and Paris. It is 15 minutes' walk east of Praça do Comércio and is served by a Metro station. There is a tourist information office in the station and a taxi rank outside the main entrance.

The impressive, modern **Gare do Oriente** is another international terminus for trains from Madrid and Paris. Although located much further north of the centre, at Parque das Nações, it has excellent links into the city by both bus and Metro.

Trains from the south and east of the city cross the Tagus via the Ponte 25 de Abril and connect with **Entrecampos** and Gare do Oriente stations. **Cais do Sodré** station serves

the resort towns of Cascais and Estoril. Use **Rossio**, **Roma Areeiro** and Entrecampos stations for trains to Queluz and Sintra. The Fertagus rail link is a commuter service to the south bank of the Tagus and Costa da Caparica. For further information *see p163* and visit the **Caminhos de Ferro** (state railway) website.

ARRIVING BY ROAD

There are seven major entry routes into Lisbon: two from the south and east, two from the north and three from the west. Those arriving from the Algarve and the south on the A2 (E1) motorway or the IC1, as well as from Madrid and the east (A6), can cross to central Lisbon via the busy Ponte 25 de Abril, or to the north-eastern part of the city via the newer Ponte Vasco da Gama. Both are toll bridges; Vasco da Gama costs considerably more.

From Oporto and the north, the A1 (E1) motorway brings you to Lisbon's north-eastern outskirts. To reach central Lisbon, follow signs indicating Campo Grande and then Centro. If you wish to head to the coastal resorts of Estoril and Cascais without entering Lisbon, turn off the A1 (E1)

on to the A9 at Alverca, 20 km (12 miles) north of the city, immediately after the toll. The A9, also known as CREL (exterior ring road), is signposted to Cascais and is also tolled.

Those arriving from Cascais and the Lisbon Coast enter via the tolled A5 motorway or the coastal N6 road, known as Avenida Marginal. From Sintra, you enter via the IC19, which links up with Avenida General Norton de Matos in the north of Lisbon. The A8 from northern Estremadura enters the city from the north. For information on driving in Lisbon *see p162*.

LISBON'S BRIDGES

One of Lisbon's most famous landmarks, the Ponte 25 de Abril, provides the main link between Lisbon and Almada, on the southern bank of the Tagus. Built in the 1960s, when cars were still a rarity in Portugal, it became a bottleneck in the late 1980s. In the 1990s more lanes were added and a rail line slung underneath in the hope of easing the congestion. The toll, which is charged only on the way into Lisbon to lessen queuing, was raised to help pay for a second bridge.

This second bridge, the Ponte Vasco da Gama (*see p81*), links Lisbon's north-eastern outskirts – Parque das Nações is right next to it – with Montijo, on the other side of the wide Tagus estuary. The toll is also charged only on the way into the city.

Getting Around Lisbon

Metro logo

An attractive city, Lisbon is a pleasure to explore, and walking can be one of the best ways to see it. However, the city is also hilly, and even the fittest of sightseers will soon tire. The trams and funiculars (*elevadores*) offer a welcome rest for the foot-weary as well as some great views. They are an essential Lisbon experience but may not always be the most efficient means of transport. For that, buses and the Metro are better choices. Driving around Lisbon is not generally recommended: the city suffers from near-chronic congestion and its street plan is full of unexpected surprises. As a result, patience is in short supply among Lisbon drivers. Taxis offer a good alternative and are relatively cheap.

Red Tours electric buggy

GREEN TRAVEL

Lisbon has, on the whole, embraced the notion of becoming an environmentally friendly city. Green initiatives are in place to help alleviate the city's chronic traffic problems. One such scheme, *Menos Um Carro* (One Less Car), launched by Carris on its website, encourages commuters to use public transport rather than drive into the city, or to consider sharing a car. Carris's online sustainable travel campaign (*Indice de Mobilidade Sustentável*) invites users to email their own ideas about how to improve Lisbon's congested transport infrastructure.

Gas-powered private vehicles that run on environmentally friendly liquefied petrol gas (LPG) are rare on Lisbon's roads due to

their relatively high fuel consumption and a lack of service stations offering an LPG option. Rarer still are expensive gas-electric hybrid cars. However, Carris is slowly introducing a fleet of LPG-fuelled buses. Alternative fuel solutions remain high on the political agenda and Lisbon Town Hall is wooing potential converts by offering free parking for 30 minutes for vehicles using these cleaner, alternative vehicles.

Increasingly, police officers are patrolling Lisbon's streets on Segways (two-wheeled electric vehicles). This eco-friendly mode of transport has also been adopted by sightseeing tour company Red Tours (Tel 211 928 852; www.redtourgps.com), which offers self-guided tours on self-drive electric buggies and Segway scooters.

The rail network in Lisbon and throughout Portugal is electrified and leaves a relatively small carbon footprint. It is also reasonably cheap to use and, for the most part, very efficient.

A number of electric trams trundle past some of Lisbon's most important cultural sights, and this "green" mode of transport offers excellent value for money.

Cycling is not popular in central Lisbon; its hilly geography simply does not make it a viable proposition. Cycle paths do exist along the Tagus river in areas such as Alcântara and Belém, and further afield at Parque das Nações and in Cascais. Some independent tourism companies, such as Lisbon Bike tour (www.lisbonbike tour.com) and Bike Iberia (www.bikeiberia.com), offer Lisbon cycle tours, but these, too, tend to avoid the capital's steeper areas.

Discovering Lisbon on foot requires a stout pair of legs and comfortable footwear, but this is one of the best ways to explore the city at leisure.

THE LISBOA CARD

Lisboa Card tourist pass

This comprehensive tourist pass allows free access to most forms of public transport (not ferries) and reduced rates on some tourist tours (including the Carris open-top bus tour, the *Colinas* tour in the red trams, and Transtejo river tours). Additionally, admission charges are waived at 27 national museums and other sights, and are reduced at a number of others (20 per cent off at the Gulbenkian Museum, for instance). It is an impressive offer, and competitively priced, but with only 24, 48 or 72 hours in which to make use of it, you might be rushed off your feet. The Lisboa Card is on sale at the airport arrivals hall, tourist offices, selected hotels, travel agents and sights, as well as in Carris kiosks (*see p159*).

PUBLIC TRANSPORT

Lisbon's public transport system provides access to all parts of the city by a variety of means: trams, lifts and funiculars, buses and the underground *Metropolitano*. The technological spectrum is vast, from early 20th-century trams and funiculars to modern Metro trains, sleek new trams and articulated buses. Buses have the most extensive network, while trams cover a smaller area but offer good sightseeing opportunities. Both are prone to delays due to traffic jams and are run, as are lifts and funiculars, by the state-owned Carris company. The Metro, run separately but also state-owned, is the most efficient form of public transport.

TICKETS

Single-trip paper tickets for buses, trams and funiculars can be bought on boarding. Multi-trip paper tickets have been replaced with electronic passes such as the *7 Colinas*, *Viva Viagem* and *Lisboa Viva* smart cards. The *Viva Viagem* card is the most practical purchase for short-term visits. It can be topped up with credit whenever necessary and provides access to the Carris network and other public transport operators. It must be validated by holding it over a validator machine. Passes can be purchased at points of travel and from Carris kiosks in many parts of the city, including at railway stations, by the Basílica da Estrela, in Praça de Espanha and by Marquês de Pombal square as well as at some post offices and newsagents.

Another option is the Lisboa Card *(see panel opposite)*, which includes unlimited free travel on the bus, tram, funicular/lift and Metro networks, and on the Sintra and Cascais railway lines. It can be purchased as a one-, two-, or three-day card and is validated on each trip by passing it over an electronic scanner.

Metro tickets are bought from machines (with multi-lingual instructions) or from ticket offices at the Metro station as reusable charge cards (there are no paper Metro tickets). The card costs €0.50 and lasts one year. A single trip costs €1.25 no matter what the zone. When purchasing your card you should keep the receipt and present it when necessary to change the card, or if it is damaged. Cards must be validated on entering the platform area by passing them over an electronic scanner to open the gate, indicated by

THE LISBON METRO AND RAIL NETWORK

KEY

— Azul Metro line
— Amarela Metro line
— Verde Metro line
— Vermelha Metro line
— Railway line
— Airport bus route
○ Interchange station

a green light. Exiting the Metro station requires the same procedure.

Children between the ages of 4 and 12, adults over 65 and students all pay half-price on public transport. Children under the age of four travel free of charge. Fines for travelling without a valid ticket are severe.

TRAVELLING BY METRO

The fastest and cheapest way to get around town is by the *Metropolitano*. Metro stations are signposted with a red M, and the service operates from 6:30am to 1am every day.

There are currently 49 Metro stations operating on four lines: the Linha Azul (Blue Line), the Linha Amarela (Yellow Line), the Linha Verde (Green Line) and the Linha Vermelha (Red Line). These lines link the Metro to major bus, train and ferry services, and provide transport from Lisbon's suburbs to the commercial heart of the city, along the north bank of the river. Plans are under way to further extend the city's Metro system, and a number of stations are currently under

construction. Although the Metro does become quite packed during the morning and evening rush hours, there are frequent trains. The system is safe to travel on, even at night time, since the stations and trains are regularly patrolled by the police. All stations have automatic gates at the entrance to the platform areas and a valid ticket must be passed over an electronic scanner both on entering and leaving the station. Metro ticket inspectors can fine you up to 100 times the value of a single-trip ticket if you are caught travelling without a valid ticket.

Automated machine dispensing Metro tickets and passes

A *Colinas* sightseeing tram

TRAVELLING BY TRAM

Trams (*eléctricos*) are one of the most pleasant ways of sightseeing in Lisbon. However, they only operate in a very limited area of the city, along the river to Belém and around the hilly parts of Lisbon. There are currently two types of tram operating in Lisbon: the charming, old, pre-World War I models and the much longer new trams with sleek interiors.

Single tickets for all rides are very cheap except for those on the red *Colinas* or *Tejo* trams, which provide special sightseeing rides for tourists and are much more expensive than the ordinary routes. These sightseeing services operate along a single giant loop throughout the year from Praça do Comércio and take in all of the major historical sights through the hilly parts of Lisbon and along the Tagus. However, it is better value to

catch either the No.25 or the No.28 tram. The former runs from the Cemitério des Prazeres in Campo de Ourique, past the Basílica da Estrela to the attractive Lapa residential district, on a steep hill facing the river. It descends to the river then runs past Praça do Comércio to where the Alfama begins, ending its route in Rua da Alfândega. No.28 shares some of its route with No.25, running via Estrela down past the Palácio de São Bento and up again to Bairro Alto and Chiado. It descends to the Baixa, passes Lisbon's cathedral, then climbs to Castelo São Jorge. It offers an excellent sightseeing tour of old Lisbon – often most of its passengers are tourists.

FUNICULARS AND LIFTS

Due to Lisbon's hilly terrain, funiculars and lifts are a convenient and popular means of getting from river level to the upper parts of the

city, particularly Bairro Alto. Although expensive in relation to distance covered, this form of transport certainly helps take the effort out of negotiating Lisbon's hills, and offers some superb views over the city.

Elevador da Bica climbs from the São Paulo area up to the lower end of Bairro Alto. Elevador da Glória goes from Praça dos Restauradores to the upper end of Bairro Alto. The walkway at Elevador de Santa Justa links the Baixa with the Bairro Alto (*see p46*). Elevador da Lavra climbs from Praça dos Restauradores up to the Hospital São José.

TRAVELLING BY BUS

Lisbon buses (*autocarros*) are usually yellow and are a bright feature around the city's streets. Most inner-city services run from 5:30am to 1am. A smaller number of night buses operate between 1am and 5:30am. The bus network is Lisbon's most extensive public transport system, and buses go just about everywhere. Their timetable suffers from Lisbon's traffic problems, which means you sometimes have to wait a long time to get on a very crowded bus. Most public vehicles are smooth-riding, air-conditioned buses that bend at the middle.

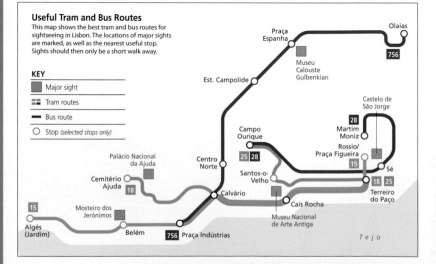

Useful Tram and Bus Routes
This map shows the best tram and bus routes for sightseeing in Lisbon. The locations of major sights are marked, as well as the nearest useful stop. Sights should then only be a short walk away.

KEY

■ Major sight

≡ Tram routes

— Bus route

○ Stop (selected stops only)

Stops are indicated by a sign marked *Paragem*, where details of the specific route are shown. The final destination is shown on the front of the bus, along with its number. Paper tickets can be bought on boarding. If using a pre-paid smart card, remember to validate it by passing it over the electronic scanner machine by the driver. Buses, trams and funiculars use the same paper tickets.

A convenient way of getting between museums and other popular sights is to hop on and off a tour bus. **Carristur** *(see Directory, p165)* runs two excellent routes – the Tagus Tour, which takes in Belém, and the Olisip Tour, which passes by Lisbon's principal musems and visits Parque das Nações. Your ticket is valid for the whole day.

A typical yellow Lisbon bus

WALKING AROUND LISBON

Lisbon is a delightful city to wander around taking in the sights, especially in the old neighbourhoods such as the Alfama and Bairro Alto. Narrow cobbled streets, picturesque buildings and alleyways provide a charming setting to experience traditional Lisbon life.

For a more contemporary backdrop, take a stroll through Parque das Nações, a riverside district east of the city centre. The area, which is totally flat and easily reached by Metro, features some of the country's most striking examples of modern architecture, and it offers a wide array of attractions, including many restaurants and cafés with views over the Tagus. Belém is another flat riverfront

Lisbon's Elevador da Glória ascending to Bairro Alto

area and one of Lisbon's most historic neighbourhoods. It was from here that the great voyages of discovery departed, and monuments in tribute to intrepid navigators abound.

Walking tours, such as the day trips organized by Inside Tours (www.insidelisbon. com) and Lisbon Walker (www.lisbonwalker.com), are a great way to get to know the city more intimately. Many tours are themed to suit individual interests, and they are always conducted in English. Private walks in Portuguese, Spanish, French, German and Italian can usually be arranged under special circumstances.

Lisbon is built on a number of hills, and unless you are fairly fit, it is wise to take advantage of public transport for the uphill climbs. The No.28 tram *(eléctrico)* goes almost all the way up to the Castelo de São Jorge; you can then walk down through the Alfama. The Elevador da Glória will take you from Praça dos Restauradores up to Bairro Alto.

Lisbon's most central shopping area is made up of the Baixa and Chiado, where pedestrianized streets are filled with shoppers, street performers and vendors, as well as a wide variety of shops, shopping centres, outdoor cafés and restaurants.

TAXIS

Compared to the rest of Europe, taxis in Portugal are relatively inexpensive, and if costs are shared between two

or more people, they can work out cheaper than travelling by bus or tram. Most taxis are beige, but a few of the older black and green cabs are still in existence. All are metered, although costs depend on the time of day.

Taxis have their "taxi" signs switched on when they are not available. Green lights indicate that the taxi is available: two green lights mean that the higher rate is being charged (10pm–6am, weekends and public holidays), one green light that the normal rate applies.

The starting rate for a taxi hailed in the street or taken at a taxi rank is €2.50. A flat rate of €1.60 is charged for any luggage placed in the trunk. The meter should always be used, although the driver might suggest agreeing on a price for long trips.

Taxis can also be ordered by phone from companies such as **Autocoope**, **Retalis Rádio Taxis** and **Teletáxis**.

A pre-paid taxi voucher, available from tourist offices, guarantees fixed taxi prices.

Driving Around Lisbon

RETIRE AQUI O SEU BILHETE

Pay-and-display sign

Using a car to get around the busy city centre of Lisbon can be daunting. Finding your way around the complex street plan isn't easy, and traffic jams don't make it any easier. Parking can be very difficult to find. Lisbon's larger roundabouts have traffic lights; on those that don't, cars travelling around the roundabout have priority over cars waiting to enter it. At all other intersections, unless there are signs or lights to the contrary, traffic from the right has priority. If it is absolutely necessary for you to drive in Lisbon, try to avoid the rush hours (roughly 8–10am and 5:30–8pm). Also, be aware that driving at weekends is much easier than during the week. Always look out for pedestrians; crossings are badly marked.

Complexo das Amoreiras, which has an underground car park

PARKING

On-street parking spaces are relatively few in central Lisbon and must mostly be paid for at parking meters. Pay-and-display parking spaces are marked by a P sign with a hand and a coin. Tickets are bought from machines along the pavement; the charge is quite low and only applies between 8am and 8pm on weekdays (and on Saturday mornings in some areas). However, there is a limit to the number of hours you can buy, and the machines don't give change, so come equipped with small coins. Illegally parked cars may be clamped or towed away, and will be released only upon payment of a fine.

Safer and longer-term parking is available in Lisbon's many underground car parks. These are marked by signs with a white P on a blue background and usually display whether there are spaces or not by means of a red full *(completo)* or green free *(livre)* light. Tickets are taken from a machine on entering and paid for before leaving. Car parks are more expensive than parking in the street. Some of the larger ones in Lisbon are beneath Praça Marquês de Pombal, Praça da Figueira, Praça dos Restauradores, Praça Luís de Camões and the Complexo das Amoreiras.

CAR HIRE

Most of the major car-hire companies have offices at the airport inside the arrivals hall *(see Directory)*. To rent a car in Portugal you must have a driving licence *(carta da condução)*. If you do not hold a driving licence from an EU member state you will need an international driving licence. Drivers must be over the age of 21 and have held their licence for at least one year.

It is usually more expensive to hire a car in summer. Most companies offer special off-peak and weekend deals. The price depends on whether unlimited mileage is included and if you want comprehensive insurance *(todos-os-riscos)*. Normally, the car is provided with a full tank of petrol; it is best to return it with the tank full, since the agency will charge to fill it themselves.

PETROL (GASOLINE)

Petrol, called *gasolina*, is relatively expensive in Portugal. Diesel *(gasóleo)* costs considerably less and is the cheapest vehicle fuel. Unleaded fuel *(gasolina sem chumbo)* comes in two types: 95-octane normal and 98-octane super. The latter is more expensive.

There are a number of petrol stations in central Lisbon, some of which are open 24 hours a day. They accept most major credit cards.

DIRECTORY

CAR-HIRE AGENCIES AT LISBON AIRPORT

Auto Jardim
Tel 218 462 916.

Avis
Tel 218 435 550.

Budget
Tel 218 495 523.

Guérin
Tel 707 272 007.

Hertz
Tel 219 426 300.

24-HOUR PETROL PUMPS

BP
Avenida Almirante Gago
Coutinho, Areeiro. **Map** 6 E1.

Galp
Avenida Engenheiro Duarte
Pacheco, Amoreiras. **Map** 5 A5.

Miranda & Ferrão
Avenida António Serpa 22,
Campo Pequeno. **Map** 5 C1.

Travelling around the Lisbon Coast

Logo for Caminhos de Ferro Portugueses

Lisbon and its surroundings offer numerous sightseeing opportunities, and the good road network means that most sights are only 30 minutes or so from the city centre. Buses, coaches and local trains are available for visiting Cascais and Estoril, buses and trains go to and from Sintra, and there are organized coach tours to the palaces and the glorious countryside around the town. There is also a frequent rail service operating from Rossio station to Sintra. To visit Sesimbra and other areas to the south of the Tagus, ferries depart from Terreiro do Paço (Estação Fluvial) and Cais do Sodré in Lisbon, and offer a more leisurely way to cross the river than the busy Ponte 25 de Abril. Alternatively, the Fertagus train also crosses the bridge on the lower level. Trains and buses can then be picked up on the south bank of the river.

High-speed train at Gare do Oriente in Lisbon

TRAVELLING BY TRAIN

The state-owned railway company, **Caminhos de Ferro Portugueses (CP)**, is responsible for operating all trains in Portugal.

There are four main rail lines out of Lisbon. The most popular ones with tourists are the line that runs from Cais do Sodré to Cascais on the coast, and the line linking Rossio station to the town of Sintra. Trains to Sintra also leave from Entrecampos, Sete Rios, Oriente and Roma Areeiro stations, and the journey takes about 45 minutes. Santa Apolónia is the main station for trains travelling north, as well as for most international arrivals.

For those travelling east or south of Lisbon, trains depart from

Gare do Oriente, Entrecampos and Sete Rios stations and cross the Ponte 25 de Abril road and rail bridge. The gleaming Gare do Oriente, near Parque das Nações, opened in 1998. It also serves as an alternative international terminus, in addition to operating as an interchange for local destinations.

To reach Estoril and Cascais, take the train from Cais do Sodré station. The journey follows the coastline and takes about 45 minutes. Check destinations on the screens at the station before you travel because some trains terminate at Oeiras, Parede or São João do Estoril during peak hours. You can also catch the train from Cais do Sodré to Alcântara-Mar, only 5 minutes away, or to Belém, 10 minutes away.

TICKETING SYSTEM

Discounts of 50 per cent are available on all CP tickets for children from 5 to 12, students (with valid ID) and adults over 65. Children under four travel free. There are also discounts for groups of 15 people or more on urban trains in the Lisbon area.

Paper tickets have been discontinued and replaced with pre-paid smart cards that can be bought at vending machines in the station. They are validated electronically by passing them over a scanner at a gate to gain access to the platforms and on leaving the station. Single, return or multiple trips can be purchased on the Cais do Sodré–Cascais and Entrecampos/Sete Rios–Sintra lines. Bicycles are carried free of charge at any time of day on the Cascais and Sintra lines but only on specially marked carriages. Passengers without a validated card will be fined.

DIRECTORY

TRAIN INFORMATION

The following numbers provide train information and apply to all **Caminhos de Ferro Portugueses (CP)** train stations and services:

Tel 808 208 208
(phoning from inside Portugal).

Tel +351 707 201 280
(phoning from outside Portugal).

www.cp.pt

Façade of Rossio station, in Praça Dom Pedro IV

TRAVELLING BY COACH

Lisbon's main coach station is **Sete Rios**. There are several private enterprises operating coach services. Each operates its own ticketing system. As a rule, you buy your ticket from the driver when you board, although it is possible to get cheaper tickets, known as *módulos* or *bilhetes*, beforehand from the relevant coach company's kiosk. As on trains, there are no group discounts, though children between from 4 to 12 pay half price.

At present, the only direct coach services between Lisbon and Cascais are run by the Scottish company **Scotturb** and **Rodoviária de Lisboa**. The hourly service goes from Lisbon airport via Campo Grande to Cascais, returning on an hourly basis as well. The two companies run one bus each, on alternate hours.

TST (Transportes Sul do Tejo) serves destinations south of the Tagus. Buses leave from Praça de Espanha (Metro Praça de Espanha) for destinations such as Costa da Caparica (1hr) and Sesimbra (1hr 45 mins).

For destinations northwest of Lisbon, contact Rodoviária de Lisboa, which operates from Campo Grande, among other places. **Rede Expressos** and **EVA** offer direct services to destinations all over the country. EVA covers the Algarve particularly well. Both are based at the Sete Rios bus terminal in Praça Marechal Humberto Delgado.

To date there is no coach link between Lisbon and Sintra. However, Scotturb operates three routes to Sintra from Cascais and Estoril. The

Ferries crossing the Tagus river

No.403 departs from near Cascais railway station every 90 minutes, via Cabo da Roca. The No.417 runs from Cascais via Alcabideche and the No.418 departs hourly from outside Estoril train station. All three buses stop at Sintra station and in the town centre. In Sintra, Scotturb also runs a service from the train station to Palácio da Pena and Castelo dos Mouros (Tue–Sun).

COACH TOURS

There are many coach tours in the Lisbon area, offering a wide choice of destinations, from a local trip around the city's sights to longer trips to other cities in Portugal such as Oporto. For those who wish to tour Lisbon, short half-day tours are available. Sintra, Cabo da Roca, Estoril and Cascais are all easily reached in a day trip. Alternatively, head southwards to Sesimbra and Arrábida, or north to Mafra. Prices depend on whether meals or special events, such as *fado* or bullfighting, are included. Most tours offer reductions to children under the age of ten. Tours can be booked directly with the tour operator,

through a travel agent or at some hotels. If you are staying at one of Lisbon's major hotels, some tours will offer a pick-up service. For coach tour companies *see page 165*.

FERRIES ACROSS THE TAGUS

Most ferry services are run by **Transtejo**. There are several different points at which you can cross the Tagus. The trips are worth making purely for the fabulous views of Lisbon. From Terreiro do Paço (Estação Fluvial) there are crossings to Barreiro (5:45am–2am daily), taking 15 minutes. Ferries also cross from Cais do Sodré to Seixal and Montijo, taking 20 and 30 minutes respectively.

Ferries owned by Soflusa operate a 15-minute service from Terreiro do Paço to Barreiro (5:45am–2am daily). From Belém, ferries go to Porto Brandão and Trafaria (7am–10pm weekdays, 7:30am–9:30pm Sat, 8:30am–9:30pm Sun & public holidays), where you can get a bus to the beaches at Caparica.

TRAVELLING BY CAR

When driving, always carry your passport, licence, car insurance and rental contract. Failure to produce these *documentos* if the police stop you will incur a fine.

Drivers and passengers must don fluorescent yellow safety vests following a breakdown or an accident. In addition, a vehicle must carry a collapsible warning triangle in the trunk to be used in the event of such an

A long-distance coach from one of the many coach companies

emergency. These items are usually supplied by the car hire company.

The speed limit for driving on a motorway is 120 km/h (75 miles/h); on an open road it is 90–100 km/h (56–62 miles/h) and within a town, 50 km/h (30 miles/h).

The road network in and around Lisbon has seen much improvement in the last decade, with the construction of new ring roads and motorways. If you are heading west out of Lisbon towards the coast and Estoril and Cascais, take the A5 motorway and try to avoid rush-hour traffic (8–10am and 5:30–8pm). To get on to the A5, follow the road out from Praça de Espanha or from Marquês de Pombal past Amoreiras. If you prefer to take the scenic coastal route (N6), follow the A5 out of Lisbon for 8 km (5 miles) and turn off at the sign to Avenida Marginal.

To get to Sintra, the best routes are either the A5 motorway or the IC19 past

Local signs giving directions to Estoril, the south via the bridge and Sete Rios

Queluz. The A5 motorway passes through small areas of countryside.

To reach Caparica, Tróia and Setúbal, south of the Tagus, you can either cross the Ponte 25 de Abril at Alcântara or take the car ferry that departs regularly from Cais do Sodré to Cacilhas. Once across the river, follow the A2 south.

ROADS AND TOLLS

Motorways around Lisbon have toll charges and most are privately owned by a company called **Brisa**. In general, they are the quickest way to travel around Portugal, as they have better surfaces than minor roads. There are also motorway rest areas where you can have something to eat and fill the car up with petrol.

There are two systems for paying tolls on motorways. Most drivers take a ticket *(título)* at the entrance and pay at the exit where the fee is displayed at the toll booth. The other system, known as *Via Verde*, is primarily for residents in the area and is not intended for general use. Drivers subscribing to this system drive through the *Via Verde* channel without stopping. Their passage is registered automatically and billed later. It is strictly forbidden for anyone who does not subscribe to drive

through the *Via Verde*, so make sure that you are in the correct lane as you approach the toll booths.

BREAKDOWN SERVICES

The local motoring association, the **ACP** (Automóvel Club de Portugal), has a reciprocal breakdown service with most other international motoring organizations. To qualify, drivers should take out European cover with their own organization.

Should you be involved in a road accident, the emergency services number is 112. If you have simply broken down, call the ACP. There are SOS phones at regular intervals along motorways. Unless you state that you are a member of an ACP-affiliated organization, a private tow truck will be sent to help you.

Breakdown assistance will try to repair your car on the spot, but if it is a more serious problem, they will tow your car to a garage. Depending on your insurance, the ACP can make arrangements for you to have a hire car until yours is repaired.

In Portugal, international rules apply to breakdowns, including placing a red warning triangle behind the car to alert other drivers. Be sure to check that you have one before you travel.

DIRECTORY

TRAVELLING BY COACH

EVA
Praça Marechal Humberto Delgado, Rua das Laranjeiras, Lisbon. *Tel 213 581 466* or 808 224 488.
www.eva-bus.com

Rede Expressos
Praça Marechal Humberto Delgado, Rua das Laranjeiras, Lisbon. *Tel 213 581 472* or 707 22 33 44.
www.rede-expressos.pt

Rodoviária de Lisboa
Avenida do Brasil 45, Lisbon. *Tel 217 928 180.*
www.rodoviariade lisboa.pt

Scotturb
Rua de São Francisco 660, Adroana, Alcabideche. *Tel 214 699 100/125.*
www.scotturb.com

Sete Rios Coach Station
Praça Marechal Humberto Delgado, Rua das Laranjeiras, Lisbon. *Tel 213 581 472 or 707 223 344.*

TST
Rua Marcos de Portugal, Almada. **Map** 5 A2. *Tel 211 126 200.*
www.tsuldotejo.pt

COACH TOURS

Carristur
Tel 213 613 913.
www.carristur.pt

Cityrama
Tel 213 191 000 or 800 208 513 (toll free).

Gray Line
Tel 213 191 000 or 800 208 513 (toll free).

Portugal Tours
Tel 213 911 000 or 800 208 513 (toll free).

FERRIES

Transtejo
Tel 210 422 400.
www.transtejo.pt

TRAVELLING BY CAR

ACP (breakdown)
Tel 219 429 113.

Brisa (motorways)
www.brisa.pt

LISBON STREET FINDER

Map references given in this guide for sights and entertainment venues in Lisbon refer to the Street Finder maps on the following pages. Map references are also given for Lisbon's hotels *(see pp118–23)* and restaurants *(see pp130–35)*. The first figure in the map reference indicates which Street Finder map to turn to, and the letter and number which follow refer to the grid reference on that map. The map below shows the area of Lisbon covered by the eight Street Finder maps. Symbols used for sights and useful information are displayed in the key below. An index of street names and all the places of interest marked on the maps can be found on the following pages.

KEY TO STREET FINDER

■	Major sight
▧	Place of interest
▤	Railway station
Ⓜ	Metro station
▤	Main coach stop
▤	Tram stop
▤	Funicular railway
▤	Taxi rank
▤	Ferry boarding point
P	Parking
ℹ	Tourist information
✛	Hospital with casualty unit
▣	Police station
✝	Church
✡	Synagogue
Ⓒ	Mosque
⊠	Post office
☀	Viewpoint
=	Railway line
=	Motorway
=	Pedestrianized street
‖‖‖	Stepped pedestrianized street
«45	House number

SCALE OF MAP PAGES 1–6

0 metres	250
0 yards	250

SCALE OF MAP PAGES 7–8

0 metres	200
0 yards	200

AVENIDA DOS

CAMPO GRANDE

AV. DOS ESTADOS UNIDOS DA AMÉRICA

5

6

COMBATENTES

AVENIDA

AV. DE BERNA

AVENIDA DA REPÚBLICA

AVENIDA JOÃO XXI

5 DE OUTUBRO

AV. ANTÓNIO A. DE AGUIAR

AV. FONTES P. DE C. MELO

AVENIDA ALMIRANTE REIS

AV. GENERAL ROCACAS

R. JOAQUIM A. DE AGUIAR

AVENIDA DA PONTE

AVENIDA DE CEUTA

AVENIDA INFANTE SANTO

4 **7**

BAIXA & AVENIDA

8

BAIRRO ALTO AND ESTRELA

C. DA ESTRELA

ALFAMA

AVENIDA 24 DE JULHO

Montijo →

Cais do Sodré

Terreiro do Paço

Barreiro →

Tejo

PONTE 25 DE ABRIL (A2 - IP1)

Cacilhas

N377

N10

0 kilometres 1

0 miles 0.5

Seixal →

Street Finder Index

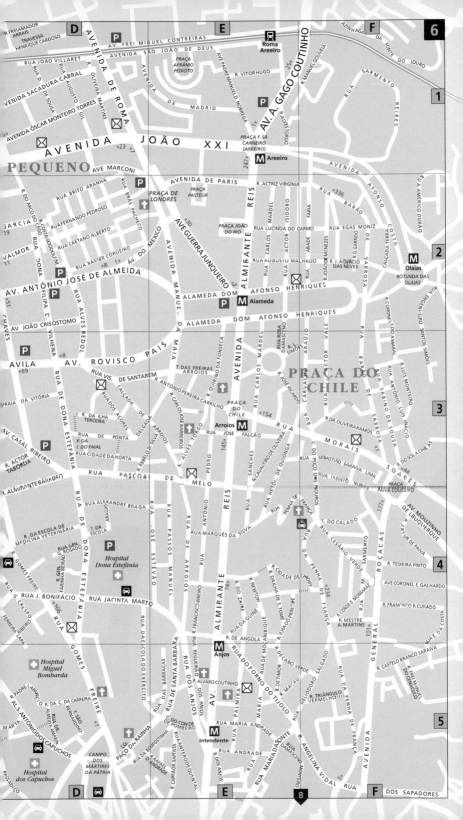

General Index

Acknowledgments

Dorling Kindersley would like to thank the following people whose contributions and assistance have made the preparation of this book possible.

Contributors

Susie Boulton studied History of Art at Cambridge University. A freelance travel writer, she is the author of *Eyewitness Venice and the Veneto*. Sarah McAlister is a freelance writer and editor for the *Time Out* guides. Her knowledge of Lisbon and the surrounding area is a result of extensive visits to the country.

Consultant

Martin Symington was born in Portugal and is a freelance travel writer. He contributes to numerous British newspapers including the *Daily Telegraph* and the *Sunday Telegraph*. He is the author of guides to *The Loire Valley* (Hodder and Stoughton), *Portugal* (AA) and *Denmark* (AA/Thomas Cook). He has also contributed to *The Algarve and Southern Portugal* (AA/Thomas Cook), *Portugal* (Insight), *Eyewitness Great Britain* and *Eyewitness Seville and Andalusia*.

Additional Contributors

Paul Bernhardt, Mark Harding, Paul Vernon, Edite Vieira.

Design and Editorial Assistance

Gillian Allan, Douglas Amrine, Gillian Andrews, Claire Baranowski, Paul Bernhardt, Uma Bhattacharya, Andrew Costello, Angela Marie Graham, Mark Harding, Vinod Harish, Mohammad Hassan, Paul Hines, Jasneet Kaur, Vincent Kurien, Esther Labi, Kathryn Lane, Maite Lantaron, Michelle de Larrabeiti, Nicola Malone, Caroline Mead, Sam Merrell, Adam Moore, Naomi Peck, Andrea Powell, Tom Prentice, Rada Radojicic, Mani Ramaswamy, Jake Reimann, Mihaela Rogalski, Ellen Root, Collette Sadler, Marta Bescos Sanchez, Sands Publishing Solutions, Azeem Siddiqui, Sadie Smith, Susana Smith, Rachel Symons, Amanda Tomeh, Tomas Tranæus, Ingrid Vienings, Fiona Wild.

Indexer

Hilary Bird.

Additional Photography

Paul Bernhardt, Steve Gorton, Matthew Hancock, John Heseltine, Dave King, Martin Norris, Ian O'Leary, Roger Philips, Clive Streeter, Peter Wilson.

Photographic and Artwork Reference

Joy FitzSimmons, Veronica Wood.

Photography Permissions

Dorling Kindersley would like to thank the following for their assistance and kind permission to photograph at their establishments: Instituto Português do Património Arquitectónico e Arqueológico (IPPAR), Lisboa; Instituto Português de Museus (IPM), Lisboa; Museu do Mar, Cascais; Museu da Marinha, Lisboa; Fundação da Casa de Alorna, Lisboa, and all other churches, museums, parks, hotels, restaurants and sights too numerous to thank individually.

Special Assistance

Emília Tavares, Arquivo Nacional de Fotografia, Lisboa; Luísa Cardia, Biblioteca Nacional e do Livro, Lisboa; Marina Gonçalves and Aida Pereira, Câmara Municipal de Lisboa; Caminhos de Ferro Portugueses; Carris; Enatur, Lisboa; Karen Ollier-Spry, John E. Fells and Sons Ltd; Maria Helena Soares da Costa, Fundação Calouste Gulbenkian, Lisboa; José Aragão, Turismo de Portugal, London; Instituto do Vinho do Porto, Porto; Simoneta Afonso, IPM, Lisboa; Mário Abreu, Dulce Ferraz, IPPAR, Lisboa; Pedro Moura Bessa and Eduardo Corte-Real, Livraria Civilização Editora, Porto; Metropolitano de Lisboa, Raquel Florentino and Cristina Leite, Museu da Cidade, Lisboa; Joao Castel Branco G. Pereira, Museu Nacional do Azulejo; and the staff at all the other tourist offices and town halls in Portugal.

Picture Credits

a-above; b-below/bottom; c-centre; f-far; l-left; r-right; t-top.

Works of art have been reproduced with the permission of the following copyright holders: *Terreiro do Paço* by Dirk Stoop 81b is reproduced by kind permission of the Museu da Cidade, Lisboa.

Dorling Kindersley would like to thank the following individuals, companies and picture libraries for permission to reproduce their photographs:

AISA: 18cr, 19tl/br, 66b; ALAMY IMAGES: Ace Stock Limited 86ca; David Angel 89tl; Peter Forsberg 127tl; John Warburton-Lee Photography/Ian Aitken 126cl; Reinhard Kliem 156br; Hideo Kurihara 11cl; Landmarks series/José Elias 40 (front endpaper br); Iain Lowson 163tr; Picture Contact/Jochem Wijnands 127c; Marka/Giovanni Rivolta 162cla; Neil Setchfield 164bl; ARQUIVO INTERNACIONAL DE COR: Neto Miranda 86cr, 87br, 87cla; ARQUIVO NACIONAL DE FOTOGRAFIA-INSTITUTO PORTUGUÊS DE MUSEUS: 19tc; Museu Conde de Castro Guimarães/Manuel Palma 14; Biblioteca da Ajuda/José Pessoa 16c; Museu Grao Vasco/José Pessoa 20bl; Museu Nacional dos Coches/José Pessoa 19bc; Henrique Ruas 64b;

Igreja São Vicente de Fora/ Carlos Monteiro 19bl; Museu Nacional de Arte Antiga/Luís Pavão 56bl/ br, 57t/c/b, 59c; Francisco Matias 21tl, José Pessoa 21tr, 56tl/tr, 58b, 59b; Pedro Ferreira 58t, 59t; Museu Nacional de Arqueologia/José Pessoa 10tc; 65c; Arnaldo Soares 144tr, 145tl; Museu Nacional do Teatro/ Arnaldo Soares 144cl; Luisa Oliveira 145tr; José Pessoa 144b, 22–23t; San Payo 17tr; TONY ARRUZA: 18c, 22–23lc.

© TRUSTEES OF THE BRITISH MUSEUM, London: 20br.

CÂMARA MUNICIPAL DE OEIRAS: 17c; CÂMARA MUNICIPAL DE LISBOA: Antonio Rafael 22cl; CAMINHOS DE FERRO PORTUGUESES: 163tl; CENTRO DO ARTE MODERNA: José Manuel Costa Alves 80tl; CEPHAS: Peter Stowell 26b; Mick Rock 128cb, 129c, Peter Stowell 26b; CHAPITÔ: 142tr; CORBIS: Arcaid/John Edward Linden 11tr; Klaus Hackenberg 34bc; Hans Georg Roth 10cla; CTT CORREIOS: 154br, 155cr CTT PORTUGAL: 154tl.

DOW'S PORT 229cra.
EUROPEAN COMMISSION: 154bl.

FOTOTECA INTERNACIONAL, Lisboa: César Soares 14bl; Luís Elvas 23b/t.

GETTY IMAGES: AFP/Michael Kappeler 19cra; AFP/ Francisco Leong 150bc; The Image Bank/Andrea Pistolesi 28-29; Stone/Hugh Sitton 88cla; GIRAUDON: 20cl; GOLISBON.COM: Mario Fernandes 149tr; GUARDA NACIONAL REPUBLICANA: 150br; CALOUSTE GULBENKIAN FOUNDATION, Lisboa: 138b.

HEMISPHERES IMAGES: Maurizio Borgese 11br; Bertrand Gardel 88br; Jean-Baptiste Rabouan 10br; IDEAL PHOTO: N. Adams THE IMAGE BANK:José Manuel 4b, 25b; Moura Machado 26c; INSTITUTO NACIONAL DE EMERGÊNCIA MÉDICA: 151t; Lisboa: 15b INSTITUTO DA BIBLIOTECA NACIONAL E DO LIVRO, Lisboa: 15b, 16b, 109bl.

JARDIM ZOOLÓGICO DE LISBOA: 84tr.
LUSA: Luís Vasconcelos 52b; André Kosters 53t; António Cotrim 145c.

JOSÉ MANUEL: 23br; MARY EVANS PICTURE LIBRARY: 23tr, 105b; METROPOLITANO DE LISBOA: 159br; MUSEU CALOUSTE GULBENKIAN, Lisboa: Enamelled Silver Gilt Corsage

Ornament, Rene Lalique, © ADAGP, Paris and DACS, London 2011, 76t/ca/cb/b, 77t/ca/cb/b, 78c/b/t, 79b/t/c; MUSEU DA CIDADE, LISBOA: Antonio Rafael 22tl/ cl/bl/br, 23c/bl; MUSEU DA MARINHA, LISBOA: 18br, 68b.

NATIONALMUSEET, Copenhagen: 20tr; NATURPRESS: Juan Hidalgo-Candy Lopesino 24t.

ORONOZ, Madrid: 18bc.

PALACIO DE PENA: 104cl; PICTURES COLOUR LIBRARY: Photolocation Ltd 89br; POLICIA DE SEGURANÇA PÚBLICA: 151cl.

RCL, PAREDE: Rui Cunha 143t; RED TOUR GPS ELECTRIC MOVE: 158tr; DIAS DOS REIS: 81tl, 152cla; REX FEATURES: Sipa Press, Michel Ginies 17b.

RUI SANTOS: www.photographersdirect.com 151cla, 161; SCIENCE PHOTO LIBRARY: CNES, 1997 Distribution Spot Image 12cl; SYMINGTON PORT & MADEIRA SHIPPERS: Claudio Capone 129cl; SOGRAPE VINHOS S.A.: 128tc, 128tr.

TAP PORTUGAL: 156ca; TIVOLI HOTELS & RESORTS: 99tl; TRANSTEJO E SOFLUSA: 164tr; TURISMO DE LISBOA: www. visitlisboa.com: 46tr, 74b, 158bc.

PETER WILSON: 30 (front endpaper tr), 44tl, 53b, 138b, 139c, 140c, 47br; WOODFALL WILD IMAGES: Mike Lane 113b; WORLD PICTURES: 25t.

Jacket
Front – PHOTOLIBRARY: age fotostock/Geoffrey Clive. Back – AWL IMAGES: Michele Falzone bl; DORLING KINDERSLEY: Eddie Gerald cla; Rough Guides/Ian Aitken clb; Tony Souter tl. Spine – CORBIS: Massimo Listri t; DK IMAGES: Peter Wilson b.

All other images © Dorling Kindersley. For further information see www.DKimages.com

SPECIAL EDITIONS OF DK TRAVEL GUIDES

DK Travel Guides can be purchased in bulk quantities at discounted prices for use in promotions or as premiums. We are also able to offer special editions and personalized jackets, corporate imprints, and excerpts from all of our books, tailored specifically to meet your own needs.

To find out more, please contact:
(in the United States) **specialsales@dk.com**
(in the UK) **travelspecialsales@uk.dk.com**
(in Canada) DK Special Sales at **general@tourmaline.ca**
(in Australia) **business.development@pearson.com.au**

Phrase Book

In Emergency

Help!	Socorro!	soo-**koh**-roo
Stop!	Páre!	**pahr'**
Call a doctor!	Chame um médico!	shahm' ooñ **meh**-dee-koo
Call an ambulance!	Chame uma ambulância!	shahm' oo-muh añ-boo-lañ-see-uh
Call the police!	Chame a polícia!	shahm'uh poo-**lee**-see-uh
Call the fire brigade!	Chame os bombeiros!	shahm' oosh bom-**bay**-roosh
Where is the nearest telephone?	Há um telefone aqui perto?	ah ooñ te-le-**fon'** uh-**keepehr**-too
Where is the nearest hospital?	Onde é o hospital mais próximo?	ond' eh oo ohsh-pee-**tahl' mysh** pro-see-moo

Communication Essentials

Yes	Sim	seeñ
No	Não	nowñ
Please	Por favor/ Faz favor	poor fuh-**vor** fash fuh-**vor**
Thank you	Obriqado/da	o-bree-**gah**-doo/duh
Excuse me	Desculpe	dish-**koolp'**
Hello	Olá	oh-**lah**
Goodbye	Adeus	a-**deh**-oosh
Good morning	Bom-dia	boñ **dee**-uh
Good afternoon	Boa-tarde	boh-uh tard'
Good night	Boa-noite	boh-uh noyt'
Yesterday	Ontem	oñ-tayñ
Today	Hoje	ohj'
Tomorrow	Amanhã	ah-mañ-yañ
Here	Aqui	uh-kee
There	Ali	uh-lee
What?	O quê?	oo keh
Which	Qual?	kwahl'
When?	Quando?	kwañ-doo
Why?	Porquê?	poor-keh
Where?	Onde?	oñd'

Useful Phrases

How are you?	Como está?	koh-moo shtah
Very well, thank you.	Bem, obrigado/da.	bayñ o-bree-gah-doo/da.
Pleased to meet you.	Encantado/a.	eñ-kañ-**tah**-doo/duh
See you soon.	Até logo.	uh-teh loh-goo
That's fine.	Está bem.	shtah bayñ
Where is/are … ?	Onde está/estão … ?	ond' shtah/ shtown
How far is it to … ?	A que distância fica … ?	uh kee dish-**tañ**-see-uh **fee**-kuh
Which way to … ?	Como se vai para … ?	koh-moo seh vy puh-ruh
Do you speak English?	Fala inglês?	fah-luh eeñ-glehsh
I don't understand.	Não compreendo.	nowñ kom-pree-eñ-doo
Could you speak more slowly please?	Pode falar mais devagar por favor?	pohd' fuh-lar mysh d'-va-gar poor fuh-**vor**
I'm sorry.	Desculpe.	dish-**koolp'**

Useful Words

big	grande	grañd'
small	pequeno	pe-**keh**-noo
hot	quente	keñt'
cold	frio	free-oo
good	bom	boñ
bad	mau	mah-oo
quite a lot/enough	bastante	bash-tañt'
well	bem	bayñ
open	aberto	a-**behr**-too
closed	fechado	fe-shah-doo
left	esquerda	shkehr-duh
right	direita	dee-**ray**-tuh
straight on	em frente	ayñ freñt'
near	perto	pehr-too
far	longe	loñj'
up	para cima	pur-uh see-muh
down	para baixo	pur-uh **buy**-shoo
early	cedo	seh-doo
late	tarde	tard'
entrance	entrada	eñ-**trah**-duh
exit	saída	sa-**ee**-duh
toilets	casa de banho	kah-zuh d' **bañ**-yoo
more	mais	mysh
less	menos	meh-noosh

Making a Telephone Call

I'd like to place an international call.	Queria fazer uma chamada internacional.	kree-uh fuh-**zehr** oo-muh sha-mah-duh in-ter-na-see-oo-**nahl'**
a local call.	uma chamada local.	oo-muh sha-mah-duh loo-**kahl'**
Can I leave a message?	Posso deixar uma mensagem?	poh-soo day-shar oo-muh meñ-**sah**--jayñ

Shopping

How much does this cost?	Quanto custa isto?	kwañ-too koosh-tuh **eesh**-too
I would like …	Queria …	kree-uh
I'm just looking.	Estou só a ver obrigado/a.	shtoh sohuh vehr o-bree-gah-doo/uh
Do you take credit cards?	Aceita cartões de crédito?	uh-**say**-tuh kar-**toinsh** de kreh-dee-too
What time do you open?	A que horas abre?	uh kee oh-rash ah-bre
What time do you close?	A que horas fecha?	uh kee oh-rash fay-shuh
This one	Este	ehst'
That one	Esse	ehss'
expensive	caro	kah-roo
cheap	barato	buh-**rah**-too
size (clothes/shoes)	tamanho	ta-**man**-yoo
white	branco	brañ-koo
black	preto	preh-too
red	vermelho	ver-**mehl**-yoo
yellow	amarelo	uh-muh-**reh**-loo
green	verde	vehrd'
blue	azul	uh-**zool'**

Types of Shop

antique shop	loja de antiguidades	loh-juh de añ-tee-gwee-**dahd'sh**
bakery	padaria	pah-duh-**ree**-uh
bank	banco	bañ-koo
bookshop	livraria	lee-vruh-**ree**-uh
butcher	talho	tah-lyoo
cake shop	pastelaria	pash-te-luh-**ree**-uh
chemist	farmácia	far-**mah**-see-uh
fishmonger	peixaria	pay-shuh-**ree**-uh
hairdresser	cabeleireiro	kab'-lay-**ray**-roo
market	mercado	mehr-kah-doo
newsagent	quiosque	kee-**yohsk'**
post office	correios	koo-ray-oosh
shoe shop	sapataria	suh-puh-tuh-**ree**-uh
supermarket	supermercado	soo-pehr-mer-**kah** doo
tobacconist	tabacaria	tuh-buh-kuh-**ree**-uh
travel agency	agência de viagens	uh-jen-see-uh de vee-**ah**-jayñsh

Sightseeing

cathedral	sé	seh
church	igreja	ee-**gray**-juh
garden	jardim	jar-**deeñ**
library	biblioteca	bee-blee-oo-**teh**-kuh
museum	museu	moo-**zeh**-oo
tourist information office	posto de turismo	**posh**-too d' too-**reesh**-moo
closed for holidays	fechado para férias	fe-**sha**-doo puh-ruh **feh**-ree-ash
bus station	estação de autocarros	shta-**sowñ** d' oh-too-kah-roosh
railway station	estação de comboios	shta-**sowñ** d' koñ-**boy**-oosh

Staying in a Hotel

Do you have a vacant room?	Tem um quarto livre?	tayñ ooñ kwar-too leevr'
room with a bath	um quarto com casa de banho	ooñ kwar-too koñ kah-zuh d' **bañ**-yoo
shower	duche	doosh
single room	quarto individual	kwar-too een-dee-vee-doo-**ahl'**
double room	quarto de casal	kwar-too d' kuh-**zahl'**
twin room	quarto com duas camas	kwar-too koñ doo-ash kah-mash
porter	porteiro	poor-**tay**-roo
key	chave	shahv'
I have a reservation.	Tenho um quarto reservado.	tayñ-yoo ooñ kwar-too-re-ser-**vah**-doo

Eating Out

Have you got a table for … ?	Tem uma mesa para … ?	tayñ oo-muh meh-zuh puh-ruh
I want to reserve a table.	Quero reservar uma mesa.	keh-roo re-zehr-var oo-muh meh-zuh
The bill please.	A conta por favor/ faz favor.	uh kohn-tuh poor fuh-vor/ fash fuh-vor
I am a vegetarian.	Sou vegetariano/a.	Soh ve-je-tuh-ree-ah-noo/uh
Waiter!	Por favor!/ Faz favor!	poor fuh-vor fash fuh-vor
the menu	a lista	uh leesh-tuh
fixed-price menu	a ementa turística	uh ee-mehñ-tuh too-reesh-tee-kuh
wine list	a lista de vinhos	uh leesh-tuh de veeñ-yoosh
glass	um copo	ooñ koh-poo
bottle	uma garrafa	oo-muh guh-rah-fuh
half bottle	meia-garrafa	may-uh guh-rah-fuh
knife	uma faca	oo-muh fah-kuh
fork	um garfo	ooñ gar-foo
spoon	uma colher	oo-muh kool-yair
plate	um prato	ooñ prah-too
napkin	um guardanapo	ooñgoo-ar-duh-nah-poo
breakfast	pequeno-almoço	pe-keh-noo-ahl-moh-soo
lunch	almoço	ahl-moh-soo
dinner	jantar	jan-tar
cover	couvert	koo-vehr
starter	entrada	eñ-trah-duh
main course	prato principal	prah-too prin-see-pahl'
dish of the day	prato do dia	prah-too doo dee-uh
set dish	combinado	koñ-bee-nah-doo
half portion	meia-dose	may-uh doh-se
dessert	sobremesa	soh-bre-meh-zuh
rare	mal passado	mahl'puh-sah-doo
medium	médio	meh-dee-oo
well done	bem passado	bayñ puh-sah-doo

Menu Decoder

abacate	uh-buh-**kaht'**	avocado
açorda	uh-**sor**-duh	bread-based stew (often seafood)
açúcar	uh-**soo**-kar	sugar
água mineral	ah-gwuh mee-ne-rahl'	mineral water
(com gás)	koñ gas	sparkling
(sem gás)	sayñ gas	still
alho	al-yoo	garlic
alperce	ahl'-pehrce	apricot
amêijoas	uh-**may**-joo-ash	clams
ananás	uh-nuh-**nahsh**	pineapple
arroz	uh-**rohsh**	rice
assado	uh-**sah**-doo	baked
atum	uh-**tooñ**	tuna
aves	**ah**-vesh	poultry
azeite	uh-**zayt'**	olive oil
azeitonas	uh-zay-**toh**-nash	olives
bacalhau	buh-kuh-**lyow**	dried, salted cod
banana	buh-**nah**-nuh	banana
batatas	buh-**tah**-tash	potatoes
batatas fritas	buh-**tah**-tash free-tash	french fries
batido	buh-**tee**-doo	milk-shake
bica	**bee**-kuh	espresso
bife	beef	steak
bolacha	boo-**lah**-shuh	biscuit
bolo	**boh**-loo	cake
borrego	boo-**reh**-goo	lamb
caça	**kah**-ssuh	game
café	kuh-**feh**	coffee
camarões	kuh-muh-**roysh**	large prawns
caracóis	kuh-ruh-**koysh**	snails
caranguejo	kuh-rañ-**gay**-joo	crab
carne	karn'	meat
cataplana	kuh-tuh-**plah**-nuh	sealed wok used to steam dishes
cebola	se-**boh**-luh	onion
cerveja	sehr-**vay**-juh	beer
chá	shah	tea
cherne	shern'	stone bass
chocolate	shoh-koh-**laht'**	chocolate
chocos	**shoh**-koosh	cuttlefish
chouriço	shoh-**ree**-soo	red, spicy sausage
churrasco	shoo-**rash**-coo	on the spit
cogumelos	koo-goo-**meh**-loosh	mushrooms
cozido	koo-**zee**-doo	boiled
enguias	eñ-**gee**-ash	eels
fiambre	fee-**añbr'**	ham
fígado	**fee**-guh-doo	liver
frango	**frañ**-goo	chicken
frito	**free**-too	fried
fruta	**froo**-tuh	fruit

gambas	**gam**-bash	prawns
gelado	je-**lah**-doo	ice cream
gelo	**jeh**-loo	ice
goraz	goo-**rash**	bream
grelhado	grel-**yah**-doo	grilled
iscas	**eesh**-kash	marinated liver
lagosta	luh-**gohsh**-tuh	lobster
laranja	luh-**rañ**-juh	orange
leite	**layt'**	milk
limão	lee-**mowñ**	lemon
limonada	lee-moo-**nah**-duh	lemonade
linguado	leeñ-**gwah**-doo	sole
lulas	**loo**-lash	squid
maçã	muh-**sañ**	apple
manteiga	mañ-**tay**-guh	butter
mariscos	muh-**reesh**-koosh	seafood
meia-de-leite	may-uh-d' **layt'**	white coffee
ostras	**osh**-trash	oysters
ovos	**oh**-voosh	eggs
pão	**powñ**	bread
pastel	pash-**tehl'**	cake
pato	**pah**-too	duck
peixe	**paysh'**	fish
peixe-espada	**paysh'-shpah**-duh	scabbard fish
pimenta	pee-**meñ**-tuh	pepper
polvo	**pohl'**-voo	octopus
porco	**por**-coo	pork
queijo	**kay**-joo	cheese
sal	**sahl'**	salt
salada	suh-**lah**-duh	salad
salsichas	sahl-**see**-shash	sausages
sandes	**sañ**-desh	sandwich
santola	sañ-**toh**-luh	spider crab
sopa	**soh**-puh	soup
sumo	**soo**-moo	juice
tamboril	tañ-boo-**ril'**	monkfish
tarte	**tart'**	pie/cake
tomate	too-**maht'**	tomato
torrada	too-**rah**-duh	toast
tosta	**tohsh**-tuh	toasted sandwich
vinagre	vee-**nah**-gre	vinegar
vinho branco	**veeñ**-yoo brañ-koo	white wine
vinho tinto	**veeñ**-yoo **teeñ**-too	red wine
vitela	vee-**teh**-luh	veal

Numbers

0	zero	**zeh**-roo
1	um	ooñ
2	dois	doysh
3	três	tresh
4	quatro	**kwa**-troo
5	cinco	**seeñ**-koo
6	seis	saysh
7	sete	**set'**
8	oito	**oy**-too
9	nove	**nov'**
10	dez	desh
11	onze	**oñz'**
12	doze	**doz'**
13	treze	**trez'**
14	catorze	ka-**torz'**
15	quinze	**keeñz'**
16	dezasseis	de-zuh-**saysh**
17	dezassete	de-zuh-**set'**
18	dezoito	de-**zoy**-too
19	dezanove	de-zuh-**nov'**
20	vinte	**veent'**
21	vinte e um	veen-tee-**ooñ**
30	trinta	**treeñ**-tuh
40	quarenta	kwa-**reñ**-tuh
50	cinquenta	seen-**kweñ**-tuh
60	sessenta	se-**señ**-tuh
70	setenta	se-**teñ**-tuh
80	oitenta	oy-**teñ**-tuh
90	noventa	noo-**veñ**-tuh
100	cem	sayñ
101	cento e um	señ-too-ee-**ooñ**
102	cento e dois	señ-too ee **doysh**
200	duzentos	doo-**zeñ**-toosh
300	trezentos	tre-**zeñ**-toosh
400	quatrocentos	**kwa**-troo-señ-toosh
500	quinhentos	kee-**nyeñ**-toosh
700	setecentos	set'-**señ**-toosh
900	novecentos	nov'-**señ**-toosh
1,000	mil	**meel'**

Time

one minute	um minuto	ooñ mee-**noo**-too
one hour	uma hora	oo-muh oh-ruh
half an hour	meia-hora	may-uh-oh-ruh
Monday	segunda-feira	se-goon-duh-**fay**-ruh
Tuesday	terça-feira	ter-sa-**fay**-ruh
Wednesday	quarta-feira	**kwar**-ta-**fay**-ruh
Thursday	quinta-feira	**keen**-ta-**fay**-ruh
Friday	sexta-feira	**say**-shta-**fay**-ruh
Saturday	sábado	**sah**-ba-doo
Sunday	domingo	doo-**meen**-go

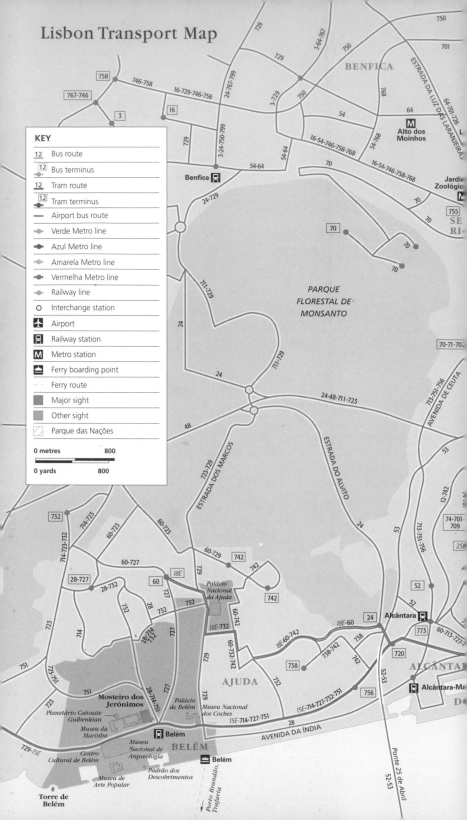

Lisbon Transport Map

KEY

12	Bus route
12	Bus terminus
12	Tram route
12	Tram terminus
	Airport bus route
	Verde Metro line
	Azul Metro line
	Amarela Metro line
	Vermelha Metro line
	Railway line
O	Interchange station
	Airport
	Railway station
M	Metro station
	Ferry boarding point
	Ferry route
	Major sight
	Other sight
	Parque das Nações

0 metres 800

0 yards 800

BENFICA

Alto dos Moinhos

Jardim Zoológic

Benfica

PARQUE FLORESTAL DE MONSANTO

Palácio Nacional da Ajuda

Alcântara

Alcântara-Ma

ALCÂNTARA

AJUDA

Mosteiro dos Jerónimos

Planetário Calouste Gulbenkian

Museu da Marinha

Centro Cultural de Belém

Palácio de Belém

Museu Nacional dos Coches

Belém

Museu Nacional de Arqueologia

BELÉM

Padrão dos Descobrimentos

Museu de Arte Popular

Torre de Belém

AVENIDA DA ÍNDIA

Porto Brandão, Trafaria

Ponte 25 de Abril